As the Fog Lifts

365 Daily Devotions

MARY RINEHART

Copyright © 2018 Mary Rinehart.

All rights reserved. No part of this book may be used or reproduced by any means, graphic, electronic, or mechanical, including photocopying, recording, taping or by any information storage retrieval system without the written permission of the author except in the case of brief quotations embodied in critical articles and reviews.

This book is a work of non-fiction. Unless otherwise noted, the author and the publisher make no explicit guarantees as to the accuracy of the information contained in this book and in some cases, names of people and places have been altered to protect their privacy.

The Living Translation (TLV)
Copyright © 1996 by Tyndale Charitable Trust

Scripture taken from the New King James Version®. Copyright © 1982 by Thomas Nelson. Used by permission. All rights reserved.

Tree of Life (TLV) Translation of the Bible. Copyright © 2015 by The Messianic

WestBow Press books may be ordered through booksellers or by contacting:

WestBow Press
A Division of Thomas Nelson & Zondervan
1663 Liberty Drive
Bloomington, IN 47403
www.westbowpress.com
1 (866) 928-1240

Because of the dynamic nature of the Internet, any web addresses or links contained in this book may have changed since publication and may no longer be valid. The views expressed in this work are solely those of the author and do not necessarily reflect the views of the publisher, and the publisher hereby disclaims any responsibility for them.

Any people depicted in stock imagery provided by Thinkstock are models, and such images are being used for illustrative purposes only.
Certain stock imagery © Thinkstock.

ISBN: 978-1-9736-1459-3 (sc)
ISBN: 978-1-9736-1460-9 (hc)
ISBN: 978-1-9736-1458-6 (e)

Library of Congress Control Number: 2018900453

Print information available on the last page.

WestBow Press rev. date: 01/17/2018

Introduction

I was raised, one of nine kids in a poor family in rural Oklahoma. We had little, besides love. Yet, I realize now the *struggle*s we experienced, were God's plan to *shape* my character. My *needs*; His *desire*, led me here.

I never intended to write a book, but God saw fit to *give* me a *Smart phone* and access to Facebook. He wanted me to use it for His glory.

Each morning, I pour my coffee and enjoy five devotional books, (listed below), along with two Bibles. I normally *read* from the NLT version, because of its simplicity. Often, I find the need to share certain Scriptures, so I use my "Scofield New Reference Bible", (NKJV), to find the *addresses* and to be able to precisely *quote* God's Word.

As I begin, each morning, I sense God's presence as I *meditate* on what I've just read. With *pen in hand*, I *jot down*, (on scrap paper), the thoughts that come to me. When I'm satisfied that this is God's *message* for the day, I copy it into my journal. Then, I put it into a *memo* on my phone. From there, it becomes a *post* on Facebook.

This has been a daily routine since the beginning of 2015. Some friends encouraged me to publish these *posts* in a devotional book. I prayed that if God intended this to happen, He would make a way.

As I am not a *polished writer*, I have my *own way* of communicating. *Professionals* may have no use for it, but it wasn't written *for them*. It was written for ordinary folks, who need encouragement.

People don't carry their Bibles, or take time to read them as they should. But they are *never without* their cell phone. I *feel free* to speak to certain needs without making people feel *uncomfortable*. (As *face-to face* confrontation would.)

May God daily use this book to bless *you*.

- "Open Windows" – A quarterly publication by LifeWay Christian Resources of the Southern Baptist Convention.
- "Grace for the Moment" – by Max Lucado
- "Voices of the Faithful" – with Beth Moore, (devotions from foreign missionaries)
- "Hearing From God Each Morning" – by Joyce Meyer
- "Jesus Calling" – by Sarah Young

JANUARY

January 1

HAPPY NEW YEAR! It's a new beginning!

Let's fast-forward and see where our direction is leading us. Look ahead 10 or 20 years.

While we reap what we sow, what will we be reaping? God has a plan for you. **"For I know the plans I have for you," says the Lord. "They are plans for good and not for disaster, to give you a future and a hope."** (Jeremiah 29:11)

Over and over in the Book of Numbers, a chapter begins with, **"The Lord said to Moses. . ."**

Each morning, as I sit with Him, He speaks to me . . . My ears don't hear Him, but my heart does.

He gives me encouragement and warnings that I feel sure He wants me to share with others, like me, who can benefit from these messages.

As I look back over them, I know they didn't come from me.

All His love is meant to go through us and on to others as we share what we've found.

I am grateful to be a go between for Him. It isn't burdensome, but delightful to be used such a way. **"Take delight in the Lord, and he will give you your heart's desires."** (Psalm 37:4)

January 2

Many think that because they go to church on Sunday, they are one of the worshippers. But, John 4:24 says, **"God is a Spirit; and they that worship him must worship him in spirit and in truth."**

We don't just physically worship Him. We bring our *hearts* before the Lord. We see our need, (Our cup is empty.) We acknowledge He has something for us and 'open ourselves' to receive it.

Worship is like *going to the table*. We need strength and sustenance. (God is our food.) **"And he answered and said, 'It is written, Man shall not live by bread alone, but by every word that proceedeth out of the mouth of God'."** (Matthew 4:4)

This food improves our *eyesight*. Gradually, we're able to see that those who spend their life partying are not the happy, (blessed) ones. We see that God's love is the seed that sprouts into peace. (That's our greatest *need*!)

We learn to trust Him as we become more familiar with His Word. We aren't free from troubles, but we find His strength to help us endure and get past them. (See Philippians 4:13).

January 3

I'm thankful for winter, because it gives me rest from the work of the summer. But I must not love my recliner so much that I allow myself to become so soft that I won't be able to work again, come summer!

Life is filled with calm and storms. We love the calm, but we need to be ready to face the storms.

First Peter 5:7-8 tells us: **"Give all your worries and cares to God, for he cares about what happens to you. Be careful! Watch out for attacks from the Devil, your great enemy. He prowls around like a roaring lion, looking for some victim to devour."**

I'm thankful for the privilege of being a mom, even with the awesome responsibility of shaping these young lives.

I see my failures, and desire that God would pick up the pieces, and fill in the gaps that my incapable hands have left.

Each of my kids have made a profession of faith, but like me, they are lacking God's wisdom to completely obey.

My prayer is that God speaks His love to them in gentle profound ways to keep them on the right path until their final destination is reached.

I relinquish my desires for them to my Loving Lord. Only He has the wisdom to guide them, the power to protect them, and the love to secure their hearts forever.

I trust His grace to be sufficient to meet any need that arises. **". . . My gracious favor is all you need. My power works best in your weakness. . ."** (Second Corinthians 12:9). I pray that He will place His eternal truths alongside their struggles, to help them trust Him, also.

January 4

I've found there's a fine line between concern and worry. When I find myself tangled in worry, I'm reminded of the Serenity Prayer.

"God grant me the serenity to accept the things I cannot change, the courage to change the things I can; and the wisdom to know the difference."

Some things are too heavy for me. I just need to allow God to work it out for me or direct me, one step at a time.

We are loaned, not given children to raise in such a way that prepares them for the future. There has to come a time of separation, when they leave our home to go to theirs.

This is a time of rejoicing for them, but not for us. It is a happy/sad day. This is what life has become. The empty nest syndrome has come. Eventually, we will become accustomed to just frequent visits. But we have all those memories. It's an important part of life.

I think God has pretty much the same scenario for our lives, except in reverse. He allows us to live away from home for a while. **"Therefore we are always confident, knowing that while we are at home in this body, we are absent from the Lord."** (Second Corinthians 5:6)

The time of separation is happy/sad for the ones we leave behind. Though there won't be visits, there will be a glad reunion day!

It's so normal to cling to our loved ones, but we must remember they were never ours. They were only *loaned* to us for a while, and for a purpose. When God calls them home, He will eventually fill that void by His grace. **"And He said unto me, my grace is sufficient for thee, for my strength is made perfect in your weakness."** (Second Corinthians 12:9)

January 5

Everything that comes to us is filtered through the loving fingers of God. Some things seem so overwhelming we think they can't possibly be God's will. The only way to make sense of it is to realize that His thoughts are completely different from ours and His ways are far beyond anything we can imagine.

"For my thoughts are not your thoughts, neither are your ways my ways, saith the Lord." (Isaiah 55:8)

It's like picking up a piece of puzzle and thinking it can't possibly fit in. But it's an important part of the picture. That's where trust comes in.

We have the *Spirit of Love* directing our lives. He sometimes stretches us to grow more than we normally would. This is painful, but necessary. He grants us the grace to endure.

"And he said unto me, 'my grace is sufficient for thee; for my strength is made perfect in weakness . . ." (Second Corinthians 12:9a)

January 6

Long before I was born, God knew who I am; what my life would be like; the choices I would make. He wrote the *book* I am reading, (living).

"You saw me before I was born. Every day of my life was recorded in your book. Every moment was laid out before a single day passed." (Psalm 139:16)

It's impossible to understand how God knows ahead what choices I will make even before I know them! We can read about this in the first chapter of Ephesians. The New Living Translation says it so plainly.

"Long ago, even before he made the world, God loved us and chose us to be holy and without fault in his eyes." (Ephesians 1:4)

I just know God has His hand on me. He is guiding me toward my eternal home, surrounded by everlasting love, peace, and joy. He allows me to make wrong choices so He can teach me the results. He forgives me and turns me in the right direction, time and time again. His love will never let me go!

January 7

We may not think about our father's name when we make poor decisions. But, we're leaving a mark on his name. Would my uncles moan, because I brought their name down, as well? This should affect our morals, and cause us to stop and think about the effects we're causing.

As Christians, we carry Christ's name. We disgrace Him by some of our actions. The awareness of this should bring us to repentance. Our salvation labels us as *Christians*. We are walking advertisements for Him.

I recently felt I was treated badly by a dental firm. I can't recommend them to anyone. They may not treat others badly, but I wouldn't want to wear their T-shirt.

"In the same way, let your good deeds shine out for all to see, so that everyone will praise your heavenly Father." (Matthew 5:16)

I'm retired and usually glued to my recliner on days like this! (Really thankful it isn't a wheelchair!)

Today will be busy. Not much time to sit and reflect on God's goodness. But grateful He goes with me where ever I go.

". . . and be sure of this: I am with you always, even to the end of the age." (Matthew 28:20)

January 8

God is a jealous God. **"Thou shalt not bow down thyself to them, nor serve them; for I, the Lord thy God, am a jealous God, visiting the iniquity of the fathers upon the children unto the third and fourth generation of them that hate me."** (Exodus 20:5)

And even our little sins hurt Him. We are flirting with His, (and our), enemy.

"Be sober, be vigilant, because your adversary, the devil, like a roaring lion walketh about, seeking whom he may devour." (First Peter 5:8)

If not confessed, these little sins add up and cause us not to desire fellowship with God. We can't get through life without Him!

We become miserable creatures. His love sustains us. He gives us rest, sees that we're not hungry, cold, sick, or even lonely.

He provides the very air we breathe and keeps our body functioning.

When we allow sin to clog our systems, we can't function as God desires. Confession of all our sin is like flushing the toilet!

"The thief's purpose is to steal, to kill, and to destroy. My purpose is to give life in all its fullness." (John 10:10)

January 9

Today, I'm in *Chapter 73* of the book God has written of my life. As I look back in *Chapter 20*, I hadn't yet experienced heartbreak and loneliness that caused me to shed enough tears to fill a bathtub. Also, until *Chapter 67*, I hadn't fought the battle with cancer that weakened my body to the point that I was a prisoner of my recliner.

As I look back on these memories, I realize they were allowed by God to shape me into the person I am today. I have confidence that God loves me and will always be with me to get me through anything He allows to come my way.

Knowing God is experiencing His love . . . so much better than just knowing about Him!

You can see a video of Niagara Falls, and realize the infinite flow and power of the water. But unless you are there, you can't smell it and feel the moisture on your face.

"And you shall know the Truth and the Truth shall make you free." (John 8:32)

January 10

When we ignore God and are too busy to listen to His Word, we leave ourselves unarmed against our enemy.

"Be sober, be vigilant, because your adversary, the devil, walketh about like a roaring lion, seeking whom he may devour." (First Peter 5:8)

Satan knows how to cloud our minds with "stinking thinking." This leads us to discouragement and depression.

God's love for us pleads with us, **"Don't copy the behavior and customs of this world, but let God transform you into a new person by changing the way you think. . ."** (Romans 12:2a)

"Who hath delivered us from the power of darkness, and hath translated us into the kingdom of his dear Son." (Colossians 1:13)

Even though we may be Christians, rescued from the power of darkness, God allows us to sit in the dark, if we choose. He is a mighty God, but He will not go against our will. He has given us the power to overcome this way of life.

". . . Those who become Christians become new persons. They aren't the same anymore, for the old life is gone, a new life has begun!" (Second Corinthians 5:17)

January 11

It's so good to bask in God's love. I don't have to worry about today. It will be busy, but He is my G.P.S. He will guide me where He wants me to go.

I pray I won't get so busy that I don't hear His voice. He will be speaking to me. May I be tuned in to the right *station*.

"**After he has gathered his own flock, he walks ahead of them, and they follow him because they recognize his voice.**" (John 10:4)

"**He lets me rest in green meadows; he leads me beside peaceful streams. He renews my strength. He guides me along the right paths, bringing honor to his name.**" (Psalm 23:2-3)

"**Lead me by your truth and teach me, for you are the God who saves me. All day long I put my trust in you.**" (Psalm 25:5)

January 12

I remember being so afraid at night, especially on week-ends, as I heard my drunken neighbors. I was alone with my small children and felt so vulnerable.

At that time, I knew God, but I wasn't aware of His continued presence. I didn't know He was personally involved in my life, but He was present to protect me and provide all my needs!

When we trust anyone or anything, they can fail us or disappear in an instant. Thank God for providing these things to help us daily, but don't depend too much on them, hold onto *Someone* who is solid and eternal.

"Anyone who listens to my teaching and obeys me is wise, like a person who builds a house on a solid rock. Though the rain comes in torrents and the floodwaters rise and the winds beat against that house, it won't collapse, because it is built on rock." (Matthew 7:24-25)

January 13

Through a Beth Moore study on Daniel, God taught me that He would deliver me from anything that may come.

He could have delivered Shadrach, Meshach, and Abednego *from* the fire. But, He chose to go *through* the fire with them. They knew they could have been consumed *by* the fire, but they knew their Eternal Home. So they were not afraid.

Every one of us will die one day. If we have found *The Way* of eternal life – Jesus, we don't have to worry when and what method God chooses.

"I am the way, the truth, and the life. No man cometh to the Father, but by me." (John 14:6)

God brought this message to me a couple of months before I was diagnosed with stage 4 ovarian cancer. He assured my deliverance in one way or another. (I couldn't lose!)

He didn't save me *from* cancer. He saved me *through* it by giving me the grace to endure it.

It would have been okay if I had been delivered *by* it, (through death). I was not afraid.

January 14

There are those in our world who are listening to the wrong voice. They truly believe they are right. But Jesus said in Matthew 7:20, **"Yes, the way to identify a tree or person is by the fruit that is produced."**

The Apostle Paul had once marched in the wrong army. He believed he was actually serving God when he killed Christians!

The Holy Spirit revealed, in a powerful way, that he was going in the wrong direction. Paul immediately turned around and offered his body as an instrument for God to use.

The radical Islamists are marching in that army. They have been trained by Satan to offer themselves to support him. How we hate their actions!

It will take God's intervention to overcome their type of thinking!

Let's make sure we're enlisted in God's army.

January 15

As God created all things in nature and provides what is needed for their survival, He also provides for us. Animals don't worry; they trust. God created good in us, but He gave us a choice.

When Adam and Eve chose to disobey God, they didn't know it, but they were playing "Follow the Leader."

God had warned, **"In the day you eat of it, you will die."** (See Genesis 2:17). (And they did. (They died to the life they had in God.) They were kicked out of God's garden, (and His kingdom).

They now walked in the darkness of sin. Satan became their leader. And they passed that inheritance down to us. But we don't *have* to live under sin's power.

"For God sent not his Son into the world to condemn the world, but that the world through him might be saved." (John 3:17)

"Who hath delivered us from the power of darkness, and hath translated us into the kingdom of his dear Son." (Colossians 1:13)

This is only true for us if we open our hearts to Him. **"Behold I stand at the door and knock. If any man hear my voice and open the door, I will come in to him and will sup with him and he with me."** (Revelation 3:20)

If He is welcome, He will move in and live with us permanently.

January 16

There are many things that can cause us to be depressed. But we don't have to go there. We can take our focus off the problem and look to the Lord.

"God is our refuge and strength, a very present help in trouble." (Psalm 46:1)

The word "temptation" can also be translated *test*, *trial*, or *trouble*. **"There hath no temptation taken you but such as is common to man; but God is faithful, who will not permit you to be tempted above that you are able, but will, with the temptation, also make a way to escape, that ye may be able to bear it."** (First Corinthians 10:13)

"Sing for joy, O heavens! Rejoice O earth! Burst into song, O mountains! For the Lord has comforted his people and will have compassion on them in their sorrow." (Isaiah 49:13)

January 17

God created the womb to be the room where a child can develop until he is able to live in our world. We think the fetus automatically grows to become ready to face the things in life. But God is at work!

The next room for the child is the family, which offers further development. He doesn't automatically develop into one with good morals. Still, God is at work, but with human influence. Not all are born into a loving, nurturing environment. But, with God's help, we can find the strength we need to become morally strong.

God allows tragedies, not to destroy us, but to help us to become hungry for Him. There are times we think, *"This is the worst thing that can happen."* But God sees from an eternal viewpoint, *"This is absolutely necessary to help you find your way."*

He promises, **"And we know that all things work together for good to them that love God, to them who are the called according to his purpose."** (Romans 8:28)

Sometimes, our difficulties are of our own making, but they are allowed to bring about the peaceable fruit of righteousness. **"For whom the Lord loveth, he chasteneth, and scourgeth every son whom he receiveth."** (Hebrews 12:6)

"Now, no chastening for the present seemeth to be joyous, but grievous; nevertheless, afterward, it yieldeth the peaceable fruit of righteousness unto those who are exercised by it." (Hebrews 12:11)

We are being prepared for the room that Jesus is preparing for us.

"There are many rooms in my Father's house, and I am going to prepare a place for you. If this were not so, I would tell you plainly. When everything is ready, I will come and get you, so that you will always be with me where I am." (John 14:2-3)

January 18

Faith helps us through tragic things - things that are bigger than we are. It's not too often our faith is tested in this way. (Thank God!)

But we need faith to get us through each day. It is hearing (with our hearts) God's voice deep inside us, guiding us, and assuring us that we can do what we need to do. Every day we face routine tasks that we don't like. Sometimes we think we can't handle them anymore. Too many times, *I can't* simply means, *I don't want to.*

The Holy Spirit living in us gives us the power to do what is necessary. When we hook our will, (*I can't.*), with His will, (*You need to, I will help you.*), we can do anything.

"I can do all things through Christ who strengthens me." (Philippians 4:13) (If my selfish attitude doesn't get in the way.)

It was our faith in God's grace that saved us. **"For by grace are ye saved through faith, and that not of yourselves, it is the gift of God—not of works, lest any man should boast."** (Ephesians 2:8-9)

We need to help God help us.

January 19

What drives us as individuals? Are we not motivated just to satisfy ourselves? Do we find pleasure in seeing others find joy and fulfillment? Sure we do. Especially those we love. When searching for the perfect gift, we want something they can continue to enjoy, more than just temporarily. We want them to think of us when they use it; to cherish both our gift and our love.

Our Heavenly Father delights in giving us gifts that bring us everlasting joy. He wants us to desire the gifts He has prepared to bring us joy that lasts.

He has given us health, family, homes, nourishment, etc., but we want more. He wants us to want more, but not material things. He wants us to walk closer to Him so He can fill our hearts with lasting joy.

"Whatever is good and perfect comes to us from God above who created all heaven's lights. . ." (James 1:17)

"Take delight in the Lord and he will give you the desires of your heart." (Psalm 37:4)

January 20

If your soul is continually troubled, something is wrong! You may be praying, but not getting the answers you want. If your problem is bigger than you, you have to turn it loose, (at the feet of Jesus.)

The cost of inner peace is total surrender. **"Not my will, but thine be done."** (See Matthew 26:39, 42, & 44). Jesus was also depressed, (V. 37), but He yielded His fleshly desires to God.

Luke 9:23 is hard to accept: **"If any man will come after me, let him deny himself, take up his cross daily and follow me."** Peace comes by nailing our human desires to the cross. God will give us His desires, (peace, love, joy, etc.)

Prayer is communicating with God; not only talking, but listening. Peace comes when we accept His will, though it may be different than ours.

"For my thoughts are not your thoughts, neither are your ways my ways, saith the Lord." (Isaiah 55:8)

Keep on talking, but listen.

January 21

My first vehicle, back in the fifties, was an old clunker. It used a lot of oil. I remember there were no self-service stations. So, when I drove up, instead of saying, "*Fill it up with gas and check the oil*", I would say, "*Fill it up with oil and check the gas.*"

There is an illustration in Matthew 25:1-13 of ten bridesmaids who took their lamps to meet the Bridegroom. Five were foolish and didn't take enough oil, so they didn't get to meet Him.

The moral of this story is: If you don't have the Holy Spirit, (oil) living in you, you won't get to be with Jesus (The Bridegroom) when He comes for us.

We know we need gas, (food, clothing, etc.) to keep us going. But does it matter that we *keep* going if we don't know *where* we're going?

"But seek ye first the kingdom of God and his righteousness and all these things shall be added to you." (Matthew 6:33)

January 22

I've gone to funerals where there was loud wailing. I could sense the agony of those left behind. I couldn't determine if their grief was so strong because they had no hope for their loved one or if they, themselves, had no hope they could get through life without them.

Regardless, their pain was great and they were dealing with it in their own personal way.

We're all alike, but we're all different. Everyone experiences great pain at a time like this, but handles it differently. I loved my sister so dearly that I couldn't imagine not having her there to share my thoughts and feelings as we communicated intimately so often.

I watched cancer take away her contagious laugh and pull me into what she was feeling. When, at last, I had to give her up, to my surprise, I found strength I had never imagined!

I couldn't feel sorry for myself. I could only sense relief and joy for her.

I deal with my grief much differently simply because I can sense Jesus' grip on my hand when I feel I'm sinking. My *Friend* helps me let go of my sister.

"Jesus wept." (John 11:35)

January 23

When we learned to walk, we weren't trained to walk in the Spirit. The physical life is all we knew. Even if we went to church, heard the gospel over and over, learned the Golden Rule, (See Matthew 7:12), and had godly parents, we didn't know that Jesus wants to be our Best Friend.

When we acknowledge His presence, and obey His voice, we are walking in the Spirit.

"This I say then, Walk in the Spirit, and ye shall not fulfill the lust of the flesh. For the flesh lusteth against the Spirit and the Spirit against the flesh; these are contrary, the one to the other, so that ye cannot do the things that ye would." (Galatians 5:16-17)

If we are walking in the flesh, we don't hear His voice, but if we walk in the Spirit, His power is there to guide us in the right direction. He has allowed us to go our own way, stumble and fall. He plans to bring us to the time and place where we're willing to lay down our toys and listen to Him.

"There is none righteous; no, not one." (Romans 3:10)

He is ready and willing to forgive us when we recognize our rebellion.

"If we confess our sins, he is faithful and just to forgive our sins and to cleanse us from all unrighteousness." (First John 1:9)

So, it's still our choice. Let's not choose to live in defeat.

January 24

Our attitude is important. It's our back-seat driver that points us where it wants to go. Momentarily, it defines who we are. But it's merely a reaction to something outside us that can change our outlook. It can build to bitterness if we let it. We can't control what happens to us, but we can control how we react to it.

This is where our faith comes in. If we leave God out of the picture, our reactions are ugly!

I'm thinking of Joseph. He didn't react with revenge when his brothers threw him in a pit and sold him into slavery. (See Genesis 37:20-27). Or when Potipher's wife unjustly accused him. (See Genesis 39:7-20).

When we seek revenge or hold a grudge, we're leaving God out of the picture.

"...**Vengeance is Mine; I will repay, saith the Lord.**" (Romans 12:19)

If we let go and let God handle it, we can keep bitterness from building to block out the flow of joy that cleanses our souls. Holding a grudge harms us much more than the one we refuse to forgive.

Do away with bitterness by letting the *Son* shine in.

January 25

A few days ago, I was trying to get rid of a small stump, (about 8" in diameter). Now, I'm not very good with a chopping axe. I visualized the place on the stump where I wanted the axe to go, but I missed my mark every time. It took about an hour of persistent effort, but it's gone.

I'm thinking that we are God's tools, created for His use.

"What, know ye not that your body is the temple of the Holy Spirit, who is in you, whom ye have of God, and ye are not your own? For ye are bought with a price; therefore, glorify God in your body and in your spirit which are God's." (First Corinthians 6:19-20)

"For that which I do, I understand not; for that which I would (aim to do)**, that I do not; but that which I hate, that I do."** (Romans 7:15)

If my axe and I worked together more often, I could be more effective. God wants to train me for His use, but I have to get *self* out of the way so He can accomplish His work.

January 26

If you've seen *"The Grapes of Wrath"*, you know what it means to be *dirt poor*.

That was *us*, when I was a child. We worked in the fields, (the whole family), chopping cotton, hoeing corn, pulling boles, then later, cutting broomcorn.

Though we didn't have much more than love, we had that! We never felt insecure. But there was no place for envy. It was like a weed; we had to chop it down as soon as it started to sprout. Nice things were just out of our league. I guess that is why, today, I'm not impressed with name brands.

The people at church think they know me, but they only know about me. They haven't seen me go bonkers, like Frankie, (the mom on *"The Middle"*). But my husband and kids have!!

You don't really know someone unless you've lived with them. You only know about them.

I fear that's the only knowledge many have of God. They really don't know Him. They only visit Him on Sunday. He wants us to abide (stay) with Him.

"If ye abide in me and my words abide in you, ye shall ask what you will, and it shall be done unto you." (John 15:7)

If we abide in Him, we know Him well enough to discern whether our desires are what will be best for us.

January 27

What's on the horizon of your day? None of us really know. Sometimes we have a smooth road ahead. Other times our road is full of potholes or we may have a steep climb ahead. It seems that just when things settle down for us, here comes something to stress us out again.

God allows this for a season. Even in nature, there are seasons. We really tire of winter, then spring comes to refresh us. We would love to have a continual spring! (That lies ahead for us!) But for now, we have today.

Some have heartaches; some have headaches; while others are enjoying time on the beach. Life conditions us for what lies ahead. At the end of each day is a time for rest. It prepares us for the day ahead. God is aware of what we will face and is busy preparing us to meet it. Also, He gave us each other. If life isn't pulling us apart for the moment, we need to be mindful of those who are being pulled apart.

We're in this together. Sometimes we can't help in the physical realm, but we can pray for them.

Jesus said in Luke 22:32, **"But I have prayed for thee, that thy faith fail not. And when thou art converted, strengthen thy brethren."**

January 28

I've been thinking of a perfect way to share an unpopular message. I'm not finding it. God just put it out there for anyone who wanted to find it.

If we really want to make our life count, (not just to find *The Way* to heaven), we must be willing to deny ourselves, (lay aside what we want and seek what He wants for us, and from us).

He said if we want to save our lives, (I think He means *find*), we must be willing to lose it for His sake. (Turn control over to Him). This is found in Luke 9:23-24.

We want to *have our cake and eat it, too*. I may be wrong, but I think it's better to have our cake, than to eat it. After all, Jesus said, **"It's more blessed to give than to receive."** (Acts 20:35)

We are to be *rivers* and not *lakes*. God blesses us so that we can bless others. We are not to hoard things or His Word.

Go into your day and share your blessings as He leads you. Speak His love to all you meet - the lovely and the unlovely. And spend some deep thought about the priorities we've set.

January 29

We carry power with us because God is in us. It's sad that many live as though God doesn't exist. They are defeated day after day by even small challenges.

In today's world, we can't live without electricity. We take it for granted until we briefly lose it. We go through the house flipping the light switch, then think, "Oh, yeah."

Wouldn't it be a shame to have that power available and never use it? Or to use it only for lights?

Because we're centered so much on our physical needs and desires, we don't see God at work in our lives. He's invisible, but so is electricity!

He's busy coordinating all our needs with those He knows we will come in contact with today. He uses us to affect others. How will my attitude and words affect my loved ones, co-workers, friends, or public workers?

Not only is God's power available, but so is my sinful nature. We all want a better world. What kind of bricks are we using in our little corner?

"The tongue is a small thing, but what enormous damage it can do. A tiny spark can set a great forest on fire." (James 3:5)

January 30

When you get a flu shot, you'll be less likely to get the flu. But even if you do, it should be milder than it may have been. People who faithfully serve the Lord still get sick and have their amount of troubles.

We can't know why God allows it, but we can know *Who* is always there to meet our needs.

Satan isn't Omni-present, (he can't be everywhere at once), like God is. But he has so many demons to do his work that it seems like it. He wants to steal our joy, kill us if he can, and destroy our lives. (See John 10:10).

But that same verse assures us that our powerful, loving Heavenly Father is always on the scene. His grace is the medicine we need. (See 2 Corinthians 12:9).

In the first 2 chapters of Job, we read that Satan has to come before that same God to get permission in order to bring his evil to us. God allows him to do some things, but limits him in order to prevent them from being so severe that they can't be used to bring about good for us. (See Romans 8:28-29).

When these things come upon us, it can shake our faith. But God knows what we can take and never allows more than we can bear. (See 1 Corinthians 10:13).

We are impatient and it seems that God doesn't bring relief quickly enough for us. The troubles we face are opportunities to exercise our faith, so James 1:2-3 tells us to face them gladly because they will build patience in us.

Hang in there! You'll be okay. . . Eventually!

January 31

My heart's desire is to speak God's love to you through what He is saying to me. I read my devotionals prayerfully, meditate on the scriptures, and wait on God's message. Sometimes I don't get the words as quickly as I'd like. God usually brings a certain person to mind and, as I pray for them, I'm able to hear Him speak to their need.

This morning He is saying to me, **"Be still and know that I am God, I will be exalted among the nations; I will be exalted in the earth."** (Psalm 46:10)

I think He is saying, "If I don't speak, you don't write."

These messages of encouragement are for His glory, not mine. Before my devotion this morning, I faintly heard, **"Behold, I set before you this day a blessing and a curse. A blessing if you obey the commandments of the Lord your God which I command you this day; and a curse, if you will not obey the commandments of the Lord your God, but turn aside out of the way which I command you this day to go after other gods, which you have not known."** (Deuteronomy 11:26-28)

God is telling me, "You know what My Word says, and *this day,* I have a specific message for you. Be sure to listen and obey."

We face choices every day. I pray today that I'll make the ones that please God.

FEBRUARY

February 1

When we look squarely into the face of anxiety, with faith in God, the anxiety melts away! (Like darkness flees when light is applied.)

You can find your way in the dark basement when the electricity is off if you have a good flashlight in your hand.

There's no greater power to work on our behalf than God, who created the heaven and the earth.

"He stretcheth out the north over the empty places and hangeth the earth on nothing." (Job 26:7)

There's no greater wisdom than God's plans for you. **"For I know the plans I have for you, says the Lord. They are plans for good and not for disaster, to give you a future and a hope."** (Jeremiah 29:11)

And there's no greater love than that which watches over you. (See John 3:16)

Only when we allow circumstances to take the forefront, can we be anxious.

"Be anxious for nothing, but in everything, by prayer and supplication with thanksgiving, let your requests be made known unto God. And the peace of God which passeth understanding, shall keep your hearts and minds through Christ Jesus." (Philippians 4:6-7)

If I want His will, He will give me the desires of my heart. (See Psalm 37:4)

Don't go into the dark basement without your flashlight!

February 2

We go to the grocery store often and keep food on hand. We are blessed to always have something to eat. We often hunger for a particular food and know just where to get it.

Our Bible is like a pantry full of spiritual food. It's full of God's promises that meet our needs. As we follow His instructions, we develop principles to live by. We have adopted these and will not deter from them. No matter what others think or say, we will always stand on these principles. They have proved to be a blessing to us, supplying stability in our lives.

We may read our Bibles often, but we don't carry them around with us, (unless we have downloaded the app.) There are *goodies* there to meet our every need. God has highlighted certain verses for us, individually. We may not know their location or be able to quote them word for word, but God brings them to our mind to speak His love to guide or comfort and encourage us at the moment He needs to help us develop further stability, (habits, etc.)

When we read His Word, we need to pause and *chew* on it for a while so it can become part of us. This reduces the stress we bring on ourselves. As we come to our Father, just to praise Him for His goodness, His mercy, His faithfulness, and to lift up the needs of others, He will guide us to find certain passages. He delights in our compassion for others and our hunger for His guidance.

We need to take time to memorize these special passages so they are always with us to meet our needs or to share with others.

"Thy Word have I hidden in my heart, that I might not sin against thee." (Psalm 119:11)

February 3

God is a Supernatural Power. He is a Spirit, (See John 4:24), not a mere human like us. Our finite brain can't hold His mysteries and mighty works.

When we read His Word, we are faced with a decision to believe it or not. God shows us continually His awesome creation and works His love and mercy in our lives.

If we want to acknowledge Him, we have no trouble believing He can do anything. **"But without faith, it is impossible to please him; for he that cometh to God must believe that he is and that he is a rewarder of them that diligently seek him."** (Hebrews 11:6)

"The fool hath said in his own heart, 'There is no God' . . ." (Psalm 53:1)

We can say all day long that we believe in God, but *do we* believe Him? Our secret motives answer that. There are very intelligent people who know much more than we do. They may even be professors in our colleges, but if they don't believe in God, and trust His leadership through His Word, they are fools!

We need to be informed, (have enough knowledge), but we have to trust God's Word to guide us so we use *that knowledge* for His glory. (This is wisdom.)

"But blessed are those who trust in the Lord and have made the Lord their hope and confidence." (Jeremiah 17:7)

Don't let the scoffing of *fools* trouble you. Just pray that God will open their spiritual eyes.

February 4

As Wednesday is *hump day*, many of us have a regular routine and pretty much know what that day will be like. But we don't know what opportunities or disappointments we may face today.

When my kids were small, I made sure they had what they needed as they headed off to school. God sees our day before we do. He already knows just what opportunities and disappointments we will face. He has prepared a lunch for us - the fruit of the Spirit: **"But the fruit of the Sprit is love, joy, peace, long-suffering, gentleness, goodness, faith, meekness, self-control. . ."** (Galatians 5:22-23)

We have what we need for the day. Jesus even goes with us and shares our *lunch* with us as we share with others

February 5

There are so many things in life that occupy our time. There are *voices*, (if you will), that call out to us to get our attention. Some are things we delight in and some are problems that need to be solved. Even routine life absorbs us. It's easy to say to God, "I love you." It's much harder to show Him!

Some of the people we love only show up when they want something. But we are like that, too. It seems there's no time for *just because*.

Fortunately, there are ways we can stay in touch, but there's nothing like those hugs!

It's good to know we have loved ones who are there for us when we really need them. And our love for them compels us to lay our plans aside to go to their rescue when they really need us.

Our Father is *always* there for us. He sees our hearts and knows the depth of our love. He understands how busy we are. But He is a jealous God.

Paul wrote in 2 Corinthians 11:2, **"I am jealous for you with the jealousy of God himself. For I promised you as a pure bride to one husband, Christ."**

God knows that some things we get involved in work as *spiritual prostitution* against His love. When we put ourselves in this position, He has to cause calamity to *wake us up*. We may think we have gotten by with it without too many problems, but "Watch out!"

"For whom the Lord loveth, he chasteneth..." (Hebrews 12:6)

We love to see children laugh and play games. But it grieves us to think of them indulging in drugs, alcohol, gambling, illicit sex, etc.

February 6

Several years ago, my daughter gave me a plaque which says, *"All the love we come to know in life springs from the love we knew as children."* I've been so blessed to have been born healthy and in a loving home. I don't even realize how much I take that for granted! I tend to think everyone has been blessed with these same opportunities to feel loved and see good as I have. But not everyone has been so blessed. I heard the gospel and responded to it as a child. Jesus has been living in me since then.

No matter what your life has been like, receiving Christ gives you a new start. **"Therefore, if any man be in Christ, he is a new creation; old things are passed away; behold, all things are become new."** (Second Corinthians 5:17)

We may not be able to walk again if we were crippled, but we will be able to compensate and adjust to that. Adjusting to emotional scars is equally difficult. Our whole outlook can be different, (unless we *parade* our scars and use them as crutches to excuse our bad attitudes.)

"No, dear brothers and sisters, I am still not all I should be, but I am focusing all my energies on this one thing: forgetting the past and looking forward to what lies ahead." (Philippians 3:13)

February 7

As I look over our church prayer list, there are those that we have prayed for long and hard. God used doctors, technology, and surgery to bring healing and they are now recovering. There are those who are going through difficulties of all sorts and those who are facing surgery.

Also, I have my own prayer list. Sometimes I'm only aware of their physical needs, not their emotional and spiritual problems. When we know someone is on the brink of death, we *wrestle* on their behalf. We are personally involved in a spiritual battle for their healing.

We are all involved in our own spiritual battle daily. We have an enemy who is constantly working to harm us. **"Be sober, be vigilant because your adversary, the devil walketh about as a roaring lion, seeking whom he may devour."** (First Peter 5:8)

Jesus told Peter in Luke 22:31-32 about this battle. He said in verse 32, **"But I have prayed for thee that thy faith fail not, and when thou art converted, strengthen thy brethren."**

Jesus prays for each of us continually and helps us fight our battles. He gives us victory to strengthen our faith and wants us to share our experiences with others to strengthen their faith.

We don't have to have earth-shaking experiences in order to have valuable testimonies that can help others. But we have to be aware of God's presence in order to see Him working so we can give Him the glory for His guidance that gives us those victories.

February 8

There are times we are bewildered and exhausted just trying to get through each day. These are times of testing. Our only hope, it seems, is to know this will surely pass.

It's like a terrible storm beating down on us. It stretches us to the breaking point! After our endurance is completely gone, we fall into the arms of our loving Savior. When we can't - *He can*!

Thank God. He's there! When we are busy trying to survive situations in life is when we need Him most. We can't find time or energy to even go to His Word for the strength, comfort, and guidance we so desperately need.

But there's night at the end of the day, *time-out*. We need this time of rest, but we need to take time to whisper a prayer for help. As we listen, God will guide us with His Word.

"But the comforter, who is the Holy Spirit, whom the Father will send in my name, he shall teach you all things, and bring all things to your remembrance, whatever I have said to you." (John 14:26)

That's why it is so important to hide God's Word in our hearts in times of peace. It is the *ammunition* we will need in our spiritual battles.

But we have the concept in our sinful nature that we don't need to fix the roof because it's not raining.

February 9

I've often wondered what traits we were born with and which ones we have learned in life. Each of us think we are right. How often do we analyze what makes us tick?

How can we know if we really *are* right? God's Word should be our guide. It's strange that if we're unwilling to change, even when we see we are wrong, we will try to find scripture that we can twist to agree with our way of thinking instead of humbling ourselves even to the Almighty God who is our maker and judge.

"There is a way which seemeth right unto a man, but the end thereof are the ways of death." (Proverbs 14:12)

Even the war on terrorism is because of these things. People have either been taught, since childhood, a doctrine they believe, or they are so empty on the inside and are filling that void with the world's thinking.

So, how important is it that we share Christ's love in order to combat the evil forces that are invading our country, neighborhood, and even our homes?

Light dispels darkness. When we walk in the light of God's love, (Jesus), we share His power to overcome this evil. Jesus said, **"I am the Light of the world; he that followeth me shall not walk in darkness, but shall have the light of life."** (John 8:12)

As we take His light with us, we are the light. (See Matthew 5:14) Even though evil is rampant in our world, we are on the winning side.

"Ye are of God, little children, and have overcome them, because greater is he that is in you than he that is in the world." (First John 4:4)

There is a greater battle than the one we fight daily. This is sharpening our commitment to lay down our lives, if need be, for what we believe.

February 10

As I was in the process of writing this morning, my husband turned on the T.V. He was watching Fox News and they were discussing a school in Florida who was teaching students an Islamic prayer! They said they weren't teaching religion, only about religion.

Since they have taken prayer out of our schools, our country has been in a downward spiral, morally.

So now, our Christian prayers are being replaced by prayers to a demonic force!

We all just go along to get along. "Don't rock the boat or they will come after you and your family." "Just wait and maybe someone will do something. " Even if they did, would we be bold enough to get behind them?

Is it worth it? Am I (*the someone*) to do something? "What? Where would I start?"

If we save ourselves and our family from the persecutions, what kind of life will we have? Maybe this is the time to apply what Jesus said in Luke 9:24, **"If you try to keep your life for yourself, you will lose it. But if you give up your life for me, you will find true life."**

They say the way to boil a frog is to put him in cold water. He won't notice when the temperature gradually increases. But he will jump out if he is put in hot water.

February 11

Even though we are zealous for the Lord, we can be deceived. We may be met by false prophets. "**. . . even Satan can disguise himself as an angel of light.**" (Second Corinthians 11:14)

What these people say may sound right and appeal to our common sense. If it aligns with what we want to hear, we may not be alert to test if it is from God. "**Dear friends, do not believe everyone who claims to speak by the Spirit. You must test them to see if the spirit they have comes from God. There are many false prophets in the world.**" (First John 4:1)

(Don't even take everything I write as truth without testing it. I am only human and can fail you, even unintentionally.)

In Matthew 4:1-11, the devil attempted to mislead Jesus in three different ways. Jesus knew to compare it to scripture. God's Word is our Rock, a stable foundation!

We can allow Satan to twist even scripture around to meet our desires if we're not alert. He used scripture in verse 6 to persuade Jesus. There are scriptures that *seem to say* something that doesn't agree with the theme that is found throughout the Bible.

For instance, the strong wording in Luke 14:26, (KJV) *seems to say* if we don't hate our family, we can't be followers of Jesus. The New Living Translation helps us to see that it means we should love Jesus so much more than family. This is still difficult for us to obey.

God is the giver of good gifts. We are not to love His gifts more than Him. Anyone or anything He has given us can become our god. Satan can use them to lure us away from Christ. We don't like to think about the loss of a loved one, but if it comes to that, will we rebound after a period of grief, because our lives are built on our *Rock*, or will our pain build *doubt* that causes us to turn our backs on Him?

February 12

It's no mistake that at this time we are studying, in Sunday School, about how God allowed Jerusalem to be destroyed and its inhabitants to be carried away as captives to Babylon!

This was done after God had tried time after time to bring His people back to Him. We, in America, are doing much the same as they were. They had accepted the introduction of other gods and had given their hearts to pleasure. They did what was right in their own eyes.

Finally, God turned them over to their own ways and allowed them to self-destruct. They had been enjoying life, having no hunger for God.

Just as He created us to seek food and water to satisfy our physical needs, He also created us to develop a hunger for Him.

If we, as His people will humble ourselves, and pray, and seek His face, and turn from our wicked ways, then He will hear from heaven, forgive our sins, and heal our land. (This is found in 2 Chronicles 7:14).

Will we force God to allow evil like ISIS, (Islamic State in Iraq and Syria) to take away our freedom? He loves us too much to allow Satan to lure us out of His hand. He has given us the freedom to choose and we have chosen to drift away from Him. He has no alternative but to allow us to self-destruct to the point we cry out to Him.

If we would judge ourselves, He wouldn't have to send judgement. (See 1 Corinthians 11:31-32).

When He judges us, He chastens us so that we won't be condemned, (to hell), with the world.

He won't let us fall from His grace. He wins this spiritual battle.

Are we His sleeping children or have we fallen for the lie that we don't really have to give Him our hearts? Or that we can fool God if we just go through the motions? (Read Galatians 6:7).

February 13

When you think of yourself as a tool that God uses or wants to use, what comes to your mind?

I guess, because I've built a few things, I immediately think of a hammer. It is useful, not only to build, but to repair. Maybe the reason a hammer comes to mind is because I don't really do much for Him; I'm just available. But when He wants to use me, I *hammer away*.

Maybe He's trying to tell me that is what I've tried to do with His gospel. (Hammer it into people's heads.)

How can I have lived 73 years before grasping a truth I should have known even as a child? Maybe it's because I'm getting too old to be used as a hammer that I have settled down to really see how God wants to use me.

For sure, He wants me to be available. And there are times when a hammer is exactly what is needed.

Today, God is showing me He wants me to be His *flashlight*. He says *He* is the light of the world. (See John 8:12). And that *we* are the light of the world, (See Matthew 5:14).

If I'm a flashlight, He is the bulb, the battery, and the switch. Without Him, I can do nothing. (See John 15:5).

You can't hammer in the dark! Meditate on these thoughts to see how God wants to use you today. If we are available, He can use us however He sees fit to help in any situation.

February 14

As we celebrate Valentine's Day, we give and receive gifts. Some are so thankful for love shown by these gifts, great or small.

Some are disappointed because they didn't receive one or that it was different than they had hoped for. While gift-giving expresses love, it isn't the giving, but the *desire to give* that truly expresses love. When you have this desire, it will show up in small ways every day.

The source of this love is God, Himself. **"God is a Spirit."** (John 4:24) **"God is love."** (First John 4:8) Therefore, God is the Spirit of Love! He is the *root* of our love. (See John 15:5).

When you get right down to it, people who reject God, are rejecting love. Their hearts are empty. They don't realize it, but they fill their hearts with other things, trying to satisfy their discontentment. These things bring happiness that only comes and goes. Also, we can have God in our hearts, but have Him pushed back in a corner so far that we don't have that contentment that lasts.

We may say, "I love God, but . . ." (I remember feeling that way.) I was a baby Christian.

I didn't feel secure in my husband's love. I knew God loved me, but He loved *everyone*! I needed someone to love just *me*. I had a lot to learn! My husband did love me; he just wasn't showing me in the way I wanted.

Maybe, that's the way baby Christians feel about God's love. If we can grab hold of the fact that God loves us *individually*, and wants our love, we can connect with the *Root of Love*, and let our love grow. We will have *true* love, not a manufactured love with a different root.

February 15

In school, we had *pop quizzes* which we all hated. They showed the teacher, (and us), what we had learned up to now. If we had known ahead of time, we would have studied harder so we could make better grades. We didn't really care about learning, we just wanted to get good grades.

We don't see life as a test, but it is filled with *pop quizzes*. Because we never know what may happen, we need to be ready to face anything. **"Study to show yourself approved unto God, a workman that needeth not to be ashamed, rightly dividing the Word of Truth."** (Second Timothy 2:15)

We can have God's truth to guide us in any situation, whether it be terror or needing the right words to encourage a friend.

"God is our refuge and strength, a very present help in trouble." (Psalm 46:1)

He goes with us to remind us of what He has taught us. **"But the Comforter, who is the Holy Spirit, whom the Father will send in my name, he shall teach you all things, and bring all things to your remembrance, whatever I have said unto you."** (John 14:26)

February 16

We want to travel life's road as an interstate highway – (our lane and their lane). We get along just fine as long as they stay in their lane and don't get in our way. Interstates are great, but we have to exit and slow down for other traffic. We become so involved in our efforts we aren't aware that others need to get to their destinations also.

A Traffic light says, "It's their turn; now it's your turn." We put undue stress on ourselves when we run late. This causes rage to build as we have to deal with other drivers. The highway isn't just for us and neither is life. When others don't yield to us, we need to yield to them. It's worth the effort.

We are all selfish and impatient. **"There is none righteous, no not one."** (Romans 3:10) We shouldn't just accept this fact, but strive to do better, as Christ lives in us. This would work better, not only for others, but also for us.

"Do nothing out of selfish ambition or vain conceit, but in humility consider others better than yourselves." (Philippians 2:3)

It has taken a lifetime to become what we are, so it will take time and effort to allow Christ to change our attitude. (Practice makes perfect.) It will never happen if we don't see the need. Peace is at the end of patience. We have our rights but sometimes it is good to yield to others out of love.

February 17

God has something to say about what's happening in our lives each day. Sometimes our days are so full that we find no time to even talk to Him about it and ask for His wisdom to deal with it. I's not that we're really that busy. It's that we think we have it under control and don't want to *bother* God with it. We can't grasp the truth that God's attention isn't turned away from something else to focus on us.

Have you ever been in a group discussion with an idea that you're eager to share, but the conversation never seems to pause long enough for you to get a word in *edge-ways*?

I think that's the way God feels about our *busy-ness*. He's our Best Friend, but He's not limited like we are. We get irritated with interruptions. But God is never interrupted. He is personally present in all our lives at the same time. That blows our mind!

No wonder we have trouble believing some things He has written in His Word.

He is *Supernatural*! There's nothing He can't do. Because we're not supernatural beings, we don't easily accept the supernatural. Satan is also a supernatural being. He interferes supernaturally to cause confusion when we begin to deal with the fact of the supernatural.

We really need to be careful not to be deceived, but God will guard our hearts and lead us into His truth if we *sincerely* seek His guidance.

"Submit yourselves, therefore, to God. Resist the devil, and he will flee from you. Draw near to God and he will draw near to you." (James 4:7-8a)

February 18

God sees our needs. He is eager to bless us. He doesn't want us to beg Him in order to change His will. He loves us and wants our very best. His best is not temporary, but deep, lasting joy and peace. We trust His answer. Often we come to Him *with a splinter in our foot*, (example). We need Him to remove it, but don't want to bear the temporary pain that is necessary to be rid of the source.

This is an example of a need we're aware we have. There are *splinters* we don't even know we have. Others can see them in us, but we can't. We can see the *ugliness* in others, but not in ourselves.

This is because we don't stand before *God's mirror*. When we do, we can see there are areas that need improvement. Real mirrors show us at a glance that we look presentable to go out in public. Or that we need an adjustment.

First Samuel 16:7 tells us not to judge someone by their outward appearance because the Lord looks at a person's thoughts and intentions.

Inner beauty is far more important. **"Create in me a clean heart, O God. Renew a right spirit within me."** (Psalms 51:10) Our compassion for others drives us to go diligently before God on their behalf. But at the same time, we secretly hope some others get what they deserve.

How marvelous it is that God's ways are not our ways! He loves everyone, not just the lovely.

"My thoughts are completely different from yours," says the Lord, **"and my ways are far beyond anything you could imagine."** (Isaiah 55:8)

February 19

As children we didn't worry like we do now. We trusted Mom and Dad to make sure we had what we needed. We knew we wouldn't get everything we wanted, so we somehow controlled our wants.

Our Heavenly Father promises to meet all our needs. **"But my God shall supply all your needs according to his riches in glory in Christ Jesus."** (Philippians 4:19)

When we really grasp that truth, we can again trust like we did as children.

The times we worried were when we knew we were going to get a spanking! Because we are sinners, we know we deserve a spanking, and want to hide from God, (even though we know we can't.)

I remember a time when my son had done something wrong and when I found out, I went after him! But he ran! I chased him for a while then gave up and warned him that he would get it when he came back.

God doesn't have to chase us but we can't *get by* with anything. **". . . Be sure your sins will find you out."** (Numbers 32:23)

When a child comes to us with a confession, we don't spank him. (Unless he continually does the same thing and thinks all he has to do is confess in order to escape punishments.) A really sneaky kid can fool his parents, but not for long. The goal of a spanking is to teach a lesson.

"Now, no chastening at the present seemeth to be joyful, but grievous. Nevertheless, afterward, it yieldeth the peaceable fruit of righteousness unto those who are exercised by it." (Hebrews 12:11)

February 20

It's hard to imagine the Book of Ecclesiastes was penned by the same man who wrote the Book of Proverbs!

We know that **"All scripture is inspired by God and is useful to teach us what is true and to make us realize what is wrong in our lives. It straightens us out and teaches us to do what is right."** (Second Timothy 3:16).

So, we know that God inspired Solomon to write both books. The *point of view* in Ecclesiastes is how a man views life apart from God. It is depressing! The book concludes with, **"Here is my final conclusion: Fear God and obey his commands, for this is the duty of every person. God will judge us for everything we do, including every secret thing, whether good or bad."** (Ecclesiastes 12:13-14)

Proverbs is full of wisdom, contrasting the way of the fool with the way of the wise. Even the fool has to eventually come to the realization that one day he will stand before God to be judged for how he lived his life. As sinners, we don't want to acknowledge God. Then we wonder why we are so depressed!

God gave us the gift of His only Son who gave His life to save us, not only from the wages of sin, which is death, (eternal separation from God), but also from living a useless, unfruitful, depressing life.

"There is a way which seemeth right unto a man, but the end thereof are the ways of death." (Proverbs 14:12)

Satan *bribes* us with fleeting pleasures to keep us in his grasp.

February 21

God speaks to us in many ways. The Bible is His *Love Letter* to us. In it he gives us truths to live by so we can have peace. He also speaks to us personally as we go through each day. He reminds us that we belong to Him.

"The Spirit himself beareth witness with our spirit that we are the children of God." (Romans 8:16)

He can even use dreams to *wake us up*. If you're like me, you don't put much stock in dreams, because so many of them are nonsense. But I vividly remember one that spoke powerfully to me:

There was a terrible storm and I fought against the awful wind and rain to get to the cellar. The lightening flashed to show me the way. When I finally was safe inside, someone asked me, "Where are your kids?" My heart sank!

Thank God, it was only a dream, but I believe God used it to make sure that even though I knew I was saved, I needed to make sure I taught my kids about God's salvation!

Also, we get storm warnings when there is one in our vicinity. We don't take all these warnings to heart. But God speaks a warning personally to us when a tornado is spotted near us, heading our way.

You've heard, "Let your conscience be your guide." God speaks personally to us through our conscience, but we can sear our conscience to the point we don't hear His warnings. That's why it is so necessary to stay close to Him and spend time in His Word.

February 22

When we have car trouble, we go to a mechanic and if we are sick, we go to the doctor. People who have studied and been trained can use today's technology to fix almost anything. We hear of birth defects that call for several surgeries to remedy the problem. We don't realize, but because of sin we were all born with *a hole in our heart*. It's a *God-shaped vacuum*. We spend our life trying to fill it. Until we accept Jesus as our Savior, we still have an emptiness that won't go away.

"Seek ye first the kingdom of God and his righteousness and all these things shall be added to you." (Matthew 6:33)

We need the Great Physician to fill that hole for us. He said in Matthew 9:12, **"They that are well need not a physician, but they that are sick."**

Cancer has no symptoms, but it is deadly! Sin has many symptoms, but others can see them in us better than we can. We think we're not so bad because we can always find others who are worse than we are. We don't want to admit how much we need our Great Physician!

February 23

I usually *read* the New Living Translation since it's easy to understand. Since childhood, I've continued to study in the KJV. But I'm also glad to have handy a NLV to help me with each verse. As Proverbs has 31 chapters, (1 for each day of the month), I was reading chapter 23 today. I read in verse 13, **"Don't fail to correct your children. They won't die if you spank them. Physical discipline may well save them from death."**

I know it's politically incorrect to spank your kids and that it often get out of control and leaves bruises that can land you in jail! But there are times when a spanking is very necessary. Some kids are so tender that a harsh word breaks their heart. You don't have to spank these kids. But there is the strong-willed child who begs for a spanking.

The truth of God's Word tell us that the pain of spanking is timely to relate to the offense of the child and will go away quickly and not leave lasting scars. When we withhold a spanking, we can actually do harm to them that may last a lifetime. As they grow up, they need to learn to obey . . . and so do we!

We need to spank our children out of love and not out of anger. (I admit I've spanked my kids out of anger. That is sin on my part.)

While their misbehavior does anger us, it is essential to use self-control.

As with many truths in God's Word, there is a *thin line* to follow. Going too far to the left or to the right is missing the mark, (sin). God guides us as we seek His wisdom daily.

Our world is getting out of control and I think some of it is due to the fact we are allowing our kids to call the shots. I'm as guilty as anyone, but as I begin to see the truth, I am responsible to share it.

"We ought to obey God rather than men." (Acts 5:29)

(Instead of ending here, I've edited this post to add that many of the problems we face today are due to the fact that we too often obey men rather than God.)

February 24

Sometimes we find ourselves between a rock and a hard place. We can't see tomorrow, but we can see the direction we are going if we have our eyes open. Somehow, we let ourselves go too far before we realize where we have come. Then there seems to be no way out!

I'm thinking of the shape we've allowed our nation to be in. But there is a parallel in many of our individual lives as well. We haven't followed God's wisdom. We've listened to the *wrong voice* that has suggested we are okay and can get away with what we are doing.

Some allow financial disaster because they trust that someone will come to their rescue if they get in over their heads. They have never had to experience bankruptcy or even jail because of their foolish decisions which have been going on for a long time.

It's strange that we can see they're heading *90 miles an hour* toward a brick wall, but they won't stop or turn in order to avoid disaster!

Just as out on the road there are caution signs and stop signs, life has these signs, also.

James addresses this in James 1:5-8: **"If you need wisdom - if you want to know what God wants you to do-ask him, and he will gladly tell you. He will not resent your asking. But when you ask him, be sure that you really expect him to answer, for a doubtful mind is as unsettled as a wave of the sea that is driven and tossed by the wind... People like that should not expect to receive anything from the Lord. They can't make up their minds. They waver back and forth in everything they do."**

February 25

Imagine watching an artist at work. He takes an empty canvas, selects his colors, and begins to paint. He is relaxed and has a finished portrait in mind. It takes a while before you can imagine what he wants to produce. Slowly you can see his intentions emerge. You admire his ability, the elegance of each brush stroke, as you begin to imagine his finished product.

But, as you continue to watch, it becomes so much more beautiful than you could imagine!

Each one of us are *God's painting*. He has a finished product in mind to enhance His kingdom. The only way we can help Him produce the final picture He desires is to stay close to Him and honor Him in all we do.

We sometimes make ugly splotches and it looks like we have ruined His plans! But He can use the dark colors we've splattered on His precious *artwork*. He incorporates them into His picture. He doesn't discard us and start over. He just uses what we give Him to produce His best in us! As we see how we've *messed up* His work, it should break our hearts as we cry, "Father, forgive me!"

"If you keep yourself pure, you will be a utensil God can use for his purpose. Your life will be clean, and you will be ready for the master to use for every good work." (Second Timothy 2:21)

February 26

You've heard the *dash* between the date of birth and the date of death on a tombstone represents one's life. Job 1:21 says, **"I came naked from my mother's womb, and I will be stripped of everything when I die. The Lord gave me everything I had, and the Lord has taken it away. Praise the name of the Lord!"**

Job was hurting because he had just lost everything, even his family! I'm amazed at his attitude! He lived in the *peace that passes understanding*. (See Philippians 4:7).

He recognized that God owns everything and only *loans* us all that we *own*. Because we have worked hard and taken care of our money to accumulate what we have, we think we did it and it is ours. Not only does God own *the cattle on a thousand hills*, (See Psalm 50:10), but He owns the very air we breathe. When Jesus said, **". . . Without me, you can do nothing."** (John 15:5) He was very aware of all He does for us. He gives us air, water, and food for strength to accomplish all we do.

Somehow, we think because we live in a sophisticated age with so much technology, we are smarter than the people were back in the days of Job. If we don't acknowledge God's soverignty, we aren't smart at all!

All of the *stuff* we work so hard to accumulate will go to someone else when we die. And much of it, they won't even want. It may go to the thrift store or even the dump!

So, what priorities should we have in our *dash*? We can only take with us the fruit of the Spirit found in Galatians 5:22-23. This fruit is given only to God's children. So, if we fail to join His family, we've lost all!

"But as many as received him, to them gave he the power to become the children of God, even to them that believe on his name." (John 1:12)

February 27

If we liken God's Word to a post on Facebook, do we skim over it lightly, not even giving it a *like*? Do we immediately agree and *like* it? Do we give it enough attention to make a *comment* by opening up a conversation with God about it? Finally, do we deem it worthy of a *share*?

We don't want to miss a post on Facebook because we want to be in the know if it comes up in a conversation with friends. How much better if we gave this much dedication to God's Word!

Let's relate Facebook posts to *seeds* in the parable of the sower in Matthew 13:3-8: **"A farmer went out to plant some seed. As he scattered it across his field, some seeds fell on a footpath, and the birds came and ate them."** (Not even a *like*.)

"Other seeds fell on shallow soil with underlying rock. The plants sprang up quickly, but they soon wilted beneath the hot sun and died because the roots had no nourishment in the shallow soil." (A *like*). **"Other seeds fell among the thorns that shot up and choked out the tender blades."** (A *comment* that - *other's comments* may cause doubts).

"But some seeds fell on fertile soil and produced a crop that was thirty, sixty, and even a hundred times as much as had been planted." (A *share* that can even go viral!)

February 28

This has been a day when I wasn't able to keep my *coffee date* with the Lord. He reminded me how different life is when the day gobbles up the time, hiding the Lord from your eyes.

I spent much of the night on the pot because of the bitter drink that prepared me for a colonoscopy. I couldn't eat or drink anything after midnight. So, there goes my coffee!

The Lord was gracious to me with a good report, but I sure missed our morning conversation.

Tomorrow will be another day at the hospital as I have my thyroid checked, but the appointment is not too early, so I will be able to keep my *date* with the Lord.

My words are empty when God isn't speaking through me.

"And the Lord came, and stood, and called as at other times, 'Samuel, Samuel!' Then Samuel answered, 'Speak, for thy servant heareth'." (First Samuel 3:10)

MARCH

March 1

We need to be reminded again what a good friend we have in Jesus. If we belong to Him, **"But as many as received him, to them gave he the power to become the children of God, even to them that believe on his name."** (John 1:12) He wants to bless us, as any loving parent would.

He doesn't withhold what He knows will work good in our lives. **"And we know that all things work together for good to them that love God, to them who are the called according to his purpose."** (Romans 8:28)

He takes His time building understanding in us. We get impatient, but He never does.

Because He is invisible to our eyes, we can forget He is there. But, it's like we have an invisible *Spiritual Superman* that can work on our behalf. We reduce Him to *"Clark Kent"* until we feel we really need Him. But *"Clark"* can see into our heart. He doesn't just visit us. He lives with us, (in us). He works *in the background*, helping us through life and we're never on our own. (Unless we tell Him it's none of His business, because *we* want to be in control).

Then, He allows us to have our own way and lets us face the consequences that He never wanted for us. That's called *education expense.*

We are allowed to *go to sleep*, spiritually, if we neglect God's Word. He has to wake us up with a trial that we wouldn't choose.

How much better to discipline ourselves to stay aware of His presence; His love; His power; and His will to guide us with His wisdom daily. Then, we can experience the precious peace and joy He desires continually for us.

March 2

I would rather write a word of encouragement that lifts our spirits and fills our hearts with joy, but this morning, my *word of encouragement* is to wake us up so we can *live in joy*.

We live in the days of *fast and convenient*. We don't want to spend time waiting or learning. We want to instantly *know*! It takes time to dig into God's Word to search for wisdom.

Today's Proverb (2) tells us in verse 12, that wisdom will save us from evil people who want to lead us astray. They want to take advantage of how gullible we are. They know we like to take *shortcuts*. So, they *bait the hook* with what will surely *catch* us. Wisdom saves us from falling for their schemes.

Also, verse 16 tells us that wisdom will save us from the immoral (woman) whose flattery can lead us into adultery.

To sum it up, wisdom causes us to be alert to *test the spirits*. First John 4:1 warns us not to believe everyone who claims to speak by the Spirit, (God's). We must test them to see if what they say lines up with what Jesus teaches. Jesus doesn't tell us to take shortcuts, but to search the scriptures diligently for God's wisdom.

Hebrews 4:12 tells us that God's Word is full of living power. It is sharper than the sharpest knife, cutting deep into our innermost thoughts and desires. It exposes us for what we really are.

We love to play trivia games to see how our knowledge measures up to others. But do we take time to look deep into our hearts to find out what we're really like? In a game, knowledge is key, but in life, wisdom is what counts. It leads us in the right direction - towards God.

March 3

I don't know how old I was when I learned what stress was! As I've stated before, we were very poor, so I'm sure Momma and Daddy dealt with it constantly. But we were sheltered from it. Momma was a worrier, but until we were grown, we never knew it.

God is our ultimate *umbrella* to protect us from stress. (He is over all.) Then, when our parents are gone, we're still under God's *umbrella*.

He tells us in 1 Peter 5:7, **"Give all your worries and cares to God for he cares about what happens to you."**

He also tells us in today's Proverb, (3), verse 5, to trust Him with all our hearts even when we don't understand.

If we honor God with our lives, we can have perfect peace. (See Philippians 4:6-7). Also, in today's Proverb, **"The curse of the Lord is on the house of the wicked, but his blessing is on the home of the upright."** (Proverbs 3:33)

Like Job, we may not always deserve the stress that comes our way, but we *do* bring a lot of it on ourselves by overspending, not consulting God before making decisions, procrastination, etc.

We see others seemingly get away with living ungodly lives and we think it's not fair. But we don't know the stress they deal with, and though they may never recognize God's authority over them, (*There's a payday a comin'!*)

"Don't be misled. Remember that you can't ignore God and get away with it. You will always reap what you sow." (Galatians 6:7) (*Either here or in eternity.*)

Too many times, we don't even try to lead those people to the Lord because we feel they won't trust Jesus. They have other things they trust. But we're not there at night when they lay their heads on the pillow and can't find rest.

March 4

We all realize that life is more than meets the eye. Raging behind the scenes is a spiritual battle. When Jesus was tempted in the wilderness, He quoted scripture. There's an arsenal of weapons in God's Word that we can use to live in victory. We just need them in our hearts - ready to use. There's no time to go get the Bible and look them up.

- *FEAR*: **"What time I am afraid, I will trust in thee."** *(Psalm 56:3)*
- *ANGER*: **"A soft answer turneth away wrath, but grievous words stir up anger."** (Proverbs 15:1)
- *DISCOURAGEMENT*: **"And we know that all things work together for good to them that love God, to them who are the called according to his purpose."** (Romans 8:28)
- *DOUBT*: **"Trust in the Lord with all thine heart and lean not unto thine own understanding."** (Proverbs 3:5)
- *BEWILDERMENT*: **"For my thoughts are not your thoughts, neither are your ways my ways, saith the Lord."** (Isaiah 55:8)
- *ENDURANCE*: **". . . My grace is sufficient for thee; for my strength is made perfect in weakness. . ."** (Second Corinthians 12:9)
- *NEED*: **"But my God shall supply all your need according to his riches in glory by Christ Jesus."** (Philippians 4:19)

There is an unending list of weapons we can use, but we need to have them handy - in our hearts!

March 5

I'm an independent sort of person, and I take for granted the blessing of being surrounded by love. I feel I can survive if I'm left alone. But I never picture myself *really* alone!

Physically, I would probably be okay, for I know how to do for myself. But I need companionship! I need people who love me.

I'm really missing fellowship with my church family right now because the weather didn't allow us to meet together last Sunday at all.

The inactivity of the winter causes me to feel useless. But the inability to share smiles and hugs really pulls me down.

Thank God, this is temporary! Spring is on the horizon! I will not be captured and held in this solitude! I will be able to enjoy the warmth of the sunshine and see the trees again turn green, decorating our world with color!

I will enjoy mowing and seeing the results I'm leaving behind - evenly mowed grass, instead of chaos.

This is the spiritual touch we need in our world today - a peaceful, well-kept, contented people who love and care for each other. Peaceful beauty. God's plan.

"If my people, who are called by my name, shall humble themselves, and pray, and seek my face, and turn from their wicked ways, then will I hear from heaven, and will forgive their sins, and will heal their land." (Second Chronicles 7:14)

March 6

As we are clad with heavy clothing to protect against the cold, we find ourselves burdened by our *shelter*. We long to throw off this outer shell and be free to enjoy again the warmth and beauty of our memories.

As life has dealt us some hard blows, we've formed a hard crust in our hearts, much like the heavy clothing. We remember more joyful and carefree times and long for them.

It's up to us as individuals to *forgive* life's damages. There are *callouses* that have been formed to protect, but they also lock out our joy!

No matter the past - it has passed. We can break through and use those experiences as *building blocks* instead of *road block'*.

Let's enjoy the spring that's ahead, (in our souls), and go barefoot, kicking up our spiritual heels in full enjoyment of this wonderful life that God intends for us.

"For I know the plans I have for you, saith the Lord. They are plans for good and not for disaster, to give you a future and a hope." (Jeremiah 29:11)

We can use the hard times as a *spiritual gym*, to build strength or we can use them in self-pity to get attention. This attitude imprisons us and robs us of the joy that awaits the one who throws off the heavy.

". . . Let us strip off every weight that slows us down, especially the sin that so easily hinders our progress. And run with endurance the race that God has set before us." (Hebrews 12:1b)

We can make up our minds to resist the depressing thoughts and to embrace the joyful. Have a wonderful day!

March 7

As you watch a small child giggle with glee, it warms your heart. You can't seem to get enough. I know the Lord delights in it also. He loves to see us laugh. He prepares little joys for us throughout our day.

Sometimes we recognize them and give Him glory. Often we take them for granted and overlook His small offerings of love.

It's not the gift, but the love behind it that should light up our days.

I'm reminded of times when my grandchildren gave me dandelions. I showed my delight and they ran to give me more. Soon, my hands were full of dandelions! I wasn't blessed because of a handful of dandelions, but of a heart full of love!

God speaks His love to us in many ways throughout each day. We can sense His presence more when we realize He is expressing His love to us through someone's simple smile and using our smiles to bless them also.

Little things mean a lot. We miss God's expressions of love when we only look for Him to do big things for us.

"I will praise the Lord at all times. I will constantly speak his praises." (Psalm 34:1)

March 8

While this isn't the beginning of spring, it is the beginning of preparation for it. As the buds begin to swell, let our hearts be filled with joy and praise for God's beautiful creation! He has wonderful things prepared for us.

Like a child hunting Easter Eggs, let us delight in finding the joys He has for us. Look, here is peace! Oh, there's joy! I found some love! As we put them in our *basket*, (heart), let's share these blessings as we go through the day!

"My son, attend to my words; incline thine ear unto my sayings. Let them not depart from thine eyes; keep them in the midst of thine heart, for they are life unto those that find them, and health to all their flesh." (Proverbs 4:20-22)

"Always be full of joy in the Lord. I say it again, Rejoice!" (Philippians 4:4)

March 9

Is there a task calling out in need of accomplishment? Maybe you've been putting it off because you lack confidence you'll be able to finish it. Sometimes we just don't know where to start or how to begin. We may have tried several times and failed, but it still haunts us.

If it's a worthwhile project that really needs to be done, we can do it! God will give us wisdom. (See James 1:5) He will give us directions.

In Luke 5:4-6, Peter had worked all night, (as a fisherman). He hadn't caught a thing! He was tired and discouraged, had put up his nets, and headed for the shore.

Jesus told him to go out again into the deep and lower his nets. Peter didn't see any use, but because Jesus said to, he was willing to try. They caught so many their nets broke!

There have been many times I have tried with all my might to accomplish a seemingly impossible task. When all my strength was gone, I realized there was no way!

But, a *voice* inside me said to try a different way, to use my mind instead of my muscles. It's amazing! Almost without fail, I've been able to get it done.

I believe the Holy Spirit was the *voice* inside. This proves Philippians 4:13 for me. If it's God's will, He will give *you* the strength, wisdom, and courage you need. Don't give up!

I don't possess anything more than you have at your disposal. I just keep trying (and praying).

March 10

Fulfillment takes time, like a financial investment for the future. If we get in too big a hurry, we may get discouraged and be robbed of a sense of accomplishment.

There are many things we want to accomplish but the key word is 'accomplish'. We simply waste our time, energy, and money if we invest in something we never finish. It is a reminder that we didn't count the cost. This is addressed in Luke 14:28-30. Verse 28 says, **"But don't begin until you count the cost. For who would begin construction of a building without first getting estimates and checking to see if there's enough money to pay the bills?"**

It goes on to say people would mock you for your foolishness. But it doesn't speak of the unfinished project mocking you. It constantly reminds you of your failure to finish. It robs you of your sense of accomplishment, (a job well done).

So, if it's worth starting, it's worth finishing.

Planning is the first step. You know it will take time, money, and energy. But it will also take patience and perseverance.

I learned patience while recovering from cancer. I wanted to be free from it *tomorrow*! But I learned to be grateful that I was going in the *right direction*, no matter how slow. To stop wasn't an option!

If you have unfinished projects mocking you, don't be discouraged. Just *begin finishing* them, one at a time, knowing it will take time, money, effort, patience, and perseverance. Even if you're not as enthused about it as you once were, you need to be rid of their *mockery*. Either chunk the whole thing or determine to finish it. And be sure to count the complete cost before you begin another project.

Have a wonderful day!

March 11

I love to watch the birds around my feeders. I watch from the sunroom with binoculars as they enjoy the food I supply. Then, I see those pesky squirrels hanging upside down, robbing from the feeders. It has been quite a challenge trying to devise a way to keep them out. No matter how crafty my ideas, the squirrels prevail!

Maybe God is trying to tell me that if I want to feed the birds, I will also have to feed the squirrels. It's just that they go through the feed so much more quickly than the birds!

Satan works even in nature to rob from us the joy God has for us. We fight him continually, but he won't go away.

God gives us hope that one day we will be free of him. Speaking in a parable of the wheat and tares in Matthew 13:30, **"Let both grow together until the harvest; and in the time of harvest, I will say unto the reapers, Gather together first the tares, and bind them in bundles to burn them, but gather the wheat into my barn."**

March 12

You're going along your usual way and everything is great - only a few minor problems. Then, *Boom*! You're diagnosed with cancer!

Now, what?? Everything is put on hold. Things that were important yesterday disappear into nothingness. You're completely absorbed in the battle for your very life. Not the life of ease and enjoyment you desired yesterday.

You push the 'pause' button and hope to be able one day to push 'play' again.

God has a way of showing us what's really important, and how much we take for granted His many blessings.

I thought I would never again go through another day without thanking the Lord for good health. And, really, I verbalize my "*Thanks*", but heartfelt joy for this wonderful blessing comes and goes. Life is a normal *gravity* that pulls us away from experiencing the joy of the Lord.

When you've lived a year on **"My grace is sufficient for you"**, (See 2 Corinthians 12:9), you get a different perspective of what it means to have a personal relationship with the Lord.

The deep truth is given to us in James 4:13-15: **"Look here, you people who say, Today or tomorrow we are going to a certain town and will stay there for a year. We will do business there and make a profit. How do you know what will happen tomorrow? For your life is like the morning fog - it's here a little while, then it's gone. What you ought to say is, 'If the Lord wants us to, we will live and do this or that'."**

March 13

The foolishness of childhood robbed me of retaining the knowledge of subjects I was taught.

Why did I hate school? Was it because I *had* to go? Maybe it's because it was indoors and I am an outdoor sort of person. Regardless, my rebellious spirit seemed to say, "You can make me go, but you can't make me learn."

This is the sort of foolishness that Proverbs speaks of.

God loves me in spite of my rebellion. His mercy has led me to live a godly life.

I remember jokingly asking someone if it was recorded somewhere in the Bible that God watches over His ignorant ones. She jokingly answered, "Sure, it's in the Book of Hezekiah." (Of course, there's no Book of Hezekiah!)

Things don't always turn out good for the foolish - only those who come to their senses and yield to God's instructions.

When we get hungry enough for knowledge and understanding, He's a great teacher. When we need a guide or counselor, we can trust He will lead us toward peace if we seek Him with all our heart.

When we acknowledge our sins before our Heavenly Father, He forgives us and cleanses us from all unrighteousness. (See 1 John 1:9).

When He died to pay the price we owed for our sins, He *traded* us His righteousness for our sins. What a bargain!

"For he hath made him, who knew no sin to be sin for us, that we might be made the righteousness of God in him." (Second Corinthians 5:21)

March 14

When I'm really, really angry, I make a lot of noise! I used to slam doors, until the window in the back door broke! Very seldom do I slam cabinet doors, but I can't say I never do. I am aware of the destruction I can leave behind so I discipline myself to keep it at a minimum. (I'm the one who has to clean it up!)

I was reading in Nahum this morning about the wrath of God. **"The Lord is slow to anger but great in power; the Lord will never leave the guilty unpunished. His path is in the whirlwind and the storm, and clouds are the dust beneath his feet."** (Nahum 1:3)

It goes on to say, He dries up rivers and causes the mountains to quake. Even rocks are shattered before Him!

His anger is righteous anger, poured out on His enemies. My anger isn't *always* righteous, but sometimes it is.

God is so good that we can't imagine His vengeance being so fierce.

We *get by* with so much folly because He is so patient. But we can get a pretty good picture of His *wrath* when we read the Book of Revelation.

James 1:17 says, **"Every good gift and every perfect gift is from above and cometh down from the Father of lights. . ."**

Years ago, when my grandson came for a visit, it wasn't long before I was asking him, "Do you want a good grandma or a mean grandma?"

I think God asks that question pretty often!

March 15

It's easy to see Satan at work in our world today. We don't even have to use our *spiritual* eyes. But he wants us to focus on him and his evil deeds. Surely we need to be aware of what's going on, but God is in ultimate control, as we read in Job 1:12, **" 'All right you may test him', the Lord said to Satan. 'Do whatever you want with everything he possesses, but don't harm him physically.' So Satan left the Lord's presence."**

Satan has to get permission to do what he wants to do.

When we know God, we know we can trust His love and wisdom, even if we can't see Him working. He shows Himself in many ways. He gives His children special faith.

Though we are like little children, who have to be told over and over again, He never gives up on us. He sometimes tests our faith in such extreme ways that we wonder if we really *are* His children, or if we just went through the motions of acceptance with our heads and not our heart. Do we have a counterfeit salvation?

But this is good. We have to *know*! Hebrews 10:38 says, **"Now the just shall live by faith; but if any man draw back, my soul shall have no pleasure in him."**

We all have doubts from time to time, but we can't live in doubt. When we are doubting, we are leaning on our own understanding. **"Trust in the Lord with all your heart and lean not on your own understanding."** (Proverbs 3:5)

March 16

Do we really believe Romans 8:28, that God works everything for our good if we love Him and are called according to His purpose?

"Stay away from the love of money; be satisfied with what you have. For God has said, 'I will never fail you, I will never forsake you'." (Hebrews 13:5)

Then, as we sincerely place our lives in His hands and determine to please Him with our words and actions, can we ever really fail?

Nothing can separate us from God's love. (See Romans 8:38-39) **"If God be for us, who can be against us?"** (Romans 8:31)

Also, **"That's why we can say with confidence, The Lord is my helper, so I will not be afraid of what mere mortals can do to me."** (Hebrews 13:6)

People have to go through God to do us harm. He only allows that if He can bring about good for us.

We can take a far different approach to life, **"Take my yoke upon you, and learn of me; for I am meek and lowly in heart, and ye shall find rest for your souls. For my yoke is easy and my burden is light."** (Matthew 11:29)

The key to this success is found in today's Proverb, **"Commit your work to the Lord, and then your plans will succeed."** (Chapter 16:3)

If we can just work for His glory and not our own, we can't fail!

March 17

As I read today's Proverb, I can almost hear my mother speaking. She must have memorized large portions of it. She quoted one verse so often, I felt she used it to rebuke me for my wrong-doing. So, I was confused by it.

"Better is a dry morsel and quietness therewith than a house full of sacrifice with strife." (Proverbs 17:1)

It finally dawned on me, just this morning, that she wasn't using it to rebuke me, but to somehow remind herself of God's presence. He saw how she struggled with a house full of unruly kids. She struggled, not only with our nonsense, but she felt she had been dealt a *dry morsel* also, as we lived in poverty. She longed for the peace that was supposed to accompany it.

I realize now that she was leaning on the Lord with all that was within her!

March 18

Raising a child is an awesome responsibility. They each have their own free will. But a parent instills in them the instructions to go the right direction. Without the parent, the child may survive and can even, with God's help, find the right way.

But, life is much easier with the guidance of a loving parent. You can teach a child to obey, just as you teach him to walk, but you can't *make* him obey! He has his own direction. You can guide him, but when your back is turned, he will go his own way.

God is our loving Parent. He teaches us and guides us. But, even *He* can't *make* us obey! We have a free will to make our own choices.

But, just as He gives birds the instinct to fly south for the winter, He instills in us to go the right direction when we reach the end of ourselves, - (no more choices - the only way to look is up!)

"But God, who is rich in mercy, for his great love with which he loved us. Even when we were dead in sins, hath made us alive together with Christ (by grace ye are saved!)" (Ephesians 2:4-5)

March 19

God told Abraham, (the Father of the Nation of Israel) in Genesis 12:3, **"I will bless those who bless you and curse those who curse you. All the families of the earth will be blessed through you."** (Jesus came to us through that family.)

We, as individuals, can choose to *bless Israel*, (be their friends), but we are part of a *nation,* who has to decide whether to bless them. It is our duty, as individuals, to spread God's promises to those we know.

Many Americans don't even know who our first president was, (and don't care.) So, they surely don't know about this portion of scripture, (and probably don't care).

In our Proverb for today, (Proverbs 19:3), we read, **"People ruin their lives by their own foolishness and then are angry at the Lord."**

The choices we make have consequences. As individuals, we *season* our communities.

"Ye are the salt of the earth. . ." (Matthew 5:13) If we make bad choices, we can't blame God when disaster hits our nation.

March 20

What forms our opinions, (beliefs)? Are they based on God's Word or merely prejudices? When my rights conflict with other's rights, who is to say whose rights prevail?

Laws are passed every day that take away a little more of our freedoms. Love can't be forced!

Let God deal with our hearts, instead of us being dragged into court to defend what we believe. Before we speak out on a matter, we need to be sure we're willing to pay the price.

For sure, there will be opposition. There is always a chance we are wrong. Those with opposing views may feel as strongly as we do and won't be swayed from their opinions.

So, we need to let it go and pray that God will reveal the truth to both of us.

"The Lord's searchlight penetrates the human spirit exposing every hidden motive." (Proverbs 20:22)

This post comes from my making a comment on a proposed amendment in Oklahoma allowing someone freedom to refuse service to gays. It opened up a *can of worms*!

Strong words were exchanged, (not by me, but by those replying to my comment.)

In the end, no one's mind was changed, but it caused me to see why I believe what I do. God will have to deal with me further if I am to change my opinion.

I'm open to His guidance.

March 21

For nine years, I tried to *fix* my husband. But he came to Christ when God *fixed me*! I was a Christian, but I didn't know how to live like one. I was that crabby, complaining wife that Proverbs speaks of. (See Proverbs 21:19).

Because I was saved as a child, and never attended church again, I remained a baby Christian. (I never grew closer to the Lord), until about age 30.

"Fire insurance" may get you into heaven, but it, alone, doesn't get you the *abundant life*, spoken of in John 10:10: **"The thief cometh not but to steal, and to kill, and to destroy; I am come that they might have life, and that they might have it more abundantly."** The secret of joy is in obedience.

Second Corinthians 5:17 says, **"Therefore, if any man be in Christ, he is a new creation; old things are passed away; behold, all things are become new."** (Maybe not *instantly*).

Many want Jesus to be their Savior, but not their Lord. This attitude robs them of the abundant life meant for them. The ones *straddling the fence* can't enjoy full fellowship with the Lord, but, at the same time, they can't fully enjoy their sins without feeling guilty.

"For whom the Lord loveth, he chasteneth. . ." (Hebrews 12:6)

March 22

Let us walk in the truth that we know and seek to know God more each day. He will lead us into more truth. There are some things we simply can't do with a clear conscience, no matter if everyone else thinks it's okay. If the Holy Spirit won't let us do it, it's wrong for us.

"Or don't you know that your body is the temple of the Holy Spirit, who lives in you and was given to you by God? You do not belong to yourself, for God bought you with a price. So you must honor God with your body." (First Corinthians 6:19)

When we accepted Christ, He redeemed us from the penalty of sin, (and has given us power over it.) We were condemned to death but Jesus paid our debt to set us free. He paid the price to buy us out of slavery to sin, (and death). We belong to Him, heart, soul, and body.

We will never find contentment until we totally surrender our all to Him. He wants us to obey Him for our own good. (As well as for His.)

As He has planned good for us, let us work with Him in order to realize the benefits. Let the *Son* shine in!

March 23

The cure for fatigue is rest. The cure for illness is medicine, (and rest). The cure for depression is focusing on the Lord and His goodness, (your blessings). He will guide you out of this maze.

Most of the time, we can find relief when we get *out of ourselves* and get involved in helping to make someone else's life better. It may be just listening to their problems and realizing we're not alone in our problems. We don't have to *stay* in our trouble.

As Forrest Gump said, *"Life is like a box of chocolates. You never know what you're going to get."*

Our God has equipped us to get through any situation. Some of our *chocolates* have licorice in them. They leave a bad taste in our mouths. We don't *have* to have a steady diet of licorice. There are other things out there.

We should have a balance in life. Most of the time, we balance work, rest, and enjoyment. We shouldn't spend too much time with only one of these needs.

For sure, these times are interrupted by sickness, difficulties, even catastrophes. But we can remember that God is always with us. He is cheering us on!

"Praise the Lord, I tell myself, and never forget all the good things he does for me. He forgives all my sins and heals all my diseases. He ransoms me from death and surrounds me with love and tender mercies." (Psalm 103:2-4)

March 24

You can't get fired from the Kingdom of God, but you can get *benched* for life! When Jesus saved us from the kingdom of darkness, He translated us into His Kingdom. (See Colossians 1:13).

He became our Lord, (*Boss*). He doubly owns us - first, He created us, then He bought us back from Satan when he lured us away from Him.

We are to honor Him as Lord and Savior. But He is also our *best Friend*! He designed a beautiful life for us and is always there to help us when we mess it up.

He gently wakes me in the morning and says, "Go get your coffee and let's sit and chat awhile. Reflect on all my blessings, remember my promises, then, tell me about your concerns before you get into your day."

It's sad that when I was younger, I didn't take time to enjoy these wonderful moments. I can talk to Jesus about anything. He wants to hear it and He can do something about what concerns me. He never scolds me for getting myself into a bind. He just gives me guidance, love, protection; really all I need, every day!

Even though He's invisible now, He's so very real! And soon I'll be able to see Him face to face!

March 25

When we were children, we knew we were accountable to our parents and teachers. Now that we're grown, who do we feel accountable to? Our bosses, for sure; maybe our spouses; maybe not.

We are accountable to God through our own conscience. But we can *sear* our conscience so that it no longer bothers us. This can put us in a dangerous position. **"It is a fearful thing to fall into the hands of the Living God."** (Hebrews 10:31)

When we work hard and do what's right, we think we *deserve* God's Blessings. But we can never put God in the position of *owing us* anything.

We don't want God's justice, because what we *really* deserve is hell. **"The wages of sin is death. . ."** (Romans 6:23a)

We want God's grace and mercy - **". . . but the gift of God is eternal life through Jesus Christ, our Lord."** (Romans 6:23b). His grace gives us better than we deserve and His mercy keeps us from the wrath we really *do deserve*.

We like to compare ourselves to the foolish ones so we look pretty good. But when we are compared to Jesus, we see how short we fall! (Thank God for His forgiveness!)

Just as we don't expect an infant to walk and talk, God doesn't expect us to act like Jesus. But He expects us to *grow* more like Him with each opportunity we experience.

"Dear brothers and sisters, whenever trouble comes your way, let it be an opportunity for joy. For when your faith is tested, your endurance has a chance to grow. So let it grow, for when your endurance is fully developed, you will be strong in character and ready for anything." (James 1:2-4)

March 26

Bad things happen, but not without the knowledge of God. If He allows it, we are assured that He will use it for good, (See Romans 8:28), even though we may not understand. (See Proverbs 3:5).

The words of an old hymn comfort us, "We'll understand it better by and by." Because we don't understand, we worry and fret.

I'm beginning to understand that I have a Wise, Loving, and Powerful *Friend* that walks every step with me through life. He will provide everything I really need and will protect me so that I come through all sorts of troubles.

I also know that one day, one of these troubles will take me out and I'll die. But I don't have to fear - it's my door to heaven!

God wants me to give Him everything but my responsibilities. For instance, I don't ask Him to babysit an infant while I run to the grocery store!

If you have a job interview, you prepare the best you can. Then, calmly trust that, if this is right for you, God will open the door; if not, He will close it. Don't be so discouraged. Just keep seeking God's will.

"Don't worry about anything; instead, pray about everything. Tell God what you need, and thank him for all he has done. If you do this, you will experience God's peace, which is far more wonderful than the human mind can understand. His peace will guard your hearts and minds as you live in Christ Jesus." (Philippians 4:6-7)

This is beginning to taste a lot more like heaven than anything I have tasted before. With God on my side, I can't fail!

March 27

It's not what we *say we believe*, but how we *react to situations* that tells what's actually in our heart. And when someone praises us, do we grab the glory, or pass it on to God?

None of us have the ability to grasp all of God's truths; the reasons behind our trials. He is constantly revealing truths, but few of them *hit home* with us.

Some people can see His message in simple events, but struggle when confronted with monumental happenings. Others can only see God in these times, but don't *get the message* in simple things.

I guess it's a lot like golf. Some are blessed to be able to hit their drives straight and long, but have trouble with their chip shots or putts. And the ones who can putt well have trouble with the long shots. (It doesn't seem fair that a 2" putt counts the same as a 300 yd. drive!)

While golf is an enjoyable pastime, we can learn a lot about ourselves as we play. How do we react when our shot goes in the water or behind a tree? Can we make ourselves do what we *know* to do? How do we treat our fellow golfers? Are we completely honest when no one saw it? Are we able to overcome a double bogey? Does a *'hole-in-one'* go to our head?

Today's Proverb is found in Chapter 27, verse 19, **"As a face is reflected in water, so the heart reflects the person."**

I see me much differently than others see me and I'm quite sure God sees me differently, also.

March 28

Our earth is awake now from its long winter's nap. It's still a bit groggy, but we see a tint of green in the trees and the redbuds are beginning to bloom! The crocus and daffodils have come and gone.

As God wakes up His earth, we have a tendency to go to sleep, spiritually. We get too busy for God. There's the mowing and trimming; the planting; and, (for sure), the enjoyment of basking in the sun! We'll make time for the games and cook-outs with the family.

We don't have to just sit inside with the Bible in our hands. God wants to go outside with us; to work and play with us. He will bring people our way who need a positive witness. We will get greater joy in blessing them than we ever could in just serving ourselves.

"Dear brothers and sisters, what's the use of saying you have faith if you don't prove it by your actions? That kind of faith can't save anyone." (James 2:14)

It's going to be a beautiful day! Let's invite God to help us use it up!

March 29

Real beauty comes from within. It grows as we come closer to God. Physical beauty fades with age.

I remember promising to love my husband, even when he grew fat and bald, and he promised to love me when I became fat and gray! You have to look below the surface for that kind of love!

It's easier to look past the physical appearance than to overlook selfish or foolish attitudes.

When Proverbs addresses the contentious wife, (21:9), which makes living with her almost unbearable, it doesn't mention whether she is physically beautiful.

We adorn ourselves to enhance our appearance, which is good. But we should spend more time cultivating our character, (inner beauty), whether we are male or female.

"Don't be concerned about outward beauty that depends on fancy hairstyles, expensive jewelry, or beautiful clothes. You should be known for the beauty that comes from within, the unfading beauty of a gentle and quiet spirit, which is so precious to God." (First Peter 3:3-4)

I believe you can have both or be completely void of either!

March 30

You see God working in your life and are thankful that He is in control... then, suddenly, you're confronted with a disappointment! One of the things you've been praising God for has been taken away!

There's a tendency to be mad at God, as all that's in you cries, "No!" But there's nothing you can do about it; you have to accept it and go on.

It's like you're riding a bus, thinking you're going to a certain place, when the driver takes an unexpected turn. He's taking you in a different direction!

Because it doesn't match your expectations, it seems wrong. Then, you realize the driver is God! You're not the driver, only a passenger, so you settle down and trust the driver.

Since God is Love, (See 1 John 4:8), and is all-wise, we can relax as He takes us where He wants.

So, we adjust our attitude of disappointment, pray for His new provision, and go forward.

"Oh, what a wonderful God we have! How great are his riches and wisdom and knowledge! How impossible it is for us to understand his decisions and his methods! For who can know what the Lord is thinking? Who knows enough to be his counselor?" (Romans 11:33-34)

March 31

Satan puts *honey* on his traps to lure us into them. God doesn't set traps for us, but uses the troubles we experience to give us a hunger for a better way of life. Our hearts naturally cry out for our Maker.

Then Satan shows up with something *more attractive* to our sinful nature. He continually seeks our attention. God speaks in a quiet, gentle voice deep inside us, telling us what is right.

When Adam and Eve ate the fruit of the Tree of Knowledge of Good and Evil, they were given a conscience to tell them right from wrong.

We know if something is wrong, but we want a taste of that *honey*! When we've finally had enough of Satan's lies and abuse, and we've accepted the gift of grace that God offers through the death of His dear Son, He begins a good work in us.

"Being confident of this very thing, that he who hath begun a good work in you will perform it until the day of Jesus Christ." (Philippians 1:6)

God empowers us to overcome the enemy. **"Ye are of God, little children, and have overcome them, because greater is he that is in you than he that is in the world."** (First John 4:4)

God works in us daily to help us grow more like Christ. **"For it is God who worketh in you both to will and to do of his good pleasure."** (Philippians 2:13)

(He gives us the desire *and power* to honor Him.)

But, for sure, Satan will never give up on us until the day of Jesus Christ. (When God calls us home.)

APRIL

April 1

This is the third time I've started over. I found Mary's words getting mixed in with God's.

I've been confused about what Jesus was saying in Matthew 5:39, **"But I say, don't resist an evil person! If you are slapped on the right cheek, turn the other, too."**

I know He doesn't want us to get beaten up by some evil person. It stands to reason then, that Jesus wants us to see that because someone gave in to Satan's temptation to cause us harm, we are not to give in to the temptation to hit back. Satan is behind the whole thing! He is pitting us against each other.

Ephesians 6:12 tells us that we aren't really fighting against evil people, (flesh and blood), but against Satan, himself.

Jesus knows we are no match against Satan, who uses disagreements as tools to tempt us to sin by taking matters into our own hands. But God is certainly a match for Satan! (See 1 John 4:4).

Jesus' answer is, **"So, humble yourselves before God. Resist the devil and he will flee from you."** (James 4:7)

God is telling us to turn the battle over to Him. When we humble ourselves before God, we are yielding our rights to God, not to the evil person.

"Dear friends, never avenge yourselves. Leave that to God. For it is written, 'I will take vengeance; I will repay those who deserve it', says the Lord." (Romans 12:19)

April 2

It's politically incorrect in America today to be a Christian and to live according to God's Word!

When Peter was commanded not to teach in Jesus' name, he responded with, **"We ought to obey God, rather than men."** (Acts 5:29)

I'm sorry, but God teaches us in Romans 1:24-27, that homosexuality is a sin! I don't hate the sinner, but the sin, because God hates it. I am guilty of sinning, also, against God.

There is a list of sins there in Romans 1:29-32. I found myself in that list.

We like to classify sins, but James 2:10 says, **"For whosoever shall keep the whole law and yet offend in one point, he is guilty of all."**

I am not proud of my sins, seeking to get laws passed so that people can't judge me for my behavior. God is my Judge and He reprimands me so that I can live a peaceful life.

If I were dragged into His court because I am guilty of sin, I would be declared, "Not guilty!", because my debt has been paid by the blood Jesus shed for me. This in no way excuses my sinful behavior. I am instructed, like the woman taken in adultery in John 8:11, **"Go and sin no more."**

April 3

Good Friday! "This is the day that the Lord hath made. We will rejoice and be glad in it." We celebrate the fact that Jesus willingly suffered so much and died for us.

If you've seen *"The Passion"*, you saw the physical agony He endured, but it wasn't all physical pain! He was carrying the sins of the whole world.

When we are dealing with the consequence of just one of our many sins, we experience guilt, depression, regret, etc. It pulls us down emotionally.

So, we can't even imagine the emotional pain Jesus was experiencing, as well. Especially when He cried out, **"My God, My God, Why have you forsaken me?"** (Matthew 27:46)

Thank God, He was willing to pay my debt! It blows my mind. **"But God commendeth his love toward us in that while we were yet sinners, Christ died for us."** (Romans 5:8)

April 4

When Jesus had been severely beaten, and mocked, they hung Him on the cross. While hanging there, in agony, He prayed, **"Father, forgive them; for they know not what they do."** (Luke 23:34)

We can't grasp His Loving Spirit! We have His Spirit living in us, but it is mingled with our selfish human spirit. Too many times, we take sides with our human nature especially when we feel we are being mistreated! We don't want to wait on God to deal with them. We want to make them pay! (And now!)

Deep in our spirit, we want to be right with God; to please Him. We certainly need His help with this. We should check out our hearts daily for hidden feelings that aren't pleasing to God.

April 5

Christ is risen! He is risen, indeed!

As we take our showers to rid our bodies of the dirt that has collected outwardly, let us also cleanse our hearts of the wrong attitudes that may have collected there. Let's go off to church, clean inside and outside to celebrate this miraculous event!

The power that raised Jesus from the dead is also there to help us overcome defeat of any sort as we sincerely pray, **"Not my will, but thine be done."**, as Jesus did. (Luke 22:42)

"Therefore, if any man be in Christ, he is a new creation; old things are passed away; behold, all things are become new." (Second Corinthians 5:17)

"For he hath made him, who knew no sin, to be sin for us, that we might be made the righteousness of God in him." (Second Corinthians 5:21) (He *traded* us His righteousness for our *filthy rags*.) (See Isaiah 64:6).

April 6

Easter is the *seed of hope* that Jesus plants in our hearts. As we struggle through this life, we long to see what the seed will become when it sprouts. **"And what you put in the ground is not the plant that will grow, but only a dry little seed of wheat or whatever it is you are planting."** (First Corinthians 15:37)

When a gardener plants an okra seed, it sprouts a green plant that looks nothing like the seed he planted. As the plant matures, it produces fruit that has many seeds in it.

That's amazing and would be unbelievable were it not for the fact that we see it often.

The disciples' hopes died when Jesus' body was buried. But when He was resurrected, their hope was renewed!

Things that seem unbelievable become evidence that Jesus gives hope when there seems to be no way.

When our human minds say, "No way", this Spiritual truth says, "*Way!*"

Jesus said in John 14:6, **"I am the way, the truth, and the life; no man cometh to the Father, but by me."**

We have many questions; He has the answers. He is the Answer!

April 7

Proverbs 7 warns about falling into the trap of the immoral woman. (For us females, it can warn us about *becoming* her). She is seductive and flattering - the perfect bait! And once you give in to her, you detest yourself, thinking you are worthless, not worthy of God's blessings. So you continue on down the path of destruction! You have no self-respect.

She isn't the only bait Satan uses to ensnare us. Then he accuses us before God. (See Revelation 12:10) He knows the flesh is weak. (We want all his goodies.)

"Watch and pray that ye enter not into temptation; the spirit indeed is willing, but the flesh is weak." (Matthew 26:41)

The bait Satan uses to lure one person is not a temptation for someone else. We all have our weaknesses. **"For all sinned and come short of the glory of God."** (Romans 3:23)

We can't let our past sins condemn us. They have been paid for and can be used as a testimony of how Jesus helped us overcome them. **"But I have prayed for thee; that thy faith fail not, and when thou are converted, strengthen thy brethren."** (Luke 22:32)

April 8

Children love to run, frolic, and play. This is their enjoyment. They have energy for it!

As children, we had a different focus. Play was good; work was awful! We were past our teenage years before we learned there should be a balance between work, play, and rest. Work provided the financial support for our play.

It's funny how that, as we got too tired, our play became work! And, as we matured, we found we had to work more and play less because life is expensive!

Also, because we became tired, we chose rest over play. In my seventies, I find that I have allowed my work to *become* my play. I have no energy for both! My enjoyment has changed from fulfilling my dreams to making myself available to help my loved ones meet their needs and enjoy their lives.

I am blessed to be content and have need for very little, so I have truly learned, as Jesus said, **"It is more blessed to give than to receive."** (Acts 20:35b)

I also love to share what Christ is teaching me. As long as I have strength, I will give it to love.

April 9

We can't keep from taking things for granted. We thank God for our health, our family, their health; all the many blessings He sends our way, and expect everything to go as usual. This is the way we have to function. Otherwise, we would be full of worry and needless concern.

When we trust our Father, we can live in peace. And if, (when), something happens to change our situation, He's there to help. We make our plans as usual, but God may see fit to change things around for us. **"We can make our plans, but God determines our steps."** (Proverbs 16:9)

God sees our needs, which may be different from what we see. **"Now we see things imperfectly as in a poor mirror, but then we will see everything with perfect clarity. All that I know now is partial and incomplete, but then I will know everything completely, just as God knows me now."** (First Corinthians 13:12)

I'm thinking of an infant who hasn't yet developed the skill to hold onto his toy or pacifier. He continually drops them and is helpless to get them back again.

We don't see ourselves as helpless, but in many ways, we are.

We need our Father to encourage us, to pick us back up again, and help us know which way to turn.

How I thank Him for His faithfulness!

April 10

Death to the caterpillar gives way to the life of the butterfly! The grave is our *cocoon*. Our life on earth is likened to the life of a caterpillar. We have limited vision because we are *crawling around* down here. We struggle through things here that will shape our future. These difficult things build inner strength and beauty for our future life. **"Dear brothers and sisters, whenever trouble comes your way, let it be an opportunity for joy. For when your faith is tested, your endurance has a chance to grow."** (James 1:2-3)

There's a reason for everything we endure. **"For I know the plans I have for you, says the Lord. They are plans for good and not for disaster, to give you a future and a hope."** (Jeremiah 29:11)

We are to carry on, waiting for the surprise God has in store for us **"No eye has seen, no ear has heard, and no mind has imagined what God has prepared for those who love him."** (First Corinthians 2:9)

April 11

Years ago, my husband and I got into a business of selling home products. We listened to motivational speakers at meetings quite often. I don't remember much about any of them, but this one stuck with me. I guess it's because it shocked me and I didn't know whether to believe it.

He said, "You're as rich as you want to be."

I thought, "No way!"

Then, as I pondered on that thought, I realized that I *could* get more if I was willing to sacrifice my time or integrity for gain. So I understood the statement could be pretty much true.

It comes to choices. Our choices determine our attitude and lifestyle. Life throws some pretty tough stuff at us. How we choose to respond determines the effect it has on us.

When Paul and Silas were thrown into prison for sharing Christ's message, they could have pitied themselves or become violent. Instead, they chose to sing praises to God. (And the prisoners heard them.) (See Acts 16:25).

Our choices affect others, as well. We determine if we will have integrity and do what is right, no matter the situation, or if we will take shortcuts or become bitter.

Self demands to be served. But in Joshua 24:15, he says, **". . . Choose you this day whom you will serve . . . but as for me and my house, we will serve the Lord."**

April 12

Our Lord, who created the Universe, is a supernatural being. He can do anything and loves us with much more than a mother's love. He knows our faults and loves us anyway. He sees the needs we see, but He also sees those we don't.

Why don't we have a closer relationship with Him? He isn't *bothered* when we call on Him. He delights in answering our prayers when they are according to His plan for us. (Perfect love).

Because we don't have perfect wisdom, we don't know if what we are asking is in His will for us. But He wants us to ask anyway, and wait for His answer.

If it is "No", or "Not yet", we can still be assured of His love and power to answer. He is like a loving mother, waiting for a call from her child. While waiting for the call, she hopes that he doesn't have too great a need. But she is willing to do all she can to help.

God already knows our need and He has the answer!

"Now unto him that is able to do exceedingly abundantly above all that we ask or think, according to the power that worketh in us." (Ephesians 3:20)

April 13

As a child, I remember finding some baby rabbits. We took them in the house to care for them. They all did fine except this one that was sick and wouldn't eat. I got a spoon of milk and tried to force it to eat, but the milk just ran out of his mouth.

I'm afraid there are those in this sin-sick world just like that poor little rabbit. They continually reject the gospel. We can't even force-feed them. We feel completely helpless as we watch them make choices that lead them in the wrong direction.

Prayer is our only tool. But it is a *mighty* tool! When we turn our loved ones over to God, that doesn't mean we stop caring. We just stop worrying.

The devil tells us that we don't love them since we no longer worry. We continue to pray, but not as fervently. We trust them to our Great Physician. He knows exactly what they need and how to handle them. He's the only One who can help.

He can send them a dream in the night that speaks truth to them, though they have no physical witness. He can raise up a close friend to gradually lead them in the right direction. He can give them a hunger strong enough to cause them to begin searching on their own.

"Bless the Lord, O my soul, and forget not all his benefits, who forgiveth all thine iniquities, who healeth all thy diseases." (Psalm 103:2-3)

April 14

God's guidance is sure. He tells us the right direction, but we don't always follow His instructions. **"And thine ear shall hear a word behind you saying, this is the way, walk ye in it, when ye turn to the right hand, and when ye turn to the left."** (Isaiah 30:21)

Then Satan comes along to cause doubt and confusion. If it is our heart's desire to bring honor to God, we can be certain He is leading us. His desire is to bring order and truth into His world.

There are times we can clearly *hear* His voice. But we must test the spirits to make sure if they are from God. (See 1 John 4:1).

Also, Proverbs 14:12 says, **"There is a way which seemeth right unto a man, but the end thereof are the ways of death."**

None of us have perfect wisdom, but if we sincerely seek God's direction, He will guide us.

"If any of you lack wisdom, let him ask of God, who giveth to all men liberally and upbraideh not, and it shall be given him." (James 1:5)

God wants to guide us in the small, temporary things, as well as the large, eternal things. His way brings peace.

April 15

I've been writing some pretty good words and have been fighting against a haughty spirit. The Lord helped me out on this yesterday!

Sometime last week, a part on our refrigerator sprung a leak and water had seeped under the carpet adjoining the kitchen tile. I had to cut the carpet back to remove the wet particle board so I could replace it with plywood. (It's a good thing the carpet is more than 20 years old and needs to be replaced, anyway!)

Needless to say, I was exhausted and my sinful nature made an appearance as I spoke harsh words to my husband, waiting impatiently for him to help me. (He was already helping me.) I just got ugly!

Our Proverb for today begins by scolding me. **"A soft answer turns away wrath, but grievous words stir up anger."** (Proverbs 15:1)

It's a good thing my husband is patient with me and can bite his tongue when I spew out angry words! Else, we would have had a *knock-down, drag out* fight.

God showed me that I'm a long way from what He wants me to be. I thank the Lord for His grace and forgiveness! (And I also thank my husband for his patience.)

April 16

If you believe in love, you believe in God. For God is love. **"And we have known and believed the love that God hath to us. God is love and he that dwelleth in love dwelleth in God, and God in him."** (First John 4:16)

When love sees a need, it provides. God sees many needs in my life. I focus on the need to find the right carpet, tile, and installation to complete the repairs I spoke of yesterday.

God is still focused on the need to build patience in my soul. He is seeking to meet all my needs.

Paul said in Philippians 4:19, **"And this same God who takes care of me will supply all your needs from his glorious riches, which have been given to us in Christ Jesus."**

I will readily accept His provision of carpet, tile, and installation at the right price, but how open will I be to accept what it takes to build patience in me?

I want to be patient. But I have developed a life-long habit to *explode on contact*!

The answer to this need will not be instantaneous! It takes a lot of work to undo habits that come so easily. They are like dust and cobwebs that come automatically, but don't disappear automatically.

April 17

Like me, I'm sure at times, you've set a goal and worked hard to achieve it. You've been successful and kept your eye on the task at hand.

Then, from nowhere, the enemy slams you with a discouraging thought. You buy into it and are ready to give up.

Then, someone comes along with a word of encouragement! The power of discouragement is devastating, but the power of encouragement can defeat it.

The encouragement can come from someone sent by God, or He can speak encouragement directly to you.

If you're waiting for *outside* encouragement, and are overcome by depression, help is just a prayer away!

"Then they cried unto the Lord in their trouble, and he saved them out of their distresses. He brought them out of darkness and the shadow of death, and broke their bands in sunder." (Psalm 107:13-14)

I realize these verses spoke to the need of the rebellious, but we don't have to be rebellious to hear (and listen to) the enemy's voice. We can be deceived for lack of wisdom.

"Oh, that men would praise the Lord for his goodness, and for his wonderful works to the children of men! For he satisfieth the longing soul and filleth the hungry soul with goodness." (Psalm 107:8-9)

April 18

God has given us another great day. Some of us will relax and bask in God's love. Some will be so busy they feel they have no time to even think about God. Others will be in the midst of a fierce spiritual battle.

If we are one of those who are basking, let us rejoice, but not forget to lift in prayer those who are in need of God's special touch today. We will need *their* prayers one day.

Physical health is always a need, but our Proverb for today says, **"The human spirit can endure a sick body, but who can bear it if the spirit is crushed?"** (Proverbs 18:14)

I've had a few problems this week, but my spirit isn't crushed! Only God can heal a broken spirit. It shatters your faith!

"The name of the Lord is a strong tower; the righteous runneth into it and are safe." (Proverbs 18:10)

April 19

I read in today's Proverb, (19:17), **"If you help the poor, you are lending to the Lord, and he will repay you."**

A need came to me this week that I wasn't physically able to handle. So, I called my brother. He isn't physically able to do much more than I can, but he knows people from his profession that he can call on.

The problem wasn't his (or even mine), but his heart is in the right place.

He took the time to get help to see if they could do something for this person.

This says a lot to me about his character. He certainly isn't perfect, as none of us are, but compassion is always a need in our world.

The realization that someone could be *playing you like a drum,* is something that keeps us from acting with compassion. There are those who are better able to help *us*, yet they show themselves as *the needy*.

As God gives us compassion, He will also give us discernment so we can use our time, energy, and money wisely to help those who are truly in need.

". . . when you did it to one of the least of these my brothers and sisters, you were doing it to me!" (Matthew 25:40)

April 20

I have two or three pair of comfortable work pants that have stains from sealing the drive-way, painting, and even from bleach. If you saw me in them, you would think, "Mary, why don't you wash those pants or maybe throw them away?"

After they are washed, they look pretty much the same. But, even if I replaced them, the new ones would look pretty much the same in no time.

Life leaves stains and scars. Sin's stains can be washed away by sincere confession. **"But if we confess our sins to him, he is faithful and just to forgive us and to cleanse us from every wrong."** (First John 1:9)

Emotional scars are not washed away. But God brings gradual healing of the wounds that caused these scars. We continue to *wear* them. If they were visible, we would all look pretty much like my pants! The scars remain to remind us of all that God has brought us through!

"Dear brothers and sisters, whenever trouble comes your way, let it be an opportunity for joy. For when your faith is tested, your endurance has a chance to grow." (James 1:2-3)

April 21

This time of the year, we are careful to be aware of the weather. We may get aggravated if our favorite T.V. program is interrupted, but we're glad if it's a threat we need to be aware of.

It's up to us, once we're warned, what we do about it. It could be disastrous to us and our whole family!

But, at the same time, we see and hear what is happening to Christians around the globe. We have heard that an electromagnetic pulse could be sent to destroy our electrical grid at any given moment and send us back to the 1800's, technologically.

We see sin eating away like a cancer destroying our freedoms and we continue to *watch our favorite show*!

Are we just unconcerned? Or, do we feel helpless to do anything about it? The greatest power we have is the power of prayer!

"If my people, who are called by my name shall humble themselves and pray, and seek my face, and turn from their wicked (programs, oh, excuse me, I meant), **ways, then I will hear from heaven and forgive their sin, and heal their land."** (Second Chronicles 7:14)

Ho, hum . . . Now, turn the show back on.

April 22

The Name of the Lord; this is our *title - Christian*. We belong to Him.

He cares constantly and faithfully for all His world, but we are special to Him. His power goes with us where we go because He is in us, (and we're in Him).

When we accepted His gift of Salvation, He put His Name on us. (His mark of ownership). His Name is our shelter. When we walk (act) in His Name, we have the assurance of His Shield.

I keep seeing a picture of a turtle in my mind. We stick our heads out and do things. That's life. Some of the things we do are for Him, but most of the things are for us.

That's okay as long as we're available and willing to obey when He calls.

The shell, (Name of the Lord, *Christian*) is our Strong Tower. **"The Name of the Lord is a strong tower; the righteous runneth into it and is safe."** (Proverbs 18:10). It protects us from what's going on around us, (Satan's activity).

The things we do in Jesus' Name honor Him. This is activity of the Holy Spirit, directing us; using us.

"This I say then, Walk in the Spirit, and ye shall not fulfill the lust of the flesh. For the flesh lusteth against the Spirit, and the Spirit against the flesh; and these are contrary the one to the other, so that ye cannot do the things that ye would." (Galatians 5:16-17)

April 23

As a picture is worth a thousand words, an action is worth so much more. Whether we like it or not, what we do tells who we really are.

Our children heard our words often, loud and clear, but they learned how to live by watching our lives. There were times they disagreed with our actions (and rightly so), and vowed never to do that.

So, we taught them good and bad. Today, we have to pray they overcome the bad.

"Even a child is known by his doings, whether his work be pure and whether it be right." (Proverbs 20:11)

We're *writing a book*, (our biography), not with our words only, but with our actions. Just like with our words, there are times we wish we could take back our actions. They are being recorded.

Once captured, they remain. We can't undo them, even though we may be forgiven. Our best effort to undo them is to overcome them with a change of heart, which can only come from God.

"People who cover their sins will not prosper. But if they confess and forsake them, they will receive mercy. Blessed are those who have a tender conscience, but the stubborn are headed for serious trouble." (Proverbs 28:13-14)

April 24

Just as Eve (spiritually) died instantly when she disobeyed God in the garden, we died instantly to the *law of sin and death* with Jesus.

"For the wages of sin is death, but the gift of God is eternal life through Jesus Christ, our Lord." (Romans 6:23)

We are new creatures, (alive spiritually), free from sin's penalty. **"Therefore, if any man be in Christ, he is a new creature; old things are passed away; behold, all things are become new."** (Second Corinthians 5:17) We were spiritually dead, (because of Eve's sin), but when Jesus died, we died with Him, to spiritual death. (We became alive, spiritually.)

"For though we walk after the flesh, we do not war after the flesh, for the weapons of our warfare are not carnal, but mighty through God to the pulling down of strongholds." (Second Corinthians 10:3-4)

We see ourselves as sinful creatures, but God sees the end from the beginning. He is taking us in the direction of holiness. That's His destination for us.

"Being confident of this very thing, that he who hath begun a good work in you will perform it until the day of Jesus Christ." (Philippians 1:6)

April 25

I see my failures every day. Some are simply because I'm selfish and some are because I can only be in one place at a time. When I am *doing this*, I leave *that* undone.

Jesus understands and calls me "Righteous." Not because of anything I do or have done, but because He gave me His righteousness when He was dying for me. **"For God made Christ, who never sinned, to be the offering for our sin, so that we could be made right with God through Christ."** (Second Corinthians 5:21)

All I had to do was accept the wonderful gift of salvation He offers. He sees my thoughts and the intentions of my heart. This sometimes makes me shudder. But He loves me, no matter what!

It's like I was a filthy stray dog in need of a home and lots of care. He adopted me into His family. He cleaned me up by His blood and made me pure.

He knows I'll *poop in the floor* often until I'm completely *house broken*. My *poop* hurts Him, (and me, because He has to discipline me). But His love remains!

"But all who believed him and accepted him, he gave the right to become the children of God." (John 1:12)

The more I realize His love for me, the more I love Him and want to please Him instead of myself.

I'm learning to *bark at the door*, instead of making messes for Him to clean up. When I do, I'm ashamed and run to Him for forgiveness. He's always there!

April 26

I didn't ask for this work that, for the moment (days) drives me. I have a deadline, (that I set). That's where I went wrong.

The carpet was ruined, though it needed to be replaced anyway. So, this was my opportunity to also replace the kitchen tile to match new carpet.

The place where we purchased the carpet will install it, but they don't do tile. So this task fell to me.

As today is Sunday, no work will be done on it. Tomorrow I have a C.T. that will take some time and the carpet will be laid about mid-morning on Tuesday.

I'm only about half finished with my tile work. I may have to finish only the part that connects to the carpet and leave the rest for another day. It will work out. It always does. But, I'm completely absorbed!

My devotion for this morning calls for rest. That's what today is for. I will rest, not only my body, but my spirit, also.

I will enjoy worship without allowing my mind to focus on my dilemma.

As Jesus is my *"Roommate"*, He knows my problem and will help me get through this.

"Thou wilt keep him in perfect peace, whose mind is stayed on thee, because he trusteth in thee." *(Isaiah 26:3)*

April 27

I am not the boss. But He's my *Friend*. When I have a need, I can trust He will come to my rescue.

But I am not to be presumptuous. I am to live wisely and not get myself into a bind, then expect that He will work things out the way I want.

He is the potter; I am the clay. His purpose for me is good.

My purpose is to bring honor and glory to Him, to allow Him to work according to His plan.

"**. . . All things were created by him and for him.**" (Colossians 1:16b)

I trust His *design* for my life. And I'm thankful that He continues His work daily. **"Being confident of this very thing, that he who hath begun a good work in you will perform it until the day of Jesus Christ."** (Philippians 1:6)

April 28

Well, I did it again! I lost my temper and showed my rear! I would like to blame physical fatigue, but it's just plain ole sin!

I post some pretty profound thoughts, but you can't put your faith in me. You can only trust the Lord, who gives me the words.

We're not there yet; still traveling toward our eternal home.

The ones who witnessed my anger were dismayed, but not devastated, by my actions. They are my family: they know me, yet love me anyway. That doesn't excuse my behavior. I owe them an apology.

What I am trying to say is that we can ruin our testimony for the Lord with one reckless moment. The mighty lion is lurking near, ready to pounce! **"Be sober, be vigilant, because your adversary, the devil, like a roaring lion, walketh about, seeking whom he may devour."** (First Peter 5:8)

April 29

When we pray, we're acknowledging God's power over us. Prayer involves us in His power and releases it as He desires. It gives God permission to work in our lives. He knows our need, but He's a *Gentleman*.

Sometimes, He's answering someone else's prayer on our behalf. I know Mom and both her parents prayed for us so often. Though they are no longer with us, their prayers still are!

When we see God answer our prayers, we feel special and pour out praise and glory to Him, as we recognize His love and involvement in our lives.

If we're not involved with Him in that prayer, we have a tendency to declare it *luck* or *coincidence*.

"Confess your sins to each other and pray for each other so that you may be healed. The earnest prayer of a righteous person has great power and wonderful results." (James 5:16)

April 30

As we see our world winding down, we are amazed at God's patience as He allows so much evil to continue!

We may have filled our lives with foolishness up till now, but it's time to get serious! Last evening Bro. Barry challenged us to make sure we have shared God's message of salvation with all our loved ones, especially our children and grandchildren.

We make many mistakes in life, but there's one that will definitely drag us into eternal hell. We may, somehow, still be alive when Satan takes the throne, (See Revelation 13:17), and declares that no one can buy or sell except they take the mark of the beast, (his *brand* of ownership).

We have to be completely sold out to Jesus or we will fall for Satan's way out of starving to death or seeing our loved ones starve!

We, ourselves, may be strong enough, because we have Christ's *brand* of ownership, but we must pray earnestly for our children and grandchildren, that they have accepted Christ and mature in Him. We don't have to fear, because our *Owner* will not allow this to happen. He will give us the strength we need, when we need it. But, what about our kids?

Prayer and our testimony, as we live a Christ-like example is our part. The rest is up to God, (and them!).

"And they overcame him by the blood of the Lamb, and by the word of their testimony; and they loved not their lives unto death." (Revelation 12:11)

Fear of death is Satan's great tool, but there's something far worse!

"O death, where is thy sting? O grave, where is thy victory?" (First Corinthians 15:55)

"For God hath not given us the spirit of fear, but of power, and of love, and of a sound mind." (Second Timothy 1:7)

MAY

May 1

How refreshing to look out and see God's handiwork as the perennials are in bloom! They were planted years ago and look better each year as they multiply.

God is so faithful to supply all our needs and also to enhance our lives with beauty. His love supplies the love we need from our family and friends. He even made us with 'built-in' heating and air-conditioning.

When we get hot, we sweat, and are cooled off by a gentle breeze. We don't like getting that hot or cold, but it's our *needs* that God supplies, not our *wants*.

I'm thinking how we complain when the weather gets cold, and in a few short weeks, we complain it's too hot!

I can just see God shaking His head, saying, "You kids are never satisfied!"

If only we could learn, like Paul, to be content. **"I know how to live on almost nothing or with everything. I have learned the secret of living in every situation, whether it is with a full stomach or empty, with plenty or little."** (Philippians 4:12)

May 2

I was at war with the squirrels that were robbing my bird feeders. I finally put chicken wire over them. It was pretty tricky getting some holes big enough for the cardinals, yet small enough that the squirrels couldn't get in.

I saw very few cardinals go in. They feared it was a trap. Even the small birds got in and out quickly. But those pesky squirrels kept trying to make the holes bigger. They succeeded!

Therefore, I took the wire off so the birds wouldn't be afraid to eat. It seems that, just as the Lord is mindful of the birds, (See Matthew 6:26), He is also mindful of the squirrels!

My plans did not succeed! **"The horses are prepared for battle, but the victory belongs to the Lord."** (Proverbs 21:31)

"A man's heart deviseth his way, but the Lord directeth his steps." (Proverbs 16:9)

(Back to the drawing board!)

May 3

The *self* in us is what sins. When things don't go our way, *self* is injured. We may seek revenge or allow pride to demand our *rights*.

As we mature in Christ, we gain more control over *self*. We become more humble and less proud; more generous and less stingy.

It takes time, practice, and wisdom to starve out *self*. The more we feed it, the more it grows, which is the opposite of what God is trying to do in our lives.

The *self* in us wants things. We give our time and money to attain them, only to find out they satisfy for just a short time.

We look for bargains that are worth a lot and cost little. Wisdom is the best bargain Christians can get.

"For the profit of wisdom is better than silver and her wages are better than gold." (Proverbs 3:14) When we spend these, they are gone. But the more we *spend* (use) wisdom, the more it is multiplied!

May 4

I work for the owner of everything. He deserves my best. He's my best Friend, my Physician, my Attorney, and my Guide. He protects me from harm and supplies all my needs.

Unlike some friends, who are sometimes busy with other things and unable to help, He is always available, dependable, and trustworthy. He has the wisdom to always know what will bring peace my way.

His love for me causes Him to work things out for my eventual good. He stretches my *spiritual muscles* so that I grow stronger when I go through difficult times. He works with me to help me accomplish all I need to do.

He comforts me when my heart is broken. He has supplied a *manual* to help me remember how much He loves me.

He's even so much more than all this to me. He paid my ransom to free me from Satan's prison of darkness under a death sentence.

How could I love anyone or anything more than Him? **"Love not the world, neither the things that are in the world. If any man love the world, the love of the Father is not in him."** (First John 2:15)

May 5

We feel secure inside our homes. The evil is *out there*. It hasn't yet seeped in full force to threaten our immediate family.

What is our correct response? Some of us are fighters. We will step outside our comfort zone to combat its onslaught. Some of us will *hunker down* in our *foxholes*, ready to pounce when it invades our home.

When we question our role, we can also ask ourselves what kind of neighbors we'd like to have. Should we not be that kind of neighbor to them?

"Do for others what you would like them to do for you. This is a summary of all that is taught in the law and prophets." (Matthew 7:12)

We are most certainly to pray, not only for our neighbors, our police officers, our military, and missionaries. The leaders of our nation are definitely in need of prayer.

If we aren't one of the fighters, let us step up as one of the prayers. **"Then if my people who are called by my name will humble themselves and pray and seek my face and turn from their wicked ways, I will hear from heaven and will forgive their sin and heal their land."** (Second Chronicles 7:14)

We have some loved ones who are completely helpless. Let us, who are capable, stand in the gap for them. And, as we pray, let us also share the gospel wherever we go, so that God's kingdom can be increased.

When one comes over to our side, (Christianity), not only is he freed from Satan's kingdom, but there is one less to *fight against* and one more to fight alongside us.

May 6

A couple weeks ago, I bought some tomato plants and transplanted them. There's a chance of storms for the next few days, so I'll cover them to protect them from high winds and hail. I'm seeing a few blooms forming that promise to become tomatoes soon, if God sees fit.

God *transplanted* me into His kingdom and watches over me with care, helping me to mature and produce fruit for Him. **"Wherefore, thou art no more a servant, but a son; and if a son, then an heir of God through Christ."** (Galatians 4:7)

That's my purpose; that I grow where I'm planted, and stand firm in His Word. **"That we henceforth be no more children, tossed to and fro, and carried about with every wind of doctrine, by the sleight of men, and cunning craftiness, by which they lie in wait to deceive."** (Ephesians 4:14)

Just as the wind and hail can damage my plants, so can my growth be stunted if I'm not firmly planted in God's Word, and committed to obey Him.

May 7

Thank God for storm shelters! A place to feel safe! When destruction is happening all around us, we can put things in perspective without hearing any preaching.

Even if, when we emerge from the storm and see we've lost everything, we can be thankful there's still hope.

It's discouraging and disappointing to have to clean up and start over. But we have the Lord, who gave it all to us and we know He will help us rebuild.

"We are pressed on every side by troubles, but we are not crushed and broken. We are perplexed, but we don't give up and quit. We are hunted down, but God never abandons us. We get knocked down, but we get up again and keep going." (Second Corinthians 4:8-9)

"No, despite all these things, overwhelming victory is ours through Christ, who loved us." (Romans 8:37)

May 8

Do we love human praise more than the praise of God? All of us love to be admired; to fit into society. We want people's praise. That's the reward we seek which drives us to dress the way we do and to do many of the things we do.

So many in our society believe that you get what you pay for. So, they look for name brands and will pay much more for them. This will impress people that you value quality. Most of the time, the best quality *is* in the name brands. But some have discovered that you may be able to get the same quality at a cheaper price or that you don't *have* to have the very best quality.

This impresses the frugal people, but not those in higher standing, (with the money). If we seek God's praise, He helps us to set our standards so that we live within our means and utilize the money wisely that He has allocated to us.

It's not *people's impressions* that should determine our standards, but God's guidance and approval.

Fear of rejection by society's elite sometimes prevents us from sharing the gospel with them.

"Many people, including some of the Jewish leaders, believed in him. But they wouldn't admit it to anyone because of their fear that the Pharisees would expel them from the synagogue. For they loved human praise more than the praise of God." (John 12:42-43)

May 9

We play games to see if we can meet the challenge and come out the winner. Some games stretch us mentally and some physically as well. Nevertheless, we voluntarily and eagerly enter into these challenges.

We go to the gym or walk miles to keep fit. But when God allows a catastrophe to come our way, we are overwhelmed and don't feel we can handle it. We try to pray it away.

Instead, we should *huddle* with our Coach to get His strategy on how to win our battle. Life is not just a game, it is war! Satan comes against us constantly. (Just turn on the news!).

God is not only our *Coach*, but He lives in us and sees our problems more clearly than we do.

He gives us strength and wisdom that we don't even know we have! **"But my God shall supply all your needs according to his riches in glory by Christ Jesus."** (Philippians 4:19)

Satan tries to overwhelm us and make us look like sissies, but, **". . . I can do everything with the help of Christ who gives me the strength I need."** (Philippians 4:13)

"But you belong to God, my dear children, you have already won your fight with these false prophets, because the Spirit who lives in you is greater than the spirit who lives in the world." (First John 4:4)

"Dear brothers and sisters, whenever trouble comes your way, let it be an opportunity for joy. For when your faith is tested, your endurance has a chance to grow." (James 1:2-3)

We don't have to go to the gym (for spiritual fitness), it comes to us.

May 10

Trust calms our hearts. This weather disturbs our peace. We worry about our safety and the safety of our family. We are concerned about losing our homes and all our belongings. They could be swept away instantly by the storm that is threatening outside our window. We are wise to take precautions; to do all we can to stay safe. But we must know that our safety is ultimately in the hands of the Lord. He gave us life and all that we have and He loves us.

"And he said, Naked came I out of my mother's womb, and naked shall I return thence. The Lord gave, and the Lord hath taken away; blessed be the name of the Lord." (Job 1:21)

We can feel safe even when the world is being torn apart around us. **"Thou will keep him in perfect peace, whose mind is stayed on thee, because he trusted in thee."** (Isaiah 26:3)

May 11

I had a wonderful Mother's Day, surrounded by all my children, my grandchildren, and some of my great-grandchildren! As usual, I received many gifts. I've never been able to fully appreciate gifts like I should. Growing up in poverty, my idea for gifts was to fill a need.

As an adult, God has seen fit to fill all my *needs*, so I've felt I have no need for gifts. I've missed the whole point of gift-giving.

It has seemed to me a waste of time and money to search for and buy something that no one needs.

I finally realized yesterday, as an old woman, that each gift was selected to express love, not necessarily to meet a need.

When I look back to see how foolish I've been, I wish I could start over as a mother with the wisdom I'm gaining daily.

God's grace has filled in what my ignorance left out while raising my children! They have become parents with more wisdom than I had at their age, and sometimes more than I have now.

I think, "How can God love me, as foolish as I am?"

Psalm 103:13-14 says, **"As a faithful father pitieth his children, so the Lord pitieth them that fear him. For he knoweth our frame; he remembereth that we are dust."**

May 12

Life is full of lessons. We've heard the expression: "You live and learn." Many times we don't try to do something for fear of failing. But God uses even our failures as learning tools.

He expects us to at least try. **"For God has not given us a spirit of fear and timidity, but of power, love, and self-discipline."** (Second Timothy 1:7)

I am amazed when I am reluctant to begin an endeavor that I've never tried to do. Satan tells me, "You can't do it."

Especially now, he tells me, "You're just an old woman, weakened by cancer. You don't have the strength and endurance you'll need. You'd better get someone else to do it."

If I feel I can afford it and can easily find someone, I turn the job over to them. But if not, it's up to me.

I pull out my *Philippians 4:13* and partner with the Lord. He speaks His encouragement to me, **"My gracious favor is all you need. My power works best in your weakness'. So now, I am glad to boast about my weakness, so that the power of Christ may work through me."** (Second Corinthians 12:9)

The job gets done!

May 13

Almost 50 years ago, I gave birth to identical twin girls. As great-grandma, I am interacting with another set of identical twins, (boys). They can be so much alike, yet so different. They each are born into the same environment, but much has happened in the womb to shape their character, though we were unaware of it.

But God has kept His eye on them from conception. **"You watched me as I was being formed in utter seclusion, as I was woven together in the dark of the womb."** (Psalm 139:15)

We see their personalities emerge as they learn to handle different situations and to interact with people.

One is patient and can wait for mommy to get his bottle ready, while the other may wail loudly!

Our heavenly Father uses mothers to love them for Him, and to teach them for Him. Though she has limits, she will do everything in her power to meet their needs. He also uses dads, but there's nothing like a mother's love!

God is not limited. He has all power to meet the needs of His children. He knows how and when to discipline us so that we can face the trials He knows are ahead for each of us.

Some of us cry loudly, waiting for Him to meet our needs. As we mature, and become more confident of His love, we learn to wait more patiently on Him.

"But if we look forward to something we don't have yet, we must wait patiently and confidently." (Romans 8:25)

May 14

As a loving parent teaches his child to color, he first gives him the crayon and shows him how to hold it without being concerned if he stays in the lines.

He patiently watches the child scribble everywhere, not expecting to see a pretty picture. It is a *wobbly beginning*. The parent has to take precautions that the crayons aren't misused and the walls become a coloring book!

As the child learns obedience, he is given greater freedom to choose his own colors and express himself in his art.

Our Father knows we will have a *wobbly beginning*. But He has a goal for each of us. Perfection is His ultimate goal - that we become like His Son. But, He is patient with us as we learn.

Sometimes, He has to take the crayons away from us and make us to *sit time out*. When we learn that He has a plan for us and we begin to obey His instructions, we are given more freedom of expression.

When we finally give Him our desires and take up His desires, He begins to see His plans for us unfold and the picture we paint tells His story.

He never turns His back on us or gets impatient when He sees us struggle. He allows us to mess up each page. But every morning, He gives us a new page, with no mistakes on it. He counts the previous *pages* as learning experiences.

"But you are to be perfect, even as your Father in heaven is perfect." (Matthew 5:48)

"He's still working on me, to make me what I ought to be."

May 15

When we become ill, we go to the doctor, who analyzes our symptoms, determines the cause, and either writes a prescription or schedules surgery.

Sometimes it just comes down to what we've been eating. **"A wise person is hungry for the truth, while the fool feeds on trash."** (Proverbs 15:14)

We can survive on junk food for a while. We love it! But, soon we yearn for *real food*.

Our world is sick. What have we been feeding on? Dirty jokes? Obscene movies? Juicy gossip?

Our great Physician has written us a prescription. But, too often, we don't get it filled. We put it aside and forget about it. Yet, we wonder why somebody doesn't *do* something.

Our *script*, (God's Word), gathers dust while we keep getting sicker.

"For the Word of God is full of living power. It is sharper than the sharpest knife, cutting deep into our innermost thoughts and desires. It exposes us for what we really are." (Hebrews 4:12)

(But, what would our *friends* think if we suddenly started living according to God's Word?) We've got a tiger by the tail!

May 16

I answered the *door* when I heard Him knock. (See Revelation 3:20) He came in to live in my heart. I didn't just clear out a *room* that I called His so I could visit Him occasionally with long formal prayers.

He shares every experience I have. (He's listening even when I'm saying things I shouldn't.)

He shares my delight when I see a beautiful expression of His creation. He reaches out His hand when I get myself into a bind where I can't go forward or backward.

He helps me make the right decision when I acknowledge His presence. **"In all thy ways, acknowledge him and he will direct your paths."** (Proverbs 3:6)

"Always be joyful. Keep on praying. No matter what happens, always be thankful, for this is God's will for you who belong to Christ Jesus." (First Thessalonians 5:16-18)

Sometimes we may think, *"This* is God's will for me??"

He's always there and He cares. If He allows it to happen, He will work it for good. (See Romans 8:28). He knows we can't understand it. (See Isaiah 55:8). That's what trust is all about.

"If you do this, you will experience God's peace, which is far more wonderful than the human mind can understand. His peace will guard your hearts and minds as you live in Christ Jesus." (Philippians 4:7)

Life is not as hard as we make it.

May 17

The serenity that comes over me when I see the awesome beauty of God's creation on a quiet, still morning brings a comforting awareness of God's presence...

That wonderful *something* that comes over me when I hear the beauty of a soft melody is God singing His love to me.

How we long for His special touch to assure us that He is with us and cares deeply for us.

"The Lord keeps watch over you as you come and go, both now and forever." (Psalm 121:8)

He is there! Look for Him.

May 18

As a child, visiting grandma, I saw her chickens pecking one of them to death! When I told Grandma about it, she said it was sick and that's the way chickens act.

I'm reminded of that when I see someone who is *sin-sick*. Instead of them being *pecked* to death, we should have compassion on them and at least pray that God would show them the error of their ways.

In Ezekiel 36:26, God said, **"A new heart also will I give you, a new spirit will I put within you, and I will take away the stony heart out of your flesh, and will give you a heart of flesh."**

As Christians, we don't immediately become compassionate like we should, but we should become more understanding as we allow God's power in us to help us overcome our faults.

When we see another Christian fail to love others as they love themselves, we have to recognize that we also fail in the same way. We are to forgive them and pray for them instead of fighting them.

"Never pay back evil for evil to anyone. Do things in such a way that everyone can see you are honorable. Do your best to live in peace with everyone, as much as possible." (Romans 12:17-18)

When gossip is being spread, do your best to share the fact that the person is *walking in darkness*, not realizing where their behavior is taking them. They need prayer, not *pecking*!

May 19

What is God's view of the tired soul who is limp with *fatigue*? When we've pushed ourselves to the brink of physical uselessness, we can't even rest for thinking of all that still needs to be done. We can't seem to muster the strength to truly praise and worship God as He deserves.

We've used God's gift of physical strength to the point where we can only *waste* the day meant to be full of blessings.

It's time to put aside all the *stuff* that's demanding our attention and just bask in God's goodness.

"But they that wait on the Lord shall renew their strength; they shall mount up with wings like eagles; they shall run and not be weary; and they shall walk and not faint." (Isaiah 40:31)

We can be revived to be useful again. When it seems like we're wasting time that can be used to accomplish much, it is essential to pace ourselves so that we can endure to the end.

God sometimes puts us in *time-out*, demanding the rest we won't give ourselves.

It's like using God's tithe for something else. This money comes to nothing. We will get a speeding ticket, the dryer will break down, or something else. We can't rob God of His part of our finances or anything that belongs to Him.

So, today, I'm voluntarily taking 'time-out' to bask in God's blessings. **"Be still and know that I am God; I will be exalted among the nations, I will be exalted in the earth."** (Psalm 46:10)

May 20

How many secrets are still hidden out there, waiting to be discovered?

In Grandma's day, it was inconceivable that you could sit in your house and see what was happening around the world. Just a few decades ago, we had to have wires for our phones and remote controls.

God knows what we're capable of, even though we don't.

"Call unto me and I will answer thee, and show thee great and mighty things, which thou knowest not." (Jeremiah 33:3)

As God knows the future, He prepares us for it. But the greatest preparation He has made for us is heaven. **"In my Father's house are many mansions; if it were not so, I would have told you. I go to prepare a place for you, and if I go and prepare a place for you, I will come again, and receive you unto myself, that where I am, there ye may be also."** (John 14:2-3)

As He is preparing a place for us, He is also preparing us for that place. **"And be not conformed to this world, but be ye transformed by the renewing of your mind, that ye may be able to prove what is that good, and acceptable, and perfect, will of God."** (Romans 12:2)

May 21

If our kids truly love us, they should love what we love. We don't have the power to give them that love, only to live in love. But, our heavenly Father has that power. He knows we have the tendency to love the world, and that loving worldly things leads to destruction.

"Love not the world, neither the things that are in the world. If any man love the world, the love of the Father is not in him." (First John 2:15)

Our Father draws us to Himself through Jesus. Jesus said, in John 6:44, **"No man can come to me except the Father, who hath sent me draw him; and I will raise him up at the last day."**

He gives us a new heart, one that loves Him and wants to please Him. **"Therefore, if any man be in Christ, he is a new creation; old things are passed away; behold, all things are become new."** (Second Corinthians 5:17)

Our new heart begins to turn away from worldly things. We look at people that live the way we did and our eyes are opened to see where it will lead.

Along with God's love comes His wisdom. Some of this comes instantly, but much comes gradually, as we walk in His direction.

"And thine ears shall hear a word behind thee, saying, 'This is the way, walk ye in it, when ye turn to the right hand and when ye turn to the left'." (Isaiah 30:21)

Obedience to God feeds the *Christian* in us and kills out the sinful desires. **"This I say, then, walk in the Spirit, and ye shall not fulfill the lust of the flesh."** (Galatians 5:16)

May 22

I am bracing myself to accept the possible ruin of my beautiful, clean carpet that I've been enjoying for about a month now.

I'm telling myself, "This is a test, this is only a test."

We're having a graduation party here tonight. It's supposed to be raining! And I just found out that, besides the 30 or so adults, there will be 10 kids . . . with red punch!

I just read in one of my devotions about a missionary who was grieving with a mother whose baby was dying. When she went to the Lord about it, He asked her why she was grieving so much more about a physical loss than about the lost souls she was sent to minister to.

Wow! My loss wouldn't be nearly as drastic as the death of a child. Much less, the devastation of a soul in hell!

Again I will post 1 John 2:15a, **"Love not the world, neither the things that are in the world. . ."**

Is there a difference in appreciating nice things and loving them? Well, anyway, my focus needs to change from me, to my purpose . . . loving people.

"The godly are like trees that bear life-giving fruit, and those who save lives are wise." (Proverbs 11:30)

It will be okay, no matter what! God is in control!

May 23

Thank you all for your concern and helpful comments. We had a wonderful time! My daughter-in-law worked tirelessly, (well, she did get exhausted!), to decorate and supply a huge variety of fruit and veggies, as well as many other delicious snacks.

We watched a great video of Jessi's life that my daughter-in-law put together for her. I know she feels very much loved!

The carpet didn't even know it survived its first party! (I will probably be the one to give it the first stain!) Another event is behind us and we look forward to many more. God is good!

"With Jesus' help, let us continually offer our sacrifice of praise to God by proclaiming the glory of his name. Don't forget to do good and to share what you have with those in need, for such sacrifices are very pleasing to God." (Hebrews 13:15-16)

May 24

There is a powerful God ruling the Universe! He knows how to get our attention! He deals with us daily to turn our hearts to Him.

He spoke to us for years through the drought. It was a slow, constant discipline, giving us every chance to see our need to seek Him with all our hearts and to put Him first.

When, corporately, we refused, He showed His power and displeasure with violent flooding. We were helpless as we saw water rising around our homes while the rain kept pouring down! We knew there was no help except that God would stop the rain!

What does God want from us? His first commandment pretty much covers it. **"Do not worship any other gods besides me."** (Exodus 20:3)

Because our hearts are empty, we seek entertainment to satisfy our need. We enjoy this time, but when it's over, we're still empty.

When we begin to obey God we find His fulfillment lasts. He gives constant opportunities to love the lost. As we help them find their way to Him, they can help others.

This multiplication plan is how God's truth can overcome evil in our world.

Our attitude will be to get busy with our obedience when the rain is pouring down, but when things calm down, we go back to life as usual. Again, we love ourselves more than God and others.

"But seek ye first the kingdom of God and his righteousness, and all these things shall be added unto you." (Matthew 6:33)

God's *kingdom* means He is *King*.

May 25

Cling to the Lord! When the rains pour down and the water rises to a dangerous level, call out to Him.

That's what I did when we had done all we could to protect our home from flooding. The forecast called for rain all night, but it had let up slightly when we went to bed.

I had calmly asked God to keep it to a sprinkle in order for the flooding to subside.

I knew He was the *only* One who could help. If He chose not to let it subside, I didn't know what would happen.

But when you trust your *Heavenly Daddy*, He will take care of you! That doesn't mean there won't be a long hard clean-up.

At our age, we don't have the energy to accomplish much, but there's no dead-line.

When things get back to normal, we'll thank God and relax, ready for what comes next.

When you stop *beating out your fire*, you look around to see that others have had it much worse than you have. Our prayers go out to them.

In 1 Corinthians 10:13, (I'm substituting the word *troubles* for the word *temptations*.) **"But remember that the *temptations* that come into your life are no different from what others experience. And God is faithful. He will keep the *temptation* from becoming so strong that you can't stand up against it. When you are tempted, he will show you a way out so that you will not give in to it."**

Oh, by the way, when we woke up, there was only signs of how high the water, that threatened, had safely risen!

May 26

When we practice allowing God to use our bodies, our time, our energy, finances, etc., as He desires, we become a *living word,* for Him.

"Let your light so shine before men that they may see your good works, and glorify your Father, who is in heaven." (Matthew 5:16)

But He also wants to use our voices so that those who are lost can see where our good works are coming from.

"So then, faith cometh by hearing, and hearing by the word of God." (Romans 10:17)

We are more uncomfortable proclaiming the way of salvation than just doing good works.

The closer we walk with God, the easier it is to *naturally* let Him use our voices. When we spend time loving people, God can turn our conversations naturally to speak for Him, (His Gospel).

We don't have to *conjure up* the words . . . just take advantage of the opportunity and let them flow!

May 27

Is it as simple as attitude?

When we *know* God, instead of just knowing about Him, we can be content with what He has given and *is giving* us.

He says He will avenge the wrongs done to us. **"Dear friends, never avenge yourselves. Leave that to God. For it is written, I will take vengeance; I will repay those who deserve it, says the Lord."** (Romans 12:19)

He says we will never understand why He allows what He does. **"My thoughts are completely different from yours', says the Lord. And my ways are far beyond anything you could imagine."** (Isaiah 55:8)

He tells us to be content with what He has given us. **"Stay away from the love of money; be satisfied with what you have. For God has said, I will never fail you. I will never forsake you."** (Hebrews 13:5)

With His help, we *can decide* in our hearts that we are going to stop complaining, take the bad with the good, and be happy regardless, because we trust His love, wisdom, and power to work in our behalf.

That doesn't mean we won't struggle in our problems and be unconcerned, but that we can trust that God will help us through it.

It will come and go, but God will still be there!

May 28

I'm sometimes confused as to how everything that happens here on earth fits into God's plans for heaven. There are some things that fit perfectly, but there are many that don't seem to have a purpose at all.

As I grow older and look back, I can see God's hand on my life as He allowed *this* and used *that* to bring me to where I am today. Those things have come into focus for me. But what He's allowing daily are still a little *blurry*.

I guess it's like looking at the under-side of a piece of embroidery. It just looks like a mess! But when you turn it over to see the right side, you can see the beautiful design!

"Now we see things imperfectly as in a poor mirror, but then we will see everything with perfectly clarity. All that I know now is partial and incomplete, but then I will know everything completely, just as God knows me now." (First Corinthians 13:12)

May 29

As I watch the twins grow and get stronger, I have the desire to help them learn.

When we put them on their tummies so they can learn to crawl, they immediately turn over on their backs again, and are as helpless as a turtle on its back!

They don't realize we're trying to help them learn. They just think we're being mean when we turn them on their tummies again and again.

I think it's pretty much the same with someone who has heard the gospel and chose to delay accepting Christ because they want to *do it their way*. They get irritated when you mention God or Jesus.

Being uncomfortable for a little while is the only way the babies will learn to crawl, and the only way a person will learn to trust Jesus instead of himself.

When he finally learns, his life is so much better, and he wonders what took him so long!

"It's like this: When I was a child, I spoke and thought and reasoned as a child does. But when I grew up, I put away childish things." (First Corinthians 13:11)

May 30

Last week's storm caused a pretty big limb to break on a tree in our yard. My husband had gotten the smaller branches off with the chainsaw, but the limb wouldn't come down. We tugged and twisted until we could see our efforts were in vain.

That's when the Holy Spirit joined our efforts by simply showing us to get a 2x4 that was nearby to put in a fork in the limb to use as a lever.

Physically, we hadn't been able to do it, but when we put our *mind* to it, we did it! Whatever you *need* to do, Satan will tell you, "You can't."

Why do we accept that? Is it because we just don't want to mess with it? Are we just *wimps*? Or do we fear failure?

I didn't want to plant a garden, but I wanted to have some okra and tomatoes. I thought, "I don't have a rototiller and I'm too old and weak to make a garden."

The Lord told me, "You can't expect a harvest if you don't plant a seed." My garden is only about 4'x8'! I planted in a spot where there was no Bermuda grass so I could dig it with a shovel. (I know Daddy is looking down and laughing!) It was too shady and wet with all the rain, so my okra never came up.

"So, then, neither is he that watereth, but God that giveth the increase." (First Corinthians 3:7)

I'll replant it once again. If God doesn't give the increase, I'll get my okra from the Farmer's Market.

What I'm saying is that our efforts don't always work, but it shouldn't be because we didn't even try.

When the children of Israel were crossing the Jordan River, they were told that when the priest's feet touched the water, the waters would part for them to cross. (See Joshua 3:13) They had to have faith to step in first.

May 31

Over and over in the Book of Numbers, a chapter begins with, **"The Lord said to Moses..."**

Each morning, as I sit with Him, He speaks to me... My ears don't hear Him, but my heart does.

He gives me encouragement and *warnings* that I feel sure He wants me to share with others, like me, who can benefit from these messages.

As I look back over them, I know they didn't come from me.

All His love is meant to go *through* us and on to others as we share what we've found.

I am grateful to be a *go between* for Him. It isn't *burdensome*, but delightful to be used in such a way. **"Take delight in the Lord, and he will give you your heart's desires."** (Psalm 37:4)

JUNE

June 1

People who believe in God have an opinion that is politically incorrect. And there are more that have a different view than those who will boldly stand up for what God's Word teaches.

So, which group is getting larger and which gets smaller?

We are accused of being narrow-minded, (because we believe that Jesus is the *Only Way* to heaven.) **"Jesus told him, 'I am the way, the truth, and the life. No one can come to the Father except through me."** (John 14:6)

They try to make us feel guilty for standing up for our view of the traditional marriage, as well as many other things God's Word teaches.

"Claiming to be wise, they became utter fools instead." (Romans 1:22)

". . . That is why God abandoned them to their shameful desires. Even their women turned against the natural way to have sex and instead indulged in sex with each other." (V. 26)

There have always been homosexuals, (Sodom and Gomorrah), but years ago, they were ashamed and *in the closet*. This is certainly not the only evidence that *we* have become a minority. Being a minority has a way of pushing you into the closet.

"For I am not ashamed of this Good News about Christ. It is the power of God at work, saving everyone who believes - Jews first and also Gentiles." (Romans 1:16)

If you were arrested for being a Christian, (which may not be too far in the future), would there be enough evidence against you to convict you?

(Pretty bold and powerful, but true!)

June 2

I used to do all sorts of crafts. Mostly, I copied other's designs. Mine never turned out quite as good as theirs, but I enjoyed anticipating the finished product.

God knew me, what He had in mind for me before I was ever conceived. **"You saw me before I was born. Every day of my life was recorded in your book. Every moment was laid out before a single day had passed."** (Psalm 139:16)

We can't conceive how God could write our lives before we were born and yet, give us the freedom to make our own choices. (He knows us so well that He knows what we will choose). He's more than one step ahead of us.

He had a finished product in mind for each of us and only allows what He can use for good. **"And we know that God causes everything to work together for the good of those who love God and are called according to his purpose for them. For God knew his people in advance, and he chose them to become like his Son, so that his Son would be the firstborn with many brothers and sisters."** (Romans 8:28-29)

He allows me to make wrong choices, but uses them, in spite of myself, to bring about His purpose. (I can take a shortcut through obedience or go the long, hard, painful way to arrive at the same destination...good!)

We are living the story that He has already written about us. When we acknowledge Him, He will direct us to take the peaceful, joyful, and fulfilling shortcut, instead of our own long, hard, and painful path. (See Proverbs 3:6)

June 3

What are the ways Satan is turning our government and judges against Christians? We're losing our rights to live out our beliefs because someone may be offended. (Their rights come before ours.)

In one of my devotions this morning, I read about a Muslim in France who has been a Christian for three years but kept it a secret for fear of losing his family.

We haven't gone that far yet, but we're gradually losing - the traditional marriage. (See Genesis 2:18-22)

(Don't speak against homosexuality, which the Bible does, in Romans 1 - that's discrimination!)

Our abortion laws go against God's law, **"Do not murder."** (Exodus 20:13). The mother's right, (not to have to live with consequences), comes before the child's right to life, (given in our constitution).

The right to even spank our children – (that's abuse!) **"Don't fail to correct your children. They won't die if you spank them."** (Proverbs 23:13)

Even our policemen are losing the right to do their jobs for fear of being labeled a *racist*.

We can't even fly our flag because someone may be offended.

Turn a few pages, and we'll be where this Muslim is, in our own country! (Afraid to say we're Christians.)

If we really trust God, can't we allow Him to fight these battles? Are we ready to suffer the consequences He allows? **"Then Peter and the other apostles answered and said, 'We ought to obey God rather than men'."** (Acts 5:29)

"For God hath not given us the spirit of fear, but of power, and of love, and of a sound mind." (Second Timothy 1:7)

Pastor Saeed Abedini has been in prison in Iran for three years for speaking the gospel. He's a modern day "Paul." I pray he is winning some of the guards over for Christ!

June 4

Have you ever wondered how God spoke to Abraham to cause him to believe in Him so strongly that he was willing to leave his country and people to go to another land? Or that he would trust God so completely that he would be willing to place his only son, (the one God had promised), upon the altar to sacrifice him?

It didn't make any sense. So, how could he know *God* was directing him?

When you've seen God answer prayer, forgive your sins, and change your heart, you learn to trust Him and you *know* when He is speaking to you. You have a peace that passes understanding. (See Philippians 4:7).

"But when you ask him for wisdom, be sure that you really expect him to answer, for a doubtful mind is as unsettled as a wave of the sea that is driven and tossed by the wind. People like that should not expect to receive anything from the Lord. They can't make up their minds. They waver back and forth in everything they do." (James 1:6-8)

I hope you've learned you can trust what I say, but I'm human and can fail you. You can only put your full trust in God. You may doubt, yourself; (that you're really hearing from God). But your close relationship with Him will tell you.

It's His love for you and your love for Him that tells you to trust. In His wisdom, He knows how to communicate to you. He has given His Word to guide us today.

June 5

When we spoil and pamper our children, are we causing them to be weak when facing the difficulties of the world? It depends on the way and how much we spoil them. They have to know they are loved!

God spoils us and wants each of us to know He *personally* loves us. He isn't disappointed when we take Him for granted. He has taught us to so depend on Him for everything we need and to know He's always there to help us through any situation. **". . . I will never fail you. I will never forsake you."** (Hebrews 13:5b)

But true love also strengthens and matures us for the battles ahead. He disciplines us. **"Don't be misled. Remember that you can't ignore God and get away with it. You will always reap what you sow!"** (Galatians 6:7)

Jesus also taught us to expect persecution. **"Remember the word I said unto you, the servant is not greater than his Lord. If they persecuted me, they will also persecute you. . ."** (John 15:20a)

It's coming! Be prepared!

As one trains for the Olympics daily, we need to grow closer to the Lord, *daily*, to get into His Word, and let it get into us. That's the way we will be strengthened, spiritually - (become aware of His presence.)

"That is why we can say with confidence, the Lord is my helper, so I will not be afraid. What can mere mortals do to me?" (Hebrews 13:6)

We're a long way from being willing to endure anything for Him. But, if we are going to be victorious soldiers of the cross, we have to get in shape.

His power, love, and wisdom provide nourishment and are the weapons we need to mature. We don't have to conjure them up. They're already there. We just have to learn to use them.

June 6

Do you have a *normal philosophy*? One pretty much like everyone else, doing the best you can, living within your means, gradually getting ahead a little at a time? Or is this too boring for you?

Life is like a long-distance race, not a sprint. We have to pace ourselves. If we spend it too fast, we'll find ourselves lacking in the end. We are wise to set our priorities. (First things first). Our money goes first to pay bills for things we need for survival, then for enjoyment.

Our goal in life should be to prepare first for eternity because it will last forever. If we use up our whole life with entertainment and enjoyment, and have not seen that life is a gift from God, not to be wasted on ourselves, we are foolish.

When we stand before God at the end, will we be able to say, with Paul, **"I have fought a good fight. I have finished my course, I have kept the faith; henceforth there is laid up for me a crown of righteousness, which the Lord, the righteous judge, shall give me at that day; and not for me only, but unto all them that love his appearing."** (Second Timothy 4:7-8)

June 7

When you obey the *letter* of the law, you do it because you feel you *have* to. But when you obey the *spirit* of the law, you do it because you know it's best.

The Sabbath was given to us because we need a day of rest physically and spiritually. If we don't take time to reflect on God's goodness, we grow more distant from Him and the, *I don't want to's*, include going to church. You find yourself going because you feel you *have* to, and eventually you quit going.

Sin has a way of turning the *spirit* of the law into the *letter*. Deep down, we want to honor God, but our flesh has a different opinion.

Paul addressed this in Romans 7:29, **"But if I,** (my flesh), **am doing what I,** (my spirit), **don't want to do, I,** (my spirit), **am not really the one doing it; the sin within me is doing it."** (My insertions are for clarity.)

Even though we're saved from the penalty of sin and deemed *righteous* in God's eyes, there's still sin in us that wants to control the *real us*, (our spirit).

So, there's a spiritual battle within us - the flesh (sinful nature) against the Spirit (righteousness). The one we feed is the one who wins in each situation.

Death is the *only end* to this battle. It is part of life, but we have to know our enemy. We have the power to overcome because, **". . . Greater is he that is in you, than he that is in the world."** (See 1 John 4:4b)

June 8

Like God, the Father, God, the Son, and God, the Holy Spirit is the Trinity, (3-in-1), we also, (our soul, the *real us*) is a trinity. Our *soul* is our mind, emotions, and will.

We also know that we are body, soul, and spirit. We are very complex creatures. Who can truly understand?

Our minds are rebellious and need discipline and training. Sometimes, even when we are praying, our minds wander from our conversation with God.

Our minds are like toddlers, getting into things they shouldn't! We have to keep constant watch over them so they don't take a word from a friend and twist it to make us angry. Or to ignore something that is for our good.

We usually can give them free reign, but there are times we shouldn't. We have the power and authority over our mind. **"And be not conformed to this world, but be ye transformed by the renewing of your mind. . ."** (Romans 12:2a)

"Let this mind be in you which was also in Christ Jesus. . ." (Philippians 2:5) When we have a bad attitude, we can do something about it. We can *change the channel*.

". . . Fix your thoughts on what is true, honorable, and right. Think about things that are excellent and worthy of praise." (Philippians 4:8)

Don't let discouragement take hold. Snap your thoughts back to good things. Leave the rest in God's hands. Not only can He handle them - He wants to!

June 9

It's an amazement to me to watch people play games on their cell phones. The games had to take a great mind to devise the *strategy*. Then, how to implement it! The designer chose *villains* to be conquered. For someone to win the game, they have to contemplate how the villains will act and take steps to conquer them. Then, they are so proud! They've spent countless hours on their *victory*.

In the end, it's only a game, wasted hours that didn't really matter. It was simply a *time-out* from the stresses of life - the real game. (A time to reload your energy supply.) The victory only boosts your ego for a very short time.

In life, your victory is essential for all eternity. The enemy is strategically placed to lead you into all sorts of problems. (Even to waste too many hours on ego.)

"Be careful! Watch for attacks from the Devil, your great enemy. He prowls around like a roaring lion, looking for some victim to devour." (First Peter 5:8)

The only way to win this game is through God's grace. **"For by grace are ye saved, through faith, and that not of yourselves, it is the gift of God - not of works, lest any man should boast."** (Ephesians 2:8-9)

God saw fit that you should hear the gospel of His great love, (that's grace). It's up to you to believe it, (that's faith). Not only did God provide His grace, but He gave you the faith to believe. Both gifts are a matter of life and death, eternally.

June 10

There's nothing sweeter than a baby! You need no other entertainment than to watch him as he learns to roll over, to hold his bottle, or try to form words. He communicates his love and trust long before he can say, "I love you"; or "Thank you."

There's a gentle joy that saturates your soul as you spend time with him before he learns to manipulate you. His cry says, "I'm hungry"; or "I don't feel good."

This is pretty much the same language we use to communicate with the Lord. We sometimes verbalize our prayers, but many times they are just *groanings*.

"And the Holy Spirit helps us in our distress. For we don't even know what we should pray for, nor how we should pray. But the Holy Spirit prays for us with groanings that cannot be expressed in words." (Romans 8:26)

June 11

When we see the leaves on a tree begin to lose their color, we know something is wrong. (Unless it is autumn.) We know that if something isn't done, it will die. The leaves will turn yellow, then fall off. Eventually, the whole tree dies.

I cling so much to the belief in *"Once saved, always saved"*, that I believe God will *kill* one of His sin-sick children instead of letting them go to hell. The key words are *"His children."* He knows which are actually His, and which are only acting like they belong to Him.

First Corinthians 11:31-32 tells me that God disciplines His children so they won't be condemned with the world. **"God did not send His Son into the world to condemn it, but to save it."** (John 3:17)

His salvation isn't temporary. Else His love and power would fail!

Once you truly become His child, His power keeps you, even though you still have a free will.

If we continue to disobey, after much discipline, He will take us out! This is the tool He is forced to use to prevent our falling. His love will never fail!

June 12

Evil is like *"The Blob."* (You have to be old to know what *The Blob* is!) It grows and grows, infiltrating more and more of our world, trying to take over everything! We can see its effects as we watch the news.

There's the violence we see in ISIS against Christianity and the more subtle approach as we are called to be *politically correct*, allowing our witness to be stifled because someone may be offended.

God's Word is our armor in this battle. **"Put on the whole armor of God, that ye may be able to stand against the wiles of the devil."** (Ephesians 6:11)

If we don't take a stand for Christ, we'll fall for anything!

"But be ye doers of the Word and not hearers only, deceiving your own selves." (James 1:22)

As we sit in our recliners, we take sides, but do we ever put on our armor?

June 13

These inspirational thoughts are in a way like manna. They are for each day. Some days there are half a dozen things I can write about. I can only choose one or two. I can't save the others for tomorrow. They are gone.

On the other hand, I sometimes have to wait on the Lord for just one thought to share.

Today, I'll share that I've been praying with someone I love for a long time. We've been waiting for our answer, which seemed so right. *It just had to be*!

But, yesterday our answer came, and it was, "No."

"What now, *Daddy*?"

A small child doesn't worry. He depends on Momma and Daddy and knows they will take care of his needs.

The Bible tells us that we are to come to Him as a little child. **"And said, Verily I say unto you, except ye be converted, and become as little children, ye shall not enter the kingdom of heaven. Whosoever, therefore, shall humble himself as this little child, the same is greatest in the kingdom of heaven."** (Matthew 18:3-4)

Our need is such that it seems that life just can't go on for my loved one! But what we can't see . . . God can!

"But my God shall supply all your need according to his riches in glory by Christ Jesus." (Philippians 4:19)

June 14

We've all been given life and what we need to live it. It's up to us what we do with what we've been given. Every day we make decisions that can show us what *god* we've put our trust in. As we *feed* these *gods*, they provide what we think we need. They have taken us to where we are today, wrapped up in the things these *gods* have provided.

Our heavenly Father knows all this and sees what our real needs are. When He says, in Philippians 4:19, that He will meet all our needs, He is speaking of our spiritual, (*eternal*) needs. He uses our physical needs to show us our spiritual situation. (Do we get bitter if He allows something we don't want?) Is He really our *God*?

Sometimes, the worst thing we think can happen is designed to show us things we can't otherwise see. He wants us to open our eyes to eternal truths.

"My thoughts are completely different from yours', says the Lord. And my ways are far beyond anything you could imagine." (Isaiah 55:8)

Do the things He allows drive us to Him in our need, or further away from Him?

June 15

When your hopes are dashed and your lights have gone out, you find yourself all alone in the darkness. All is quiet and sullen. Then, slowly, the light begins to shine, like the sun coming up, reminding you that you're not alone. One who loves you very much is with you.

He begins to soothe your pain and bring encouragement. He has told you so often that He has a plan and will work everything out for good. (See Jeremiah 29:11 & Romans 8:28-29).

But you can't see it. Even though you have a free will, at this point, you have no choice but to trust the Lord.

If He doesn't change the situation, He wants to change us, (inside out). The direction He has for us is something we've never considered.

We will become a channel of blessing with a testimony that will bring encouragement to all who have fallen into this hole we find ourselves in.

"When he, the Spirit of Truth is come, he will guide you into all truth...he will show you things to come." (John 16:13)

June 16

There are people today who are facing giants like I was six years ago when I was diagnosed with stage-4 ovarian cancer. God had prepared me to receive this news calmly. He had worked a miracle in my heart before He worked one in my body!

He had just taught me through Beth Moore's Bible study on Daniel that He was with Shadrach, Meshach, and Abednego as they faced the fiery furnace. Beth brought out the fact that they weren't afraid to die. They knew that if they died, they would be with the Lord, so they couldn't lose!

They knew they would be delivered, either *from* the flames, (They wouldn't get thrown into the fire.), *in* the flames, (Which they were.), or *by* the flames, (They would die.) Either way, they would be victorious!

"If we are thrown into the blazing furnace, the God whom we serve is able to save us. He will rescue us from your power, Your Majesty. But even if he doesn't, Your Majesty can be sure that we will never serve your gods or worship the gold statue you have set up." (Daniel 3:17-18)

When I heard my terrible news, I was immediately reminded that I couldn't lose.

If your faith is in God, and you *know* He's in control, no matter what comes your way, you *can't lose*.

God will strengthen your faith through it or He will end your need for faith by taking you home.

"What shall we say to these things? If God be for us, who can be against us?" (Romans 8:31)

June 17

As we consider Presidential candidates for our next election, we hear promises that we can say, "Amen" to. But what is that *thing* that would cause us to actually vote for them?

We hope we can trust them to follow through with their promises. A candidate is only as good as their character.

Like us, they hope their faults are not uncovered and only their best is seen. We can be fooled by what they say, even if they profess to be Christians.

If I were smart enough to lead this great country, could I trust myself to do what I know is right? Would I be prejudiced or seek this power to even lead me to forsake God?

Bringing it down to a personal level, 1 Corinthians 11:31-32 would say, **"For if I would judge myself, I should not be judged"** (by God). **"But when I am judged, I am chastened of the Lord, that I should not be condemned with the world."**

How often do I take personal inventory of my soul? (Judge the *real me*?)

June 18

Thank God for giving us power over sin! I still have the picture in my mind of the flood we had about 3 weeks ago and how helpless we were to do anything about it.

We find ourselves in positions of helplessness in various situations. But, when we can't - *God can!*

Satan is powerful, cunning, and sly. But he is not all-powerful! He catches us off-guard, lies to us, and coaxes us to do what we know isn't right. Then he goes before God and accuses us of our wrong-doing. "**. . . who accused them before our God, day and night.**" (Revelation 12:10b)

God has given us a *power tool* – prayer - that is more powerful than the evil thoughts that come our way. It is our *light switch*. When we turn it on, the darkness flees.

The only problem is - Satan has a way of almost hypnotizing us so that by the time we realize this is wrong, we are so weak that we don't even want to pray and ask for help.

To prevent this *hypnotic state*, we have to keep our minds filled with praise for God, reminding ourselves of His promises, and offering ourselves for His use. This helps us to stay aware of His presence. "**So humble yourselves before God. Resist the devil and he will flee from you.**" (James 4:7)

It's harder for Satan to *knock the slats* out from under one who stays close to God. "**Draw close to God, and he will draw close to you. . .**" (James 4:8a)

God allows disappointments to come our way to test our faith, showing us what we're made of.

If we put our fists up against God, we have fallen into *Satan's trap*!

June 19

We can instantly become Christian, but we don't *instantly* become *Christ-like*. **"Train up a child in the way he should go and, when he is old, he will not depart from it."** (Proverbs 22:6)

Many of us have not been trained as Christians. We have acted and reacted with little or no thought of Christ. It's hard to break all those years of no training!

Now that we have become Christians, we need to fight our *own will* daily, training ourselves to allow God's will to help us become *Christ-like*. (See Philippians 2:5-8)

Some days, we do great, but other days we act like we've never been saved!

Not only are we fighting against *no training*, but we have that natural instinct that wants to sin.

We see our own struggles, but can't believe other people act the way they do!

Instead of retaliating in anger or getting our feelings hurt, we should understand their plight, forgive them, and pray for them.

"And be ye kind one to another, tenderhearted, forgiving one another, even as God, for Christ's sake hath forgiven you." (Ephesians 4:32)

We're all in the same boat. Let's row in Christ's direction, instead of each one in his own.

June 20

Job said in Chapter 14:1-2, "**. . . How frail is humanity! How short is life, and how full of trouble! Like a flower, we blossom for a moment and then wither. Like a shadow of a passing cloud, we quickly disappear.**"

No matter how much we learn or how wise we become, we are like a small ant in the face of a giant. We have no power; we have no right.

We are clay in the Maker's hand. All we can do is yield our lives to Him. Whether we understand or not makes no difference.

The only way to peace is to accept His wisdom and trust His great love for each of us. This not only gives us daily victories, but we win in the end!

June 21

Trusting God feels so good! There are so many uncertainties out there that can bring fear and even terror. Something as small as having to tackle an unfamiliar task makes us afraid.

We gain strength and courage when we pause to acknowledge God's assurance.

I remember when my kids were young, there was a fierce storm one night. I was looking out the kitchen window, watching the large trees bending low, first one way, then, the other. It was an awesome sight!

One of the twins asked, with wide eyes, "Mama, are you scared?"

I said, "No."

She said, "I'm not either."

This is the way it is for us when we trust our Heavenly Father. We can know He is there with His loving care and the power to conquer anything. He knows what needs to be done.

"Take my yoke upon you and learn of me; for I am meek and lowly in heart, and ye shall find rest unto your souls." (Matthew 11:29)

June 22

God hates sin! It is an infection that causes sickness in our souls.

It seems cruel for God to tell King Saul in 1 Samuel 15:3-4, "**. . . Now go and completely destroy the entire Amalekite nation - men, women, children, babies, cattle, sheep, camels, and donkeys.**"

If they didn't utterly destroy all of them, they could infect the nation of Israel with their idolatry.

Also, I read this morning about one in the church in Corinth that was sleeping with his father's wife. Paul told the church, "**. . . Don't you realize that if even one person is allowed to go on sinning, soon all will be affected? Remove this wicked person from among you so that you can stay pure.**" (First Corinthians 5:6b-7a,)

Physically, we are careful to avoid infection, and to treat it quickly. Why do we allow, (even embrace) spiritual infection?

We experience pain with physical infection, but there is temporary pleasure with spiritual infection.

Hebrews 11:25 speaks about Moses, when it says, "**. . . He chose to share the oppression of God's people instead of enjoying the fleeting pleasure of sin.**"

This temporary pleasure leads to death. "**For the wages of sin is death, but the gift of God is eternal life through Jesus Christ our Lord.**" (Romans 6:23)

It's like trying to rid your garden of Bermuda grass. If you leave just one nodule, it will spread, threatening to take over.

We must evaluate our *secret sins* and expose them to the light of God's Word so they can be exterminated.

Satan tells us, "You'll never be perfect. So, why even try?"

Try telling that to a serious athlete! We must strive to be all we can be for God's glory. That takes *self-sacrifice*.

June 23

The little girl is very shy. She withdraws when you speak to her. She hasn't learned to trust you. How different it will be when she learns that you love her!

That's the way we are with God. Our relationship with Him can be as close as we want it to be.

He approaches us, but we draw away, missing out on all that He desires for us.

"But when the Holy Spirit controls our lives, he will produce this kind of fruit in us: love, joy, peace, patience, kindness, goodness, faithfulness, gentleness, and self-control..." (Galatians 5:22-23a)

How He longs for a closer relationship with us!

June 24

There are a lot of "*Thou shalt not's*" in God's Word. These are as necessary as the stop signs on our highways. They are not there to rob us of our desires, but to protect us and keep us pure. When you need to wipe your face, you want to use a clean rag.

We should keep our lives clean for God's use, not only to be blessed by Him, but to prevent having to deal with the consequences of disobedience.

I've often wondered how missionaries are able to spread the gospel in areas that are hostile to Christ. God revealed to me that their main purpose is to love people.

When we take time to love people, they are more receptive to what we say.

We are drawn to Christ by His love for us. **"Greater love hath no man than this, that a man lay down his life for his friends."** (John 15:13)

"*Love*" is a word that is over-used. It means much more than infatuation.

In John 21, Jesus asked Peter, **"Do you love me?"** Each time Peter responded with, **"You know I love you."** Jesus replied **"Feed My sheep."** (See John 21:15, 16, & 17).

God gives us the *feed* to share as we encounter different *sheep*.

The food He supplies is *love*.

As we take time to love people, it's easy to glorify God by giving Him credit for every good gift that He has given us. (See James 1:17).

If we are thankful and recognize the good we have is from God, it is natural to give Him the glory.

June 25

When we go to the doctor, we don't begin by telling him that he is the best doctor around and that we have full confidence that he will be able to find the reason for our problem and fix it.

But if we did, he may have a greater desire to give us special attention.

We don't have to *build up* our heavenly Father when we bring our problems to Him. But if we begin our prayers with praise, focusing on the majesty of the *One* we are talking to, we would know He is able and willing to handle the situation... *"And the things of earth will grow strangely dim in the light of His glory and grace."*

As soon as we have spoken our need, we should pause and listen. If nothing comes to us, He is saying, "I'm working on it, just wait." He will speak His love and concern for us.

"Look at the birds. They don't need to plant or harvest or put food in barns because your heavenly Father feeds them. And you are far more valuable to him than they are." (Matthew 6:26)

If God's answer doesn't come quickly, we know He is mindful and working *in the background*.

We are so busy we don't feel we have time to wait on Him. It's like we are starving, but don't have time to eat. We may have to *eat on the run*, (listen for God while we go on about our day.)

He may take longer than we desire, but He has perfect timing and He is coordinating our needs with those around us. (We're not the only ones He's concerned with.)

June 26

Christ saw our need and reached out to save us, even when we didn't even *like* Him. (See Romans 5:8).

He shined His Light to show us the way to life.

Someone who isn't a Christian doesn't want to hear about Christ because he is convicted of his sinful ways.

He wants to keep going his way until he *knows* he has to turn around.

When we reach a *dead-end*, and the only way to look is *up*, we finally accept what has been right all along.

The wisdom of God and His patience allows His love to work in our behalf, to draw us to Him.

As C.S. Lewis says, *"God whispers to us in our pleasures, speaks to us in our conscience, but shouts to us in our pain."*

In the pleasure of seeing His handiwork, God whispers, "I am here."

When we know we're doing wrong, but want to do it anyway, He says, **"Be not deceived, God is not mocked, for whatsoever a man soweth, that shall he also reap."** (Galatians 6:7)

When we refuse to listen, He shouts to us *with pain*. Because He loves us, He cannot allow us to live the way we want to. (See Hebrews 12:6)

"For I reckon that the sufferings of this present time are not worthy to be compared with the glory that shall be revealed in us." (Romans 8:18)

God is so good! His love is everlasting!

June 27

We are *loaned*, not *given*, children to raise in such a way that prepares them for the future.

There has to come a time for separation, when they leave our home to go to theirs.

This is a time of rejoicing for them, but not for us. It is a *happy/sad* day. This is what life has become.

The *empty nest syndrome* has come. Eventually, we will become accustomed to just frequent visits. But we have all those *memories*.

It is an important part of life.

I think God has pretty much the same scenario for our lives, except in reverse. He allows us to live away from home for a while. **"Therefore we are always confident, knowing that while we are at home in this body, we are absent from the Lord."** (Second Corinthians 5:6)

The time of separation is *happy/sad* for the ones who are left behind. Though there won't be visits, but there will be a glad *reunion day*!

It's so normal to cling to our loved ones, but we must remember they were never ours. They were only *loaned* to us for a while, and for a purpose.

When God calls them home, He will eventually fill that void by His grace. **"And he said unto me, my grace is sufficient for thee, for my strength is made perfect in your weakness."** (Second Corinthians 12:9)

June 28

I've not recently gone through devastating trials, but I don't know what may be just around the corner.

Life goes on! No matter how tragic any event is, (unless it kills you), life continues.

It may shake us to the point that we don't even want to go on, but we have to reevaluate life itself. We have to adjust, (which takes time.)

"We can make our plans, but the Lord determines our steps." (Proverbs 16:9)

"The thief cometh not but to steal, and to kill, and to destroy; I am come that they might have life and that they might have it more abundantly." (John 10:10)

One day, we'll be able to laugh again. That's God's will for us. (To recover and become even stronger.)

June 29

Why is it that when we know what is right, we continue to search for another way?

There are a lot of "Yeah, but's . . ."

I remember sharing Christ with a distant cousin. He was living as an Orthodox Jew. After I had shared that Jesus said in John 14:6, **"I am the way, the truth, and the life; no man cometh unto the Father, but by me."**, he responded with, "Yeah, but there may be another way and I'm gonna find out."

That just goes to show, "You can lead a horse to water, but you can't make him drink."

I guess that's the choice people make when they want to be *politically correct* instead of going in God's direction. **". . . Professing themselves to be wise, they became fools."** (Romans 1:22)

"For this cause God gave them up unto vile affections; for even their women did exchange the natural use for that which is against nature. And likewise also, the men, leaving the natural use of the woman, burned in their lust one toward another, men with men working that which is unseemly. . ." (Verses 26-27a)

That is *sin*!

But we all sin, and God doesn't see that one sin is *bigg*er than the other. (Sin is sin, *missing the mark*.)

But, when your sin pushes to even make a law (that goes against scripture) and declares that I accept it, that is going too far!

God hates sin, but loves the sinner. His love wants to turn us away from our sin. (No matter how politically correct!)

June 30

Yesterday, I was out of my routine and it felt like I was being led blindfolded through the day.

I wasn't able to *report in* and get my *marching orders*. I felt like I had left the Lord at home.

My time with the Lord is like a meeting with the *Boss*.

I don't know what He has lined up for me, but He assures me that He'll be right there with me to instruct me, to protect me, and to supply me with all I need to complete each task.

He was with me all day yesterday, as usual, but somehow, I couldn't sense His presence. This is most important for me!

He supplies the confidence that I am doing what is right, and His approval grants me peace.

Today, my routine will again be interrupted, but I've met with my Lord for instructions and the assurance of His presence.

I don't know what will happen, but I'll be with *the One* who does!

He wants me to handle what I can and He'll do the rest.

He created the world from nothing, but He supplies me with everything I need to go through the activities of the day.

"And this same God who takes care of me will supply all your needs from his glorious riches which have been given to us in Christ Jesus." (Philippians 4:19)

Also, **"For I can do everything with the help of Christ who gives me the strength I need."** (Philippians 4:13)

I thank God that He is in charge of this day. (And my life)

July 1

I remember hearing that the way to trap a monkey is to put bait that is bigger than the width of the bars, in a cage. When the monkey grabs it, he can't get it out, but he won't let go of it, even for his freedom.

I don't know if this is true, but it is a perfect picture of us and our *secret sins*. (We just don't have them, *they have us!*) We don't want to turn loose. They are more important to us than anything else.

It may be that we have a reputation with unbelievers or carnal Christians, who admire us, and our pride won't allow us to surrender this to God. We fear that we may lose these *friends* because they will be disappointed if our behavior or attitude is changed. (The dirty jokes cease, or the snide remarks stop.)

But we can be sure that God's way is best. Bringing honor and glory to God is more gratifying than this.

"And ye shall know the truth, and the truth shall set you free." (John 8:32)

Also, **"For the Lord has redeemed Israel from those too strong for them. They will come home and sing songs on the heights of Jerusalem. They will be radiant because of the many gifts the Lord has given them - the good crops of wheat, wine, and oil, and the healthy flocks and herds. Their life will be like a watered garden, and all their sorrows will be gone."** (Jeremiah 31:11-13).

This speaks of material blessings, as well as the joy in their soul. I cherish the joy in my soul so much more than the material blessings. (Although I am extremely grateful for them, also).

July 2

Boy! First Corinthians 15 is packed full of truths and explanations! It helps us see God's design for the human race. **"For our perishable earthly bodies must be transformed into heavenly bodies that will never die."** (Verse 53).

Just as we watch an artist begin his painting or drawing, we have no idea what he has in mind. But slowly, we begin to *think* we know. We may change our mind several times before it becomes clear. Now, only the special details, and it is finished.

When we were young, we were so busy exploring and experimenting that we had no idea what God had in mind for us. Only when we're *almost done*, does it begin to become clear. We realize this life will soon end and we get serious about building our relationship with Christ, as He puts His finishing touches on our life.

For all these years, we have shunned and even feared death. More each day now, we embrace it and long for the finished touch to be applied. Then we will be like Christ and live with Him forever! (See verse 49).

This was in God's mind before He even touched His brush to the pallet. **"He saw me before I was even born. . ."** (Psalm 139:16a)

July 3

I just heard Lee Greenwood sing, "*God Bless the U.S.A.*" I was moved to love and appreciate our wonderful country! It brings tears to my eyes when we sing "*The Star Spangled Banner*", and I realize the battles that have been fought to assure that "*our flag was still there*"!

It is sad to know there are American citizens who have even enlisted to fight against our great country! This is what happens when love for God is not instilled at a young age. **"Train up a child in the way he should go and, when he is old, he will not depart from it."** (Proverbs 22:6)

The *tares*, (weeds), have grown up among the wheat. **"But while men slept, his enemy came and sowed tares among the wheat, and went his way."** (Matthew 13:25)

Not only have the parents failed these people, but we, as friends and neighbors, haven't been the right examples, either. They have a free choice, so we are not completely to blame. But when we see a youngster drifting, we should take notice and try to be a positive influence in his life.

I realize the *tare* is one from its seed, so this may not be the best example. But it *paints the picture* that there are people living amongst us who need nourishment to keep them from acting like *tares*. (They don't produce any fruit and only seem to sap the nutrients from benefitting other plants).

"It's none of my business", we may say. But our neglect will show up when we reap what we have sown. (See Galatians 6:7).

July 4

When we seek purpose, we look way beyond where we are and what we're doing. But, we are in the process of fulfilling Gods purpose for us, (for our lives).

We are still in training but as we learn, we are to take note of each lesson. It is a *piece of puzzle* that, when put together with others, will make up the picture that God saw even before we were in the womb.

When we make mistakes or even rebel against God, *He knew we would* and even uses it to bring about His ultimate purpose.

His will is that we be born, that we live, and that we die. We have no choice in the beginning and the end of our life. But we have many choices in the *living* part of life.

We can think of ourselves as plants that scatter seeds. What kind of seeds are we scattering?

We know that God's purpose for Jesus was that He'd be born, (in Bethlehem); that He'd live (for 33 short years) in the region of Israel; and that He'd die a horrible death in order to pave the way for us to be with Him in eternity. And that His Great Love be preached world-wide. We condense this to say, "Christ died for us."

Christ's *seeds* were *love*. **"Greater love hath no man than this, that a man lay down his life for his friends."** (John 15:13)

His purpose for us is simply that we scatter His seeds of *love*.

"These things I command you, that ye love one another." (John 15:17) (See also, Matthew 28:19-20).

July 5

There's a difference in *love* and *acceptance*. Because God saw how much our world needed to be rescued from our sin, He sent His Son.

If He had merely accepted our behavior, there would have been no need for a Savior.

But, because He saw our need, He came. He knew they would call Him names and even kill Him!

Love came to help us be acceptable.

Some label our beliefs as *bigotry*. But we can't go against God's Word.

When Jesus teaches in Matthew 7:12, **"Do for others what you would like them to do for you. This is a summary of all that is taught in the law and prophets."** He is teaching us how to show His love.

No one wants to be rebuked, at the moment, when they're doing wrong. But the scenario is like that of an animal caught in a trap. You want to rescue him, but you know he will fight you. (He may even call you names!)

Does love just shrug its shoulders and walk on? (No.)

But only God can save someone. He desires to use us, but sometimes all we can do is pray for them.

"Confess your sins to each other and pray for each other so that you may be healed. The earnest prayer of a righteous person has great power and wonderful results." (James 5:16)

July 6

Somehow, we have to get *outside ourselves* to see what God's will is for our lives. When we are so focused on what we want and what feels good to us, we can't see or care about anyone else.

That's like being *homebound*. There's a whole world out there that God wants to love through us. We're only one piece of His great *puzzle*!

The acronym for JOY is *Jesus* (first), *Others*, (next), then (finally), *You*.

We have it all wrong when we think things should always go the way we want.

I think Paul had it right when he said in Philippians 4:11-12, **"Not that I was ever in need, for I have learned how to get along happily whether I have much or little, I know how to live on almost nothing or with everything. I have learned the secret of living in every situation, whether it is with a full stomach or empty, with plenty or little."**

We may think we have the right attitude, but what does Christ see when He rides with us as we drive to work or to the doctor's office? Are we *road-hogs*'? How do we react to *road-hogs*?

Maybe there are only times that we slip into the wrong attitudes, but maybe they are a way of life. What looks ugly on someone else, looks ugly on me, too.

"Be kindly affectioned one to another with brotherly love, in honor preferring one another." (Romans 12:10)

July 7

One afternoon, I was enjoying time with one of the twins in the porch swing. I was singing, "*Sing, sing, sing a little song. . .*" He seemed to really be enjoying it.

A few days later, he was fretting because he was tired and fighting sleep. I tried talking to him, but he paid no attention. Then I started singing, "*Sing, sing, sing a little song. . .*" Immediately he stopped crying and looked at me as if to say, "Oh, yeah, I remember." (His attention was brief).

That's a simple illustration of how we can get a different perspective in our struggles by directing our thoughts to God's presence, His goodness, and mercy. We can remember His promises.

There has to be a particular time when He spoke His love to each of us in a powerful way that brought peace and contentment to us, a beautiful memory. (Or one of His many promises).

Recalling memories like this can instantly work the *magic* that happens when we flip the light switch "on."

"Remember your promise to me, for it is my only hope. Your promise revives me; it comforts me in all my troubles." (Psalm 119:49-50)

July 8

Our prayer life is like a kid in a candy store. We ask, even beg, God for answers. When He gives us our desires, we thank Him, but beg for more! I guess that's human nature.

Some of our prayers are for miracles other people need. They are heavy-duty needs that only God can meet.

I'm thinking especially of two particular people today. One's need is visible. It is for physical and financial health. The other one is invisible. It's a deep spiritual need.

Both people's needs are completely up to them and God. I don't know how they will turn out. But, though I am deeply concerned, I recognize God's love, His wisdom, and His power is at work in both their lives.

I can only wait, trust, and keep on praying. God's heart isn't heavy for them. He knows the answers. He wants to ease my burdens, as well as theirs, as I beg for the miracles they need.

"Come unto me, all you who labor, and are heavy-laden and overburdened, and I will cause you to rest. (I will ease, and relieve, and refresh your souls.)" (Matthew 11:28). (I believe this verse is from the Amplified Version). I got it from a Joyce Meyer devotional.

We have to be alert that our *concerns* don't turn into *worries*. (That's when we take God's job upon ourselves). We can't handle it.

July 9

God doesn't change His plans for our lives. He has a perfect will, but He knows we sometimes get in His way. His *permissive will* allows us to make our own choices.

I'm thankful for His patience. As I deal with stubborn people, I eventually get frustrated and just walk away. But God is faithful and never leaves us. He uses our mistakes as learning tools.

He desires that we learn from *cause and effect*; from history; from His Word. He knows we will learn, one way or another, sooner or later, with great pain or little. His love guides us, protects us, and patiently teaches us.

"Take my yoke upon you. Let me teach you, because I am humble and gentle, and you will find rest for your souls." (Matthew 11:29)

We know His way is best. . . **"All scripture is inspired by God and is useful to teach us what is true and to make us realize what is wrong in our lives. It straightens us out and teaches us to do what is right."** (Second Timothy 3:16)

As we grow physically, we should also grow and mature spiritually.

"Then we will no longer be like children, forever changing our minds about what we believe because someone has told us something different or because someone has cleverly lied to us and made the lie sound like the truth." (Ephesians 4:14)

July 10

Something new! We all long for something new. We get tired of things so quickly. If only we could turn back to the time we received the *old*. It was new and we were grateful for it. But now, we take it for granted. Sure, we're still thankful that we have it instead of nothing. But we view it as *next to nothing*.

God has His loving arms around us, protecting us and giving us everything we need in life. He not only gives us His love, but He supplies us with people who love us; those we love!

How empty life would be if there was no one to shower with love! We have a deep need to receive love, but just as deep a need to give it.

Love is something you give away, and the more you give, the more you have to give. We can't hoard it.

It reminds me of the manna that God gave the children of Israel in the wilderness. (See Exodus 16:16-20). Whatever wasn't eaten in one day rotted and became useless.

If we don't keep loving, we forget how to love and become selfish, (and rotten!)

We even take for granted the new life God gave us when we accepted Christ and joined His family. "**. . . Those who become Christians become new persons. They are not the same anymore, for the old life is gone. A new life has begun!**" (Second Corinthians 5:17b)

If we don't praise Him for His goodness daily and share His great love every day, even our *new* life becomes 'old' to us.

July 11

When one becomes a candidate for office, he is sold out for what he believes in. He gives all he has for the cause.

In the process, it's easy to get side-tracked, thinking the end justifies the means. I doesn't matter *how*. The important thing is that he wins!

But when the responsibility is his, he may find out the power isn't! He has to be loyal to those who helped him get there. He may even discover that some only *supported* him in order to control him. Now *he* is in their control.

Is his cause still all-important to him? Is he willing to risk becoming a *nobody* again in order to stand for what he still believes is right, in the face of all the corruption he faces daily?

The price of our freedom cost Christ His life! We are His. **"Or don't you know that your body is the temple of the Holy Spirit who lives in you and was given to you by God? You do not belong to yourself, for God bought you with a high price. So you must honor God with your body."** (First Corinthians 6:19-20)

There is no wicked *in the process* involved here. Christ saw our dilemma and came to our rescue.

Our body was never ours. We *were* a slave to sin that leads only to death. *Now*, we are God's *slave* to be used for His glory. We were in the wrong army; now we are in the right one.

July 12

We have a creek in back of our property. It is usually dry, but with several days of rain recently, logs and debris washed up against a fence that crosses it. As a result, water backed up further than it ever has. It didn't threaten our house, but we knew with more rain in the forecast, we had to *unclog the dam*.

Sometimes things pile up in our personal relationships that also need to be *unclogged*.

This is evident in one of my relationships. Things haven't been right for years. I felt it couldn't be any worse, so I *threw in another log*, hoping to at least have my say.

The Lord quickly convicted me that I had acted in the flesh. I had a choice. I could either say, "Oh, well, the damage is done." Or, immediately jump in to at least retrieve this *log*.

I felt terrible, so I asked forgiveness.

I don't think it changed anything, but my conscience is clear once again.

We all mess up and need forgiveness. Pride is the monster that stands in our way.

"Judge not, and ye shall not be judged; condemn not, and ye shall not be condemned; forgive, and ye shall be forgiven." (Luke 6:37)

We need to forgive, but we all need forgiveness, as well.

God is gracious! **"He forgives all my sins and heals all my diseases."** (Psalm 103:3)

July 13

Whether we like it or not, our lifestyles declare our allegiance. Do we find ourselves on the throne? Do we view ourselves the same way God views us?

"As God's messenger, I give each of you this warning: Be honest in your estimate of yourselves, measuring your value by how much faith God has given you." (Romans 12:3)

Tattoos label us for life. I would never get one and I hope you wouldn't either. But, if I had a tattoo, it would declare God's ownership.

Our purpose on earth is not to serve ourselves, but others. When we serve others, we are serving God.

The "Dead Sea" is called that because it is the lowest point on earth. What flows into it stops there. It doesn't flow out.

Whatever God gives us is not for us only. He means for us to share it for His glory.

I love the idea of *"Pay it Forward."* It expresses appreciation for one who has used his resources for the good of others. And it encourages further participation in sharing God's goodness. This sharing should bring honor and glory to God from whom it came.

July 14

Several years ago, our family of five, on vacation, went up Pike's Peak. We were all packed in our little Chevette, which had a 4-speed manual transmission.

Soon we had to shift to 3rd, then to 2nd. There was an outlook about half-way where we stopped to enjoy the view.

I looked way up the mountain and saw a motor home still traveling *up*. It looked like a little toy!

I remember the stress as I felt I was helping to *push* us up that mountain. When we had to shift to 1st gear, I thought, "Oh, no! Soon we'll be rolling backwards down this mountain!"

There was a gift shop at the top where I saw a shirt with this message, "I survived Pike's Peak." I thought, "They need to sell those at the bottom!"

Unlike Pike's Peak, we can't see where God is taking us. We're sometimes amazed at how far we've come. But, with confidence, we know that He will take us the rest of the way.

When we get there, we'll be in awe at the beautiful view!

"Surely goodness and mercy shall follow me all the days of my life, and I will dwell in the house of the Lord forever." (Psalm 23:6)

July 15

You can't dictate generosity or dependability. It has to come voluntarily from the heart.

The people who want the job, but not the work, are also the kind who want Jesus to be their Savior, but not their Lord, (Boss).

We all want the benefits, that's human nature, but we must be willing to give of ourselves to the One who supplies. We must accept the authority that is over us.

We've all seen the teenager who wants the free rent, food, and clothing, but doesn't think he has to obey his parents. Or the employee who takes the paycheck and all the benefits, but calls in sick to shirk his duties, then complains of all he has to endure to be employed.

This is a chronic illness in the individual. They see others with this attitude who seem to get by with it and think, "Why not me?"

But there is an absence of stress when we accept our responsibilities and submit to the higher authority.

Of course, as a nation we find ourselves under the authority of one who doesn't see that he, too, is under the *One* who allows his abuse of power for a purpose that we don't understand. One day, God will say, "Enough!"

But in the meantime, we need His grace to help us be the kind of person that willingly pulls his own weight.

Will we hear the Lord say, **"Well done, thou good and faithful servant. Enter thou into the joy of thy Lord."** (Matthew 25:21)

Or will it be, **"And then I will profess unto them, I never knew you; depart from me, ye that work iniquity."** (Matthew 7:23)

July 16

I had a good audience yesterday as he twins lay in the floor of the sunroom after playing in the pool. Their mom wasn't feeling well, so I watched them for a while.

As they lay on their backs looking at me, I decided to tell them a story. I couldn't believe how intently they listened! They will be 10 months old tomorrow.

This shows me that though they haven't yet learned to use their arms to help them crawl, they are mentally ready to learn and can be taught.

As one of my devotions and my scripture reading today was on giving, I wondered if generosity is something you can teach or a trait you're born with.

We can teach all we want, but if the child isn't receptive, it is for naught. (But we are still responsible to teach.) God will help them learn. He wants us to give willingly.

When we are truly grateful, we will want to be a blessing to others.

This can't be forced; it has to come from the heart.

"You must each make up your own mind as to how much you should give. Don't give reluctantly or in response to pressure. For God loves the person who gives cheerfully." (Second Corinthians 9:7).

In order to give cheerfully, we have to learn to be grateful. God's lessons can seem cruel sometimes, but they fulfill their purpose. We don't appreciate something until it's briefly taken away.

July 17

God loves for us to laugh and enjoy life. When we go on a vacation, we should enjoy the *trip* as well as the destination. But we have to be careful where we are and keep our eyes open for danger. Our plans may be interrupted.

There is a secret to enjoying life even while on our eternal journey. We keep our eyes on our *Guide*!

Satan wants to distract us and get us side-tracked so that we forget where we're going and act like we've already arrived.

As we journey, we encounter people who may be used as *angels* to help us on our way. Others could be used as *demons* who wish to lead us astray.

"For we are not fighting against people made of flesh and blood, but against the evil rulers and authorities of the unseen world, against those mighty powers of darkness who rule this world, and against wicked spirits in the heavenly realms." (Ephesians 6:12)

At the same time, *we* could be used as *angels* to help others find their way. Or could it be that we are allowing Satan to use us to further his demonic plans?

"Therefore, let us not sleep, as others do, but let us watch and be sober-minded." (First Thessalonians 5:6)

July 18

When I go before the Lord in prayer, I know He is powerful, far more powerful than I can imagine! I know He loves me (and others) much more than I can ever understand! I know His wisdom formed the whole world and keeps it together!

Therefore, if I should ask something of Him that isn't granted, it isn't because of any lack in Him, but because it doesn't align with His purpose or timing.

I am to pray like Jesus did in the garden for what I desire, but also, yield to God's will. (See Luke 22:42).

I don't understand why God teaches us to pray, no matter what. **"Ask, and it shall be given you; seek, and ye shall find; knock, and it shall be opened."** (Matthew 7:7) Because there are clearly times He has to say, "No."

Maybe it's a way to draw us closer to Him Maybe it's a way to test our faith and teach us to trust Him, no matter what. **"And the peace of God, which passeth all understanding, shall keep your hearts and minds through Christ Jesus."** (Philippians 4:7)

If I ever understand this perfectly, I'll be sure to pass it on to you.

July 19

A miracle is *a supernatural happening*. We think of them as rare. But how *natural* is it that the earth hangs on nothing, stays in place, and does what it is designed to do? The only explanation is God is at work.

"Where were you when I laid the foundations of the earth? Tell me, if you know so much. Do you know how its dimensions were determined and who did the surveying? What supports its foundations, and who laid its cornerstone?" (Job 38:4-6)

God is at work continually, but we don't see His efforts, only the results. When a person's heart and mind are changed, God is at work. He's still in the *miracle business*. He still changes and sustains lives.

The *nonsense* we see all around us is visible. We can't deny it. But the quiet, invisible, miraculous things God does are more powerful.

In our finite minds, we limit Him. We reduce Him to *one of us that is more powerful*. It's difficult for us to believe that Jesus actually walked on water, that He healed deadly diseases, and that He came back to life after He was dead and buried.

He is not *one of us that is more powerful*. He is a Supernatural Being, and it's not difficult for Him to work miracles.

He cannot be manipulated by our prayers. He will do what is according to His plans. Sometimes this pleases us, sometimes it doesn't.

July 20

How can I ever thank the Lord for all His blessings, naming them one by one? That would take forever and I'm sure I would forget to mention many of them!

But, first of all, I'm thankful that I'm His. I have a sense of belonging; never feeling completely alone or unloved.

I'm thankful that His plans included me, and that He drew me to Him as a small child who understood nothing except that He died to make a way for me to know Him.

Love and acceptance is the foundation He gave me to build my life on.

I have made many mistakes (and still do), and even rebelled against Him, but He never gave up on me. He patiently dealt with me and continued to guide me, even chastening my stubbornness.

I've always known it was for my good because He gave me the faith to trust His love. (See Ephesians 2:8-9)

His plan for me has been in operation though I haven't always seen Him at work.

Each morning, I awake to a new day to see that He has protected me while I slept. I take this for granted, along with most all of His many blessings so much of the time.

He is all I will ever need - *The Giver*! Because I personally know Him, I have His gifts abundantly showered upon me!

"Whatever is good and perfect comes to us from God above, who created all heaven's lights. Unlike them, he never changes or casts shifting shadows." (James 1:17)

July 21

Beware of physical fatigue! It can dull our minds and hinder our prayer lives. It can rob us of gratitude. We may no longer even sense God's presence and hear His voice directing us to live for Him.

God created nights so we could rest. The wise will take advantage of these opportunities.

A tired body can't function as well as it should to open our minds for inspiring thoughts. Sickness sometimes works in the same way.

We can try to ward off fatigue and sickness, but sometimes life just has a way of getting us down.

"Always be full of joy in the Lord. I say it again, 'Rejoice'!" (Philippians 4:4)

Can you hear it? Can you do it? Rest and allow yourself time to reflect on God's goodness, on all He has done for you.

"Draw close to God, and God will draw close to you. . ." (James 4:8a)

"Come unto me, all ye that labor and are heavy laden, and I will give you rest." (Matthew 11:28)

Did you sense that I am preaching to me?

July 22

How evil did God allow the world to become before He destroyed it with a flood? **"Now the Lord observed the extent of the people's wickedness, and he saw that all their thoughts were consistently and totally evil. So the Lord was sorry he had made them, it broke his heart. And the Lord said, I will completely wipe out this human race that I have created. . ."** (Genesis 6:5-7a)

I don't think they had T.V.s in those days so that everyone could see all the evil. We see so much that our hearts are hardened to the pain and heartbreak of the families who are personally affected by each senseless murder. I don't have to go into any further details, you see it!

How depraved do we have to become before God finally says, "Enough!"?

He knows, and only He knows. **"However, no one knows the day or the hour when these things will happen, not even the angels in heaven or the Son himself. Only the Father knows."** (Matthew 24:36)

In the midst of all the wickedness are those Jesus still wants to save.

"He said unto His disciples, 'The harvest is so great, but the workers are few. So pray to the Lord who is in charge of the harvest; ask him to send out more workers for his fields'." (Matthew 9:37)

July 23

We read in Matthew 6:33, **". . .and he will give you all you need from day to day if you live for him and make the Kingdom of God your primary concern."** (NLT)

This simply states that if we are truly committed to Christ, He helps us to be committed to our spouse, our children and our responsibilities at work and at home.

Without His Lordship, we are *spinning our wheels*. We work and strive, but it seems we never find real happiness.

We may even become millionaires or trusted leaders in our community, but we will still feel empty. Nothing can fill that *God-shaped vacuum* except Christ, not only as our Savior, but as our *Lord*.

It's like when you're hungry for something, but nothing sounds good.

It's a shame when a young person hears this message and responds with, "Yeah, but. . ."

This foundation should be discovered early in life so that all that is built on it has meaning.

In a wedding ceremony, we vow our commitment to each other, expecting happiness, but if Christ isn't first, the disappointments that come may overpower our commitment to each other.

As *Lord*, He directs our lives in such a way to help us overcome the problems that He allows.

If we know He is in control, we can endure anything. (See Philippians 4:13).

"Each time he said, my gracious favor is all you need. My power works best in your weakness. . ." (Second Corinthians 12:9a)

So when you can't, *God can*!!

July 24

I'm so thankful to be living peacefully - in America, where I don't have to fear rockets being hurled at our home. And in a neighborhood where I can sleep at night without fear that someone may, at any time, break down our door. (Though this is more likely than rockets.)

I don't fear that a policeman will come to arrest me or any of my loved ones.

Though life is uncertain and, at any given time, tragedy may strike, I don't live in fear of it.

I know that I can't depend on being healthy for the rest of my life. But I can depend on God's grace to help me endure whatever He allows to come my way.

My *bottle of pills* is a full supply of God's promises that I have hidden in my heart. My *handgun* to protect against intruders is the knowledge that God is always with me, no matter what, and one of *my little pills* tells me that He won't allow anything to come my way that I, (*He*), can't handle. He will make a way for me to escape. (See 1 Corinthians 10:13)

Because I'm human, I know I'll let God down from time to time and I'll also disappoint my loved ones, but God has His hand on my life and I know I'll recover, and so will my family. That's peace!

Now, if I were trusting myself, there would be no peace! **"I know I am rotten through and through so far as my old sinful nature is concerned. No matter which way I turn, I can't make myself do right. I want to, but I can't."** (Romans 7:18)

I don't have to *walk* according to the flesh because Christ freed me from slavery to it, but I still choose to walk in that direction, from time to time, because I'm still a sinner!

Thank God for forgiveness!

July 25

Sarah and Abraham had received God's promise of a son. They waited and waited, but it didn't happen; so they devised a plan to *help God out*.

God's plan was for them to wait for Him to do something out of the ordinary so they would definitely know it was from Him.

We hate to wait! But we can't run ahead of God. We somehow get the idea that praying is a waste of time. God has given each of us prayer assignments that call for us to stop all *activity* and focus on Him. (But we have things to do, we don't have time to wait.)

God wants to involve us in His work so we can see His activity in our lives. He is faithfully working on our behalf daily, but much of what we have been praying for hasn't happened. He asks us to pray, and wait, and *trust*.

"Rest in the Lord, and wait patiently for him; fret not thyself because of him who prospereth in his way, because of the man who bringeth wicked devices to pass." (Psalm 37:7)

God has a great inheritance for us. **"And since we are his children, we will share his treasures - for everything God gives his Son, Christ, is ours, too. But if we're to share his glory, we must also share his suffering."** (Romans 8:17)

Jesus *waited* on the cross for God's victory. What we endure while we're waiting is not so bad!

July 26

I know my husband was wringing his hands, trying to come up with something I would eat. I had been diagnosed with stage four ovarian cancer. And chemo had destroyed my taste buds. Even the sweets I had always craved tasted bitter. I also had difficulty drinking enough liquids to stay hydrated.

I learned that I could go to the emergency room to get the fluids I needed. But they couldn't fix my appetite.

The doctor told me, after I had lost one third of my body weight, that he would have to put a feeding tube down my throat or directly into my stomach; or I would have to force myself to eat. . .or I would die!

When that truth sunk in, I began forcing myself to drink the shakes my husband made with *"Boost"* and a scoop of yogurt ice cream. He gradually added another scoop, until it was up to four scoops! (Pretty sneaky!)

I lived on that and Malt-O-Meal, and little else, for 5 or 6 months.

I've never related my physical condition to the spiritual condition of a lost person who has no appetite for God.

I believe prayer saved me! My family prayed long and hard for me. My dear church family, along with members of different churches, faithfully lifted my need to the Lord.

Even though there was little hope, I'm still here after more than six years! *God is so good*!

Now, we need to keep praying for our loved ones who have no appetite for the Lord. As long as there's life, there's hope!!

God can use a variety of ways to open their eyes. **"And he spoke a parable unto them to this end, that men ought always to pray, and not to faint."** (Luke 18:1)

July 27

If life isn't rewarding and there's no peace and contentment in our souls, even in the face of our troubles, we don't have enough of God.

When we fully trust Him, we *know* He will see us through our problems. The only ones that have true power over us are the ones we cause. God uses these problems to teach us that we can't fool Him.

"Don't be misled. Remember that you can't ignore God and get away with it. You will always reap what you sow!" (Galatians 6:7)

We can't find fulfillment with a *little of God*. Satan has successfully fooled many into thinking they have Christ in their hearts because they invited Him in. The only problem is that they never really opened the door when He knocked.

"Look! Here I stand at the door and knock. If you hear me calling and open the door, I will come in and we will share a meal as friends." (Revelation 3:20)

We can't just *sit in our recliners* and *say* "Come in." If we are hungry for God to change our lives, we have to give them to Him. There's no *in-between*!

"Then he said to the crowd, 'If any of you wants to be my follower, you must put aside your selfish ambition, shoulder your cross daily, and follow me. If you try to keep your life for yourself, you will lose it. But if you give up your life for me, you will find true life'." (Luke 9:23-24)

We want to keep our *fun* and *friends*, yet find fulfillment in our same lifestyle. It's not going to happen! We have to become new persons, inside-out. **"What this means is that those who become Christians become new persons. They aren't the same anymore, for the old life is gone. A new life has begun!"** (Second Corinthians 5:17). (I realize I have beat this drum before, but this bears repeating!) Too many people are living defeated lives.

July 28

We need shelter from the storms, the bitter cold, the scorching heat, wild animals, criminals, those who seek our souls, etc. As long as we have shelter, we feel safe. Nothing can harm us. The danger is *out there*.

Self-sufficiency and pride are false shelters, like an umbrella on a windy day. We think we're smart and will be okay with our own philosophy . . . until that huge *gust of wind* destroys our *shelter*.

There is only One *Shelter* that can withstand anything that comes against it. **"But as for me, how good it is to be near God! I have made the Sovereign Lord my shelter and I will tell everyone about the wonderful things you do."** (Psalm 73:28)

"For the Son of Man is come to seek and to save that which was lost." (Luke 19:10)

A wise person will run *to* the Lord, not *from* Him.

July 29

We all have a desire to learn. Sometimes other desires keep us from pursuing knowledge of God.

As we seek to know Him, He opens our understanding little by little.

He uses situations in our life to express Himself to us. He has given us His Word, the Bible, to speak to us.

But when we don't understand what He is saying, He shows us a *live demonstration*.

(Many times we just don't get it.) Lately, I've watched the twins struggle as they are learning to crawl. They get so close, then get frustrated. (Actual crawling is delayed for another time.)

There are many things that compete for our attention. Just as we desire to help infants learn, so also does God desire to help as He watches as we struggle. He is willing to help, if we will let Him.

"And ye shall seek me, and find me, when ye shall search for me with all your heart." (Jeremiah 29:13)

July 30

Life is full of calamities. Sometimes we don't recover from one before another one hits!

It seems as if we're like a log floating down the river with no power of our own. We bang against things and things bang against us. Sometimes we even get hung up on a sandbar and can't go anywhere.

No matter what comes our way, we know, and can rest assured that God has His eyes on us and we're never left unattended. When we take advantage of His faithfulness, His wisdom and His power, we know we will be okay.

When we're *washed up on a sandbar*, it feels good that we're not being buffeted on every side, but we also know that we're not getting anywhere. We have to get washed back *in the river* to reach our destination.

"Furthermore, because of Christ, we have received an inheritance from God, for he chose us from the beginning, and all things happen just as he decided long ago." (Ephesians 1:11)

We'll get through each calamity and everything will be fine because God is in control, not us.

July 31

Even if we're not wearing a shirt that *advertises* that we are a Christian, there are those in our circle of friends, in our family, and in our church that know we profess to be Christian. The trouble is that someone is always watching our lives. Even when we wish they weren't.

We are *Ambassadors* for Christ, representing Him in our world. But we aren't always careful to act like a Christian should. Therefore, our witness goes against Christianity. We're telling the world that Christ doesn't make that much difference.

I realized this one day when I was in a hurry and getting impatient as I was in line behind someone who had misunderstood the price of an object. They had to call for a manager to come and clear it up. I looked down to see I was wearing my shirt with *Jeremiah 29:11* printed on it.

This quickly convicted me to settle down!

"Let your light so shine before men that they may see your good works, and glorify your Father, who is in heaven." (Matthew 5:16)

AUGUST

August 1

(The Lord woke me up in the night to tell me this):

Life is about right and wrong, (honoring God).

Selfishness and pride are like weeds in the garden . . . when left unattended, they take over and destroy the whole soul. There are *seeds of selfishness* in each of us that sprout into sin as we *do that which is right in our own eyes.* (Leaving God out of the picture).

When a person lives like this, he becomes more depraved, and fails to teach his child. Then, his children have nothing to pass on to their kids; and on, and on. . .

This is the way life had become when Josiah was king.

(They had forgotten God).

But Hilkiah found the Book of the Law of the Lord that had been neglected for many generations.

God had told the people, through Jeremiah, that destruction was coming.

"So now, I am filled with the Lord's fury. Yes, I am weary of holding it in. I will pour out my fury over Jerusalem, even on children playing in the streets, on gatherings of young men, and on husbands and wives, and grandparents. Their homes will be turned over to their enemies, and so will their fields, and their wives. For I will punish the people of this land, says the Lord." (Jeremiah 6:11-12)

Imagine this happening to America!

We can, (and are supposed to) enjoy life, but we *must* honor God first and foremost! (And teach our children!)

"I will not send the promised disaster . . . until after you have died and been buried in peace. . ." (Second Chronicles 34:28)

We may escape, but what about our kids and grandchildren?

August 2

There's *fun and games*; then there's life. We need to sort them out.
"There's a time for everything, a season for every activity under heaven." (Ecclesiastes 3:1)

We need to recognize just what our lives are built on. Integrity is all important! (This is what we would do if no one would ever know.)

My sister just dropped by unexpectedly. Here I sat, (in my recliner), (in my gown), (at 9:30 a.m.)!

I had just read Matthew 24, where Jesus warns that He will come unexpectedly, as a thief in the night.

I pray that I'll be reading my Bible, instead of being deeply involved in what society deems important.

But, now, it's time to get up from here and get busy with things that *think they're important*!

Since I know what's *really* important, I am glad that I've put God first.

He instructs us in Zephaniah 2:2, **"Gather while there is still time, before the judgement begins and your opportunity is blown away like chaff. Act now, before the fierce fury of the Lord falls and the terrible day of the Lord's anger begins."**

August 3

Advice, unheeded, can guide no one. Medicine, not taken, can cure no one.

Why do we writhe in pain when there's a cure?

"Is there no balm in Gilead; is there no physician there? Why then is not the health of the daughter of my people recovered?" (Jeremiah 8:22)

Deep down, in the sub-conscience, some need *sympathy* more than a cure.

May God reveal this truth to them, else misery will be their lot in life!

". . . The Lord has appointed me to bring good news to the poor. He has sent me to comfort the broken-hearted and to announce that captives will be released and prisoners will be freed." (Isaiah 61:1b)

"But for you who fear my name, the Son of Righteousness will rise with healing in his wings. And you will go free, leaping with joy, like calves let out to pasture." (Malachi 4:2)

August 4

I *flounder* continually and it bothers me. Since I am with me all day, I have to deal with my failures. No one can do that for me. Some are small and need only to be slightly recognized.

But some are heart-wrenching, as I realize how *filthy my rags truly are*!

"We are all infected and impure with sin. When we proudly display our righteous deeds we find they are but filthy rags. Like autumn leaves, we wither and fall. And our sins, like the wind, sweep us away." (Isaiah 64:6)

My *laundry* piles up constantly, but if I want to be blessed and to be a blessing to others, who may grope for the truth that God has revealed to me, I have to keep a good supply of *detergent*!

"But if we confess our sins he is faithful and just to forgive us and to cleanse us from every wrong." (First John 1:9)

God, who created us, knows that life gets us dirty. He doesn't throw rocks at us when we sin. He just reaches out His hands, helping us up, and gives us the strength and courage to get over the *skins and bruises* of each fall.

He could lock me away in a nursing home, so I wouldn't fall so often. But He uses my *scars* to teach me to walk more carefully.

It's astounding how He faithfully keeps everything in the universe going, and yet can focus on me and my ailments!

I am assured of His love . . . but I know it's not because of how good I am, but because of how great my need for Him is, (and how great He is!)

August 5

I understand darkness and turmoil, the need to run away, trying to escape heartache and despair.

I was a baby Christian when I experienced all this. There was no peace and contentment for me. I knew God loved me, because He loves everyone. But He seemed so far away. I couldn't sense His presence.

That was a terrible storm that lasted 9 years!

When I finally came to a *dead end*, and could only look up, God whispered the "Serenity Prayer" to me.

Suddenly I realized I couldn't handle this and gave it all to God.

I told Him that I had messed up the beautiful life He had planned for me, and asked Him to just take my life, because I didn't have the faith that, even He, could fix it.

He simply *sat at the foot of my bed* and asked me questions that caused me to understand the root of my concern.

It was a *Lifeline* that I grabbed hold of and haven't turned loose since.

I had no idea that anyone could ever be content and have peace in the midst of battle, especially me!

The only time I go back in memory to this painful time is when I see someone struggle, in a similar way.

I am driven to pray for them and try to encourage them.

"He comforts us in all our troubles so that we can comfort others. When others are troubled, we will be able to give them the same comfort God gave us." (Second Corinthians 1:4)

Now, I know the plans He has for me. (See Jeremiah 29:11).

August 6

God watched closely as He formed us in the womb. (See Psalm 139:15)

He had a plan that He was *building* in us. He couldn't tell us about this plan because we couldn't understand His language. Even now, we can't hear His directions clearly.

"I had to feed you with milk and not with solid food, because you couldn't handle anything stronger. And you still aren't ready." (First Corinthians 3:2)

The more we grow as Christians, the more clearly His plan comes into view. It's more about *being* than *doing*.

We can get a glimpse of our progress as we examine our attitudes. **"For you are still controlled by your own sinful desires. You are jealous of one another and quarrel with each other. Doesn't that prove you are controlled by your own desires? You are acting like people who don't belong to the Lord."** (Verse 3)

Until we understand that it's *not about me*, (what I want), but about how God wants to use me, we will continue to be jealous and fight against each other.

Life is not a *popularity* or *beauty contest*. It's has more to do with the *kitchen cabinet*.

We are like *dishes* to be filled, so people who are hungry for the Lord can be fed.

As God fills our plate, we need to keep ourselves clean, so we can be useful. (And not pile up in the sink with other *dirty dishes*.

August 7

My *own understanding* was ruling in my heart. I had learned a lot from life and thought I knew the way to handle most things.

But, when I opened my heart's door to invite Jesus in, the battle inside me began.

He brought His wisdom. He didn't *kick* my old nature out completely. But, it was no longer *on the throne*, ruling me.

Gradually, God led me toward His will. He still allows me to fail, so He can show me that His way is far better.

Peace and contentment can replace struggles and worry. When I step aside and let Him do His will in every situation, it turns out good.

(If it doesn't go like I wanted, it's not *my fault*, it's *God's fault*).

From my perspective, it may not look good, but God never fails!

He can, (if I let Him), bring victory in every situation.

When we trust our own understanding, we can be led astray.

"There is a path before each person that seems right, but it ends in death." (Proverbs 14:12)

It may not be physical death, but the death of a victory.

August 8

I was working with one of the twins in the pool, tying to help him overcome his fear of the water.

He had his *floaties* on, but hadn't yet learned to move his feet and arms to keep his body upright, so he could relax.

Finally, he allowed me to hold onto one hand, as we *walked* around in the pool. (But he didn't use his arms.)

When I released him completely, he panicked! (Though I was right there, with my eyes on him, and speaking my love for him).

I immediately took him out of the pool. When he stood safely on the deck, he was ready to get back in the water.

As God teaches us to trust Him, we sometimes panic.

It takes time for us to realize that He is right there and will not take His eyes off us.

"Don't be afraid, for I am with you. Do not be dismayed, for I am your God. I will uphold you with my victorious right hand." (Isaiah 41:10)

We have trusted our own selves all our lives, so it is fearful to turn our trust over to a God that we can't see.

But, when we finally learn to open our spiritual eyes, we can see Him working in our lives, and sense His presence as He speaks His love to us.

He has great things in store for us!

August 9

We love our children and spoil them so easily! We show our *love* by our gifts.

But just over the horizon, they will face *battle*!

If our love has softened them, so that they don't know how to suffer and endure, they will be defeated. This will be our doing!

Wisdom teaches us to balance love with discipline, (suffering).

"No discipline is enjoyable while it is happening - it is painful! But afterward, there will be a quiet harvest of right living for those who are trained in this way." (Hebrews 12:11)

As an athlete trains for the Olympics, he has to endure suffering. He keeps his eye on his goal.

"Yet what we suffer now is nothing compared to the glory he will give us later." (Romans 8:18)

We complain when we have to go through trials, but God knows what He's doing!

"Dear brothers and sisters, whenever trouble comes your way, let it be an opportunity for joy. For when your faith is tested, your endurance has a chance to grow." (James 1:2-3)

August 10

In the parable of the farmer, in Mark 4:14-20, where do I fit in?

Sometimes I hear God's Word, but I can't comprehend its meaning or application.

It's soon forgotten, (snatched away by Satan).

There are times when I hear and realize what it means. It sounds good, but I never put it into practice.

At other times, I am determined to apply its truth to my life, (and I do - for a while).

Then, other priorities seem to absorb my time and desires. It isn't able to really change my life.

I continue to struggle, (just like an unbeliever).

Only when I set my heart on it, does it have the power to change my attitude and become a part of me.

In other words, I have to *acknowledge* that it's God's will and desire to use it in order to bless me and others.

I have to seek His will over mine. **"Then he said to the crowd, if any of you want to be my follower, you must put aside your selfish ambitions, shoulder your cross daily, and follow me."** (Luke 9:23)

The *shouldering my cross daily* means that I have to keep *killing* my own selfish desires.

If I let them have their way, I'll be defeated.

Satan desires to destroy me, and he will use every tactic to persuade me to put my desires ahead of God's will.

". . . because the Spirit who lives in you is greater than the spirit who lives in the world." (First John 4:4b)

August 11

When we pray, we should listen more than we talk. **"My dear brothers and sisters, be quick to listen, slow to speak, and slow to get angry."** (James 1:19a)

Jesus already knows what we need, but He wants us to hear some things that will be a big blessing for us.

No matter what we are saying, or asking, He is saying, "Come."

You may be fighting something so big that you feel that you've come only 2 feet in a mile-long *dark tunnel*.

But listen, and you will hear Him saying, "Come."

If tomorrow, you've only come one foot further, don't be discouraged. (You're going in the right direction), and you can still hear Him saying, "Come."

He's not in a hurry, (though you might be). He has all the time in the world, and a solid plan to bless you.

As we draw closer to Him, (even if it's only one slow step at a time), earthly things will grow dimmer and eternal truths will become clearer.

"Turn your eyes upon Jesus. Look full in His wonderful face. And the things of earth will grow strangely dim in the Light of His glory and grace."

(I didn't find the word, *come* in my concise concordance,) but a few references came to mind: Matthew 11:28; Luke 9:23; & Mark 1:17.

August 12

The scripture in one of my devotionals this morning, was Habakkuk 3:17-18: **"Even though the fig trees have no blossoms, and there are no grapes on the vine; even though the olive crop fails, and the fields are empty and barren; even though the flocks die in the fields, and the cattle barns are empty, yet will I rejoice in the Lord. I will be joyful in the God of my salvation."**

The author of my devotional paraphrased this to address her circumstances.

I, too, will paraphrase it:

"Although I am old, and life wears me out; even though there are troublesome repairs to be made and not enough money to hire them done; even though my prayer list is long, with the needs of my loved ones who are suffering, yet will I praise my Lord, for His gifts are many!"

"He allows me to live in a country where I can freely worship with other believers."

"He is gracious to speak His love to me and to offer His grace in my times of need."

"He has supplied a wonderful, loving family, and a safe, comfortable home."

"But, most of all, He drew me to Him for the salvation that He purchased for me, and is presently preparing my home with Him in heaven."

"He has miraculously cured me from cancer and given me a testimony of His faithfulness in numerous acts of mercy and grace."

I could go on forever! He is a *Great and Mighty God*!!

August 13

When you watch kids play together, it brings joy to your heart. You can sense their pleasure.

If it doesn't bring a smile to your face, it brings one to your heart.

I believe that people can sense the joy you have in a close relationship with Jesus. It brings joy to their heart also, but if our heats are not filled with that joy, (even in trouble), we broadcast our discontentment and bitterness to others. (Maybe ignorantly, without realizing it).

Our lives can be refreshing, like one who wears a pleasant-smelling cologne, or we can carry an awful odor!

I'm not really talking about actual smells, but *attitudes*.

"When I refused to confess my sins, I was weak and miserable, and I groaned all day long." (Psalm 32:3)

Our bad attitude causes us to *stink*. No one wants to be around that! We just need to take a bath!

"But if we confess our sins to him, he is faithful and just to forgive us and to cleanse us from every wrong." (First John 1:9)

"When doubts filled my mind, your comfort gave me renewed hope and cheer." (Psalm 94:19)

Now, we have a better fragrance and are more pleasant to be around.

"For I have given rest to the weary and joy to the sorrowing." (Jeremiah 31:25)

August 14

Our faith in God helps us to see life from a different perspective. We have lived our whole life *chained* to a *human viewpoint*.

We have now become new creatures. **"What this means is that those who have become Christians become new persons. They are not the same anymore, for the old life is gone. A new life has begun!"** (Second Corinthians 5:17)

We *were* children of darkness; we *now* are children of Light!

"For he has rescued us from the one who rules in the kingdom of darkness, and he has brought us into the Kingdom of his dear Son." (Colossians 1:13)

We have passed from (eternal) death to (eternal) life!

We should no longer have the same perspectives or priorities.

"That is why we live by believing and not by seeing." (Second Corinthians 5:7)

Our hope is in the Lord, not in ourselves; not in our family or friends; not in our paycheck.

After all, God is the One who has supplied all these.

You might say, they were *training wheels*, until we could walk by faith.

He may see fit to take them away at any time, but we will still be okay. Because we have *Him*.

He is *God*! He is *there*! He is *love*! He is *guidance*! He is *strength*! He is *ours*!

August 15

This will seem harsh to so many who have accepted Satan's lies.
They will cry out, "You don't understand!"
I pray they'll find out that they're the ones who haven't understood.
If we have accepted Christ as our Savior, He is our *"Eternal Foundation."*
He came to live in our hearts and has adopted us into His family. Our body is His temple, (house). (See 1 Corinthians 6:19)
He cleaned our house and desires that we keep it clean. He plants truths in our heart, (which rules our body).
Since we are His children, Satan has no business *jerking us around*.
". . . Whatever you prohibit on earth is prohibited in heaven, and whatever you allow on earth is allowed in heaven." (Matthew 18:18)
We allow Satan to lie to us and we even make his lies *our gods*, (by bowing before them as we *trade* sympathy for victory).
When we say, "We can't help it!" have we applied Philippians 4:13?
Which spirit do we believe? It's our choice!
I'm sorry if the truth hurts.
"And you shall know the truth, and the truth will set you free." (John 8:32)

August 16

"I think I can . . . I think I can . . . I think I can."

"I know I can't . . . I know I can't . . . I know I can't."

"I'm sure He can . . . I'm sure He can . . . I'm sure He can!"

I would love to get rid of this *me that* keeps following me around.

I'm so thankful that Jesus loves me more than I do!

He sees all that I see, yet He sees a completed picture that I can't see.

Some days I sense that victory is just around the corner; other days, I'm reminded just how far away I am!

It's hard to see me like Jesus does. **"Now we see things imperfectly as in a poor mirror, but then we will see everything with perfect clarity. . ."** (First Corinthians 13:12a)

I'm in my *cocoon*, struggling to become that beautiful creature! And there's ugliness as I deal with stress.

But each failure teaches me where my strength truly is.

". . . My power works best in your weakness. So now I am glad to boast about my weaknesses, so that the power of Christ may work through me." (Second Corinthians 12:9b).

If I could consistently live as I know I should, I would become proud. **". . . Even though I have received wonderful revelations from God. But to keep me from getting puffed up, I was given a thorn in my flesh, a messenger from Satan to torment me and keep me from getting proud."** (Verse 7)

God so wants to guide me in His way that He deliberately lets me *step in poop,* when I walk ahead of Him!

August 17

Satan's desire is to put a barrier between us and hope. Hope is *always* there!

Just as God is faithful to bring the sun up each morning, He supplies hope!

Some days the clouds cover the sun so we can't see it or feel its warmth. But it's *always* there!

God makes a way when there seems to be no way!

Instead of searching for a way, we should look to Him. He *is* the Way! (See John 14:6).

He does so many things that we can't see or understand. But that doesn't limit Him or His ability!

He may work in a different way than we desire or expect, but He is working . . . everything for our good. (See Romans 8:28)

How dare we say to our Maker, "You're messing up"! He's the Architect who designed everything, (and keeps it going). Who are we?

He has a purpose. (See Jeremiah 29:11)

One day we won't need hope, but now, it's our anchor!

Hang onto hope when all seems impossible. **"He replied, 'What is impossible from a human perspective is possible with God'."** (Luke 18:27)

August 18

Sometimes we have to struggle, but there are times that we struggle when we don't have to.

For instance, our outside faucet has been leaking for quite some time and is getting worse.

I'm always *the repairman*, and I dread the task at hand.

There's another solution. It will cost and I will have to trust that they will do the job well.

There's *One* who desires to handle all our stresses and He doesn't charge a dime! Why don't we turn to Him for guidance?

He's not going to do the actual work for me, but He can supply the help I need, whether it is His guidance, or the strength and courage to tackle it myself.

I know that He has allowed this problem so He can, *again*, prove that He is faithful.

It matters not whether the problem is great or small, He will supply our needs. **"And this same God who takes care of me will supply all your needs from his glorious riches, which have been given to us in Christ Jesus."** (Philippians 4:19)

(I may have mentioned this before, but I still haven't taken care of the leak!)

August 19

The sands of life shift constantly, but our *Rock* provides the stability we need. (See Luke 6:48-49).

Life is so uncertain. We worry about all the *what ifs,* and it takes us nowhere, (except to fatigue), because it keeps us awake at night.

I've learned to finally ask myself, "What's the worst that can happen?" This is what I fear, but when I face this fear and look into the face of the One who (may) allow this to happen, I find out that He's still there. (The world is still turning around!)

I will have to place my hand in His and ask, "What now?"

He will grant me guidance and courage as I need it.

To highlight His faithfulness, I will refer to the problem, (the puny little need), I mentioned yesterday - my outside faucet.

In my post, I asked, "Why don't we turn to Him for guidance?" He asked me, "Yes, why don't you?"

As I pondered the question, He showed me a different way to repair the leak!

I had to simply do the *first thing* first. When I chiseled away the mortar, so I could replace the faucet, I found that I could simply pull the pipe our far enough to get a grip on it, to keep it from twisting.

I had it in my mind that I would have to crawl under the floor and go through a big ordeal!

"For I will turn their mourning into joy and will comfort them and give them joy for their sorrow." (Jeremiah 31:13b, NASB)

August 20

In the days of our school years, we could hardly wait to graduate - to get on with life.

We didn't realize that we would always be in *the school of life*.

I hope we never stop learning. I've often made the statement, "Some people live and learn; others just live!"

Our greatest accomplishments are lessons learned from our mistakes.

We've suffered the consequences, which lead us in another direction.

Sometimes, we have to learn the same lessons over and over.

God won't let us *pass* to the next *grade,* until we've conquered the lessons of this grade.

He wants us to progress, but each lesson equips us for the next. If we haven't conquered the *trust issue*, we'll keep experiencing this test, (in different situations).

Once we've truly learned that we can trust God in *any* situation, we can *graduate* to *peace and contentment*.

From time to time, there will be a *pop quiz,* to make sure we still *trust*. If we're not there, we will be demoted.

"I am not saying this because I am in need, for I have learned to be content, whatever the circumstances. I know what it is like to be in need, and I know what it is like to have plenty. I have learned the secret of being content in any and every situation, whether living in plenty or in want." (Philippians 4:11-12)

Paul's *graduation gift* was Verse 13, **"I can do everything through Him who gives me strength."**

August 21

As we minister to our family, we gain knowledge and experience needed to minister to others. Home is our first *mission field*.

When we look to God and ask for His plans, instead of ours, we will succeed. Our family shares this success. There is joy, peace, and laughter, instead of strife and complaints.

In "Jesus Calling", Sarah Young writes, *"Do not worry about what other people think of you. The work that I, (Jesus) am doing in you is hidden at first. But eventually blossoms will burst forth and abundant fruit will be borne."*

We can't see what a small deed like preparing a meal or making a bed may be accomplishing in God's Kingdom. But our family needs to see these acts of love and service, as God uses us in His *hidden* work.

"Work hard and cheerfully at whatever you do, as though you were working for the Lord rather than for people." (Colossians 3:23) (They may not ever appreciate it).

August 22

I was impressed with the devotion in "Open Windows" today. It showed a comparison between a chameleon and a butterfly.

One changes on the outside to blend in with its environment, (in order to hide its true being), while the other goes through a transformation on the inside, and emerges as a new creation.

Of course, the scripture reading was, **"And be not conformed to this world, but be ye transformed by the renewing of your mind, that ye may prove what is that good, and acceptable, and perfect will of God."** (Romans 12:2)

Satan has a lie that causes many to *take a shortcut* that *looks* like salvation, when actually, these people have only *gone through the motions*.

They've follow instructions, but they've never given themselves to God, in exchange for the new life He offers.

My sister has just gone through a *remodel* of her bathroom. She had to be willing that her old tub be torn out, (destroyed) in order for a new shower to be installed.

This was a big decision, not only because of the cost, but because of the inconvenience and vulnerability of trusting that the job be completed to her satisfaction and in her time frame.

When we accept Christ as our Savior, we also have to trust Him as *Lord*, (*Boss*).

If we don't surrender the *old*, we can't experience the *new*.

We'll only be *chameleons* with no power to live the peaceful, abundant life that Christ died to supply.

I pray that this post will convey the power of God's Word to change the lives of those who have fallen for Satan's deception. (See Hebrews 4:12)

August 23

Generations ago, we lived a simple life, nurturing our children, honoring the Lord.

We were so blessed! But we didn't know it. We didn't give God praise for these blessings.

We looked around and envied our neighbors. They wore nicer clothes, drove better cars, and lived in beautiful homes.

We wanted these things for our kids, so we *traded away* the time we spent with them.

We made the *nice things* our *gods*. We didn't realize that we were actually *offering our children* as sacrifices to them.

We haven't passed the simple life on to our kids. They don't know that the Lord is the source of everything good; of all that we'll ever need. (See Matthew 6:33).

We've been scammed!!

Our most important *assignment* is to please God with our lives. When we seek to do this, He brings peace, strength, and encouragement, as He guides us daily.

We're so blinded by the *things we can see* that we don't seek the Invisible Power that supplies the most important things. (For now and for eternity.)

We are simply *souls* that God has allowed to exist.

How can we bring our focus back to the simple life? (Loving God and loving each other), instead of running the *rat race* without any significance?

"Enter in at the narrow gate; for wide is the gate, and broad is the way, that leadeth to destruction, and many there be who go in that way." (Matthew 7:13)

August 24

As we travel through life, we encounter trials, (*battles*) that leave us in need of help.

We may find ourselves *awaiting surgery*. (To allow healing to begin).

Or we may, at the moment, be in the *operating room*, actually going through a painful procedure. (To bring about some good - see Romans 8:28).

This process will either transport us on into eternity, or we will find ourselves in the *recovery room*.

In extreme instances, we will spend some time in *ICU*, as our critical needs are met.

But after this process, we will continue our recovery in our *hospital room*.

Though it has been a difficult struggle, we will finally be released, strong enough to *go home* and ready to conquer yet another *battle*, (normal life).

These *exercises* are common to everyone. **"But remember that the temptations"**, (troubles) **"that come into your life are no different from what others experience. And God is faithful. He will keep the temptation from becoming so strong that you can't stand up against it. . .He will show you a way out so you will not give in to it."** (First Corinthians 10:13)

(He's our *Spiritual Trainer*). We *can* receive the strength we need to overcome Satan's tactics.

The *offensive weapon* we have is the *Word of God*. **"Put on salvation as your helmet, and take the sword of the Spirit, which is the Word of God."** (Ephesians 6:17)

We can *whoop* the devil because we're God's children. (See 1 John 4:4).

August 25

When despair has us in its grip; when there's absolutely no way we can win, and we have to give in to the inevitable...*There's God*!

We win when we yield to Him! Peace settles in like a fog. We're *okay*! We're in His loving hands. This is His plan.

We can know that what we need, (and don't have), will be given to us at just the right time. (See Philippians 4:13 & 19).

We can trust the One who keeps the earth on its axis.

It's not about us, our strengths, desires, or wisdom.

We are His *pawns* in His *chess game*. He uses us, and the trials that He allows, to spread His truth to the world.

"Acknowledge that the Lord is God! He has made us, and we are his. We are his people, the sheep of his pasture." (Psalm 100:3)

To God be the glory! Great things He has done, is doing, and will continue to do!

August 26

There's a powerful message in "Open Windows" today about guarding our heart.

"It's where God works and it's the target of the enemy."

The devotion mentioned the Titanic, and the main point was that "a whole ocean of water can't sink a ship . . . unless it gets inside!"

It is essential that we pay attention to our thought process. Because negative thoughts *infect* our very being.

They *will* come, but we must resist them and *replace* them with praise.

We get spiritually lazy and just allow them to invade. Then, we are overwhelmed by life itself, because these negative thoughts are like *weeds* that sap the *health* of our soul.

God tells us what to think about when Satan tries to poison our thoughts. "**. . . Fix your thoughts on what is true and honorable and right. Think about things that are pure and lovely and admirable. Think about things that are excellent and worthy of praise.**" (Philippians 4:8)

It takes spiritual *effort* to put up a *road block* against these *naturally flowing*, destructive forces. But they *mess up* our whole outlook on life, and cause us to dwell on "Woe is me!"

The Bible says we are dead to sin . . . (but sin is not dead!) It pounds on the door of our heart continually, trying to gain entry.

August 27

When we pray for someone to be healed, we think, "This is surely God's will. He is good! He is loving and compassionate! He is able!"

But pain and death are some of His *tools* that cause us to fall on our knees before Him.

When we do, some of us confess our need for salvation, as we see our loved ones facing eternity.

We know, as long as there is life, there's hope. But after death, all hope (to change) is gone.

Those of us who are already saved, seek to know God better. As we seek understanding, we are drawn to His Word and communication with Him through prayer.

We can read in Isaiah 55:8, **"My thoughts are completely different from yours . . . and my ways are far beyond anything you could imagine."**

"For I know the plans I have for you . . . they are plans for good and not for disaster, to give you a future and a hope." (Jeremiah 29:11)

"Come unto me. . ." (Matthew 11:28)

"My grace is sufficient for you. . ." (Second Corinthians 12:9)

"You both precede and follow me. You place your hand of blessing on my head." (Psalm 139:5)

"I am Alpha and Omega, the beginning and the ending . . . who is, and who was, and who is to come, the Almighty." (Revelation 1:8)

He is *love*. (See 1 John 4:8) And He knows what *love* is doing. (We don't.)

August 28

How thankful I am for love and laughter!

Wouldn't life be dark and dreary without it?

Sometimes love makes us laugh. It produces the *nutrients* that help us grow.

The direction we are to grow is toward God and the ones who need love most.

Love sometimes demands more than we like to share. We seem to think it weakens us to give of ourselves and show love to those who *really* need it. But it's the strength that keeps us going.

(Without love, where would we go?) And what would be the use of *going*?

It's the *fuel* that helps us function. Love doesn't allow us to concentrate on ourselves continually. It thrives when we're blessing others.

Jesus called it *"Light."* **"Don't hide your light under a basket! Instead, put it on a stand and let it shine for all."** (Matthew 5:15). He wasn't talking about our own love, but His. His love *lights* our way.

It seems that we all *take turns* needing love from others. God fills our heart to overflowing when we're not *stingy* with it.

August 29

"Why didn't I do that?" or "Why did I say that?"

Some of our failures or harsh words haunt us. They came and went so quickly that we didn't have a chance to even think.

We are as bewildered as the ones we wronged!

Our best response is to humble ourselves and ask forgiveness.

The ones we wronged may not be willing to freely forgive us, but we must forgive ourselves.

An immature Christian, (That's all of us!) will act like an immature child.

We have to *learn* not to be selfish or arrogant. We can't possibly overcome all our faults quickly, but we can make progress.

"We do this by keeping our eyes on Jesus, on whom our faith depends from start to finish. . ." (Hebrews 12:2a)

As we grow closer to the Lord, we grow further from our sinful nature.

Hopefully, today, we'll be different than yesterday. (Even if only so slightly that it can't be measured.)

But, just as a toddler has to be *trained* not to wet his pants, victory will gradually come, (with God's help).

Forgiving ourselves can be compared to dealing with grief, (though there's a process to go through), we have to turn it loose. Like releasing a balloon, (never to recover it). We can release our grief, while keeping our memories.

Jesus cast our sins as far as the East is from the West. (Infinity)

"As far as the East is from the West, so far has he removed our transgressions from us." (Psalm 103:12)

We can't be content with what we were yesterday or we'll never grow, but we can be free from that haunting guilt.

August 30

We encounter God unexpectedly. Do we recognize Him?

He is in the people we meet and the situations we deal with daily. He sees how we act and react.

"Thereafter, Hagar referred to the Lord, who had spoken to her, as "the God who sees me!" For she said, I have seen the one who sees me." (Genesis 16:13)

God knows where we are and He desires to build His character in us.

"If you're happy, (and you know it), then your face will surely show it!" If we're grateful, (and we know it), then our heart will surely show it!

He not only sees our body, He sees our need, (for love, for comfort, for strength, for encouragement. . .)

He's all these things for us. His name is **"I AM!"** (See Exodus 3:14).

"And I will give you a new heart with new and right desires, and I will put a new spirit in you. I will take out your stony heart of sin and give you a new obedient heart." (Ezekiel 36:26)

He gave us this power and He's teaching us how to use it.

August 31

I saw a video on Facebook of a man using a chainsaw on a large stump to form a beautiful creation of 3 raccoons, climbing the stump, and a fox.

The video was *time-lapsed*, so I could quickly see every action, without realizing the time and effort spent.

How could he look at a stump and see his finished project in his mind?

He chiseled away everything that didn't belong, as he visualized the beauty of his finished work.

When God looks at us, He doesn't see a *stump*, but the *purpose* of His creation.

We only see the stump and feel the pain of all that is being *chiseled* away.

Our complaints are heard far and wide! All the while, God is silently creating His *work of art*.

"And I am sure that God, who began the good work within you, will continue his work until it is finally finished on that day when Jesus Christ comes back again." (Philippians 1:6)

"For God knows his people in advance, and he chose them to become like his Son, so that his Son would be the firstborn, with many brothers and sisters." (Romans 8:29)

"Yet, what we suffer now is nothing compared to the glory he will give us later." (Romans 8:18)

SEPTEMBER

September 1

The truth of this world is that the spirit needs the body in order to perform its tasks. That's why God left us here after He saved us. He is a Spirit. **"For God is Spirit, so those who worship him must worship in spirit and truth."** (John 4:24)

He uses our bodies to meet the needs of others. **"And the King will tell them, "I assure you, when you did it to the least of these my brothers and sisters you were doing it unto me!"** (Matthew 25:40)

We are to no longer serve only ourselves, but others. **"Then he said to the crowd, 'If any of you wants to be my followers, you must put aside your selfish ambition, shoulder your cross daily, and follow me'."** (Luke 9:23)

He bought us out of slavery to sin. **"For God bought you with a high price. So you must honor God with your body."** (I Corinthians 6:20)

We are the *tools* He uses to accomplish His will here on earth. When we finish our work, He has a great *retirement plan* for us.

". . . No eye has seen, no ear has heard, and no mind has imagined what God has prepared for those who love him." (I Corinthians 2:9b)

September 2

Lay's Potato Chips claim, "Bet'cha can't eat just one." as a temptation to try. It's better if you're on a diet, to say, "You're right. So I won't even try."

It's harder to stop, once we indulge, than to abstain altogether. Look at any sin - gossip, drinking, smoking, etc. Once we start, we're hooked!

Paul said in 1 Thessalonians 5:22, **"Abstain from all appearance of evil."**

I guess, in the example of Lay's claim, if it looks like a potato chip, stay away from it! (Of course, we know there's nothing wrong with a potato chip.) Thank Goodness!

James gave us the answer to this dilemma, **"Submit yourselves, therefore, to God, resist the devil, and he will flee from you."** (James 5:7)

September 3

Anger causes one to act impulsively. We just do something without really thinking about it. It's what's in us coming out, like a broken water spout, spewing everywhere. I guess that's more than just anger, that's a temper tantrum!

I've had more than my share of them. (I can almost hear my kids saying, "*Amen!*")

What comes out is from the pits of hell! Stress builds and finds the weakest point.

Back when we were dealing with a drinking problem, I would threaten to leave and never come back. He would just plead for me to sleep on it, saying things would look better in the morning. He was so right! But I was immature and advice didn't come easily to me.

As I sit here *having coffee with the Lord*, He just showed me Psalm 30:45, **"Sing to the Lord, all you godly ones! Praise his holy name. His anger lasts for a moment, but his favor lasts a lifetime! Weeping may go on all night, but joy comes with the morning."**

Things may not change, but God can give us a different perspective *in the morning*. Resting in Him allows us to remember that He has a plan and that He is allowing each situation in order to speak to us. He's there and He cares!

September 4

We don't know our destination here on earth as we travel through life. **"We can make our plans, but the Lord determines our steps."** (Proverbs 16:9)

I get a picture in my mind of me watching an ant, with a load of food, heading for home, much like us coming home from the grocery store.

Most of the time, he is unhindered. But, what if I placed a large object in his way?

I can't know if he is cussing a blue streak or merely saying to himself, "Oh, well, I guess I'll go this way."

God doesn't just place things in our path to frustrate us. He has a plan for our good. (See Romans 8:28)

Before we were saved, we weren't searching for God. **"No one has real understanding, no one is seeking God. All have turned away from God; all have gone wrong. No one does good, not even one."** (Romans 3:11-12)

But God is seeking us! **"For the Son of Man is come to seek and to save that which was lost."** (Luke 19:10)

He still seeks us for fellowship. We're His children and He wants to spend time with us. But, it's like this week-end. I want our family to get together for a cook-out and fellowship. But, I realize that life makes demands on them and they are very busy.

I don't want a cook-out to be a burden on them. Since we get together often, I can give up a week-end. But we really do *have* to get together often!

September 5

This message is strictly for me. But I invite you to listen in.

As we travel down the road or street, we pass many houses. A family lives in each one. It's impossible, in town, to visualize who lives in each house. But in rural areas, we may have time to wonder about each family, what their lives may be like, and maybe even to pray God's blessing over them.

But most of the time, we're much too busy or preoccupied to be concerned.

Also, we come in close contact with people every day. But we only see their bodies. We don't take time to care who *lives there*.

If we're waiting in line, we may be able to strike up a conversation and learn a little about them. If the wait is long enough, we could even find out if we're *kin*, (brothers and sisters in Christ).

I have never been a *people person*. The scripture in "Open Windows" this morning is James 2:8, **"If ye fulfill the royal law according to the scripture, thou shalt love thy neighbor as thyself, ye do well."**

In another devotion, **"Yes, if you cry out for discernment, and lift up your voice for understanding, then you will understand the fear of the Lord, and find the knowledge of God."** *(*Proverbs 2:3 & 5)

God is telling me that each person is valuable to Him and that I should care about them.

September 6

We say we trust God, but do we tithe? People have a lot of different views about it. Some have their finances so tied up with earthly pleasures that they feel they can't afford it.

Others think they can obligate God to bless them if they give to Him. (See Malachi 3:10).

We're His children and He has blessed us in so many ways. When we recognize that, we truly want to honor Him for His goodness and mercy. **"Honor the Lord with thy substance and with the first fruits of all thine increase; so shall thy barns be filled with plenty, and thy presses shall burst out with new wine."** (Proverbs 3:9-10)

We can look at tithing as *paying the rent*. It is what we owe God. **"Will a man rob God? Yet ye have robbed me. But ye say, 'How have we robbed thee?' In tithes and offerings."** (Malachi 3:8)

Offerings are gifts but the tithe *belongs* to Him.

If we don't tithe, we aren't trusting God to supply what we truly need. We want to take the *rent money*, and spend it on ourselves.

September 7

God guides us by His love. When He has to correct or rebuke us, it isn't to shame us and make us feel guilty. He wants us to feel good about ourselves.

Many times when we hear a sermon, we feel bad but we don't really try to change. That's not the intended purpose.

"There is therefore, now, no condemnation to them who are in Christ Jesus, who walk not after the flesh, but after the Spirit." (Romans 8:1)

Christ wants to free us from a life of guilt and bring us into a life of joy as He guides us.

"And thine ears shall hear a word behind thee saying, 'This is the way, walk ye in it. When ye turn to the right hand, and when ye turn to the left'." (Isaiah 30:21)

When watching a toddler heading for disaster, we attempt to turn him in another direction, not to ruin his fun, but to protect him. He shows his frustration, but he is immature.

When we know we're doing wrong, our rebellion shows that we are immature.

"As for God, his way is perfect. All the Lord's promises prove true. He is a shield for all who look to Him for protection." (Psalm 18:30)

For our good, we should seek to follow Him. **"In all thy ways, acknowledge him, and he shall direct thy paths."** (Proverbs 3:6)

September 8

Let's visualize ourselves in *the courtroom of life*.

There's an Eye Witness. **"Nothing in all creation can hide from him. Everything is naked and exposed before his eyes. This is the God to whom we must explain all that we have done."** (Hebrews 4:13) (Or *though*t, see Verse 12)

Before our case is presented, the penalty has been paid. **"That is why we have a great High Priest who has gone to heaven, Jesus the Son of God. Let us cling to him and never stop trusting him."** (Verse 14)

Our High Priest is also our Defense Attorney. **"This High Priest understands our weaknesses, for he faced all of the same temptations we do, yet he did not sin."** (Verse 15)

We don't have to fear as He presents our case before the Judge. **"So let us come boldly to the throne of our gracious God. There we will find grace to help when we need it."** (Verse 16)

In John 19:30, we reflect as the payment was being made on the cross for our penalty. **"When Jesus had tasted it, he said, 'It is finished'. Then he bowed his head and gave up his spirit."**

We now walk away, free from any condemnation, because all has been paid on our behalf! (See Romans 8:1)

Our gratitude should constrain us to return His great love. We can't out-give God, the more we give to Him; the more He pours out His blessings on us.

What an awesome God and loving Friend!

September 9

It's good that we don't have to live this life alone. We have the gift of someone who cares. For some, it is a spouse. For others, it is children, a sister or brother, a mom or dad. For some, it may be a neighbor, a co-worker, or someone at church, etc.

Even someone that is homebound with no family has a caretaker of some sort.

We need each other. When we are weak, they are strong; when they're weak, we're strong.

It's our responsibility to keep ourselves strong so that we can help those who need physical help, or encouragement or comfort.

"For where two or three are gathered together in my name, there am I in the midst of them." (Matthew 18:20)

We may think we can't help because we, ourselves are in need. **"Study to show thyself approved unto God, a workman that needeth not to be ashamed, rightly dividing the word of truth."** (Second Timothy 2:15)

Praise God for providing someone for each of us!

September 10

It's a dangerous thing to keep *playing church*, just going through the motions, for whatever reason.

When we sit in church Sunday after Sunday, claiming to know God, yet there's no joy - something is seriously wrong!

Our lives are not proclaiming the victory of the cross. Instead, they are saying, "I know all that, but it's not enough."

I was reading in Hebrews this morning. **"For it is impossible to restore to repentance those who were once enlightened - those who have experienced the good things of heaven and shared in the Holy Spirit, who have tasted the goodness of the word of God and the power of the age to come - and who have turned away from God, it is impossible to bring such people to repentance again because they are nailing the Son of God to the cross again by rejecting him, holding him up to public shame."** (Chapter 6:4-6)

Jesus gave all He had, even His life, to set us free from the chains of life – (sin). If we're so *married* to sin that we choose any part of it over the truth of God's love, heaven help us!

We cringe when we read, **"Thou shalt have no other gods before me."** (Exodus 20:3). We know how much we love even our grandchildren. The test is:

If they were taken away from us or had to suffer drastically, would that cause us to turn away from God, or run to Him? (That tells us if they are our *gods*!)

September 11

I'm in God's hands. Therefore, I am totally secure. Troubles come and go, and Satan always nips at my heels. But he can only threaten. He can cause me to worry, but I have a Savior who loves me and controls all things. Therefore, I can have peace.

His grace has brought me through multiple *impossible* situations.

I'm not holding onto Him, He is holding on to me. My strength is small, but His never fails! He has an appointed time to call me home. Until then, He sustains me.

May I be sensitive to His voice so that I'll be a useful instrument for His purpose? (Whatever that may be.)

Looking back, I'm *amazed*! Looking ahead, I'm *confident*. Sitting here, I'm *content*. His presence is so precious!

I'm saying today what Jesus cried on the cross, **"Father, into Thy hands, I commend my spirit."** (Luke 23:46b)

September 12

Peter had no idea the type of battle he would be facing when he declared his allegiance to Jesus in Mark 14:31, **"But he spoke the more vehemently, if I should die with thee, I will not deny thee in any way. . ."**

He thought it would be a physical battle. That's why he cut off the servant's ear. (See verse 47) He knew if it came to that, he would be willing to die for his Lord. But he was *blindsided* by the enemy. It was a spiritual battle instead!

Our insight isn't much different. We read in 1 Timothy 6:10, **"For the love of money is the root of all evil, which, while some coveted after, they have erred from the faith, and pierced themselves through with many sorrows."**

Yet we find ourselves giving up so much in order to attain more of that stuff! The problem is that we need money in order to survive. But as we gain *survival*, we see that *more* can give us more comfort, more recreation, etc.

Without realizing it, we're marching in the wrong direction. This *race* causes us stress that builds, which destroys our health.

A millionaire still hasn't *arrived*. He strives to become a billionaire!

Wisdom gives us contentment when we've reached *enough*. We have enough when we don't *need* any more.

Now, *want* is a different story! I don't *need* to *want* more!

"But seek ye first the kingdom of God and his righteousness, and all these things shall be added to you." (Matthew 6:33)

September 13

When one smokes, there is a smell that permeates the whole house and everything in it. When you walk in, or come close to the person, there's no doubt about the source of the odor.

A sweet smell isn't an odor, it is a *fragrance*. Christ's presence is like a sweet smelling rose.

"How fragrant your cologne, and how pleasing your name! No wonder all the young women love you!" (Song of Solomon 1:3)

We don't smell it with our nose, just like we don't hear His voice with our ears. When we spend time with Christ, His fragrance permeates our soul. We can be like an air freshener when we walk into a room, much like when we bring His light into the darkness if we're filled with His love.

"Let your light so shine before men that they may see your good works, and glorify your Father, which is in heaven." (Matthew 5:16)

We are not to bring judgement of condemnation. That's out of our realm of authority. Only God has that right.

(*"Except for the grace of God, there go I."*)

A sweet fragrance is like the *balm* in Gilead. **"Go into Gilead and take balm, O Virgin, the daughter of Egypt; in vain shall thou use many medicines; for thou shalt not be cured."** (Jeremiah 46:11)

September 14

As it is football season, maybe we can get a better picture of our mission in God's kingdom. God, as the *Coach*, calls the plays, (gives us assignments). He guides us.

"Trust in the Lord with all thine heart, and lean not unto thine own understanding." (Proverbs 3:5)

He gives us the strength to carry out His plan. **"My grace is sufficient for thee; for my strength is made perfect in weakness. . ."** (Second Corinthians 12:9a)

He uses others on the team to assist (pray for) us as we combat the enemy.

Even if we feel we're alone out on the field, we'd be amazed if we could see all the *fans* cheering for us. **"Wherefore, seeing we are compassed about with so great a cloud of witnesses, let us lay aside every weight, and the sin which doth so easily beset us, and let us run with patience the race that is set before us."** (Hebrews 12:1)

God is not only our *Coach*, He is a *Player-Coach*, who is out on the field with us. He is blocking for us, opening a hole for us to run through so we can advance the *ball*, (gospel).

"When thou passeth through the waters, I will be with thee, and through the rivers, they shall not overflow thee; when thou walkest through the fire, thou shalt not be burned, neither shall the flame kindle upon thee." (Isaiah 43:2a)

When we hand the ball off or pass it, we are involved in the *touchdown* (salvation).

While we'd like to be the hero, we all know who the *Hero* really is. He not only saved us, but created us to be on His team.

"For whom he did foreknow, he also did predestinate to be conformed to the image of his Son. . ." (Romans 8:29a)

September 15

Sometimes the devil says, "Yes", while God is saying, "No." And sometimes God is saying "Yes", when the devil says, "No."

How can we know who is saying, "Yes"?

If we don't know God's Word very well, it is confusing. By His Word, we can distinguish His voice. **"My sheep hear my voice, and I know them, and they follow me."** (John 10:27)

Many times Satan disguises himself as an *angel of light*. (See Second Corinthians 11:14).

He offers us something that outwardly looks or sounds good at the moment, but can lure us away from God. (Much like a stranger offering candy to a child.)

We really need to keep our eyes on God and stay close to Him. He is our protection from that *roaring lion* in 1 Peter 5:8.

Also, Satan can use those who *profess* to be Christians. They speak about God, but they don't belong to Him. **"Beware of false prophets, who come to you in sheep's clothing, but inwardly they are ravening wolves."** (Matthew 7:15)

It's dangerous to go to the wrong church. Anytime we hear a message that doesn't line up with the rest of the gospel, we need to be diligent to study its direction. (Where it may lead.)

The situation with Jim Jones, in Guyana, is the perfect illustration of this truth.

Life is too precious to *play* with. Not only can our foolish or immature decisions get us into trouble, but our children may follow us into that same trap!

September 16

We don't see missionaries as *heroes*, but many of them serve among radical Islamists - those who have sprouted into terrorist groups like ISIS. These missionaries have the courage of Green Berets or Navy Seals. They have to work covertly in order to stay alive.

Their mission is not to kill the enemy, but to save him! God, alone, is their shield. They don't take Him for granted or neglect His guidance. They realize they need His power and protection, as well as His wisdom in order to keep breathing so they can share the gospel with those who hate them.

"But I say unto you, love your enemies, bless them that curse you, do good to them that hate you, and pray for them who despitefully use you, and persecute you." (Matthew 5:44)

These missionaries have truly placed their lives in God's hands. They have their eyes fixed on Him and listen carefully as He unfolds His plans for each day.

When they have doubts and become discouraged or afraid, they express this to their Leader, so they can be assured, **". . . I will never fail you. I will never forsake you. That is why we can say with confidence, The Lord is my helper, so I will not be afraid. What can mere mortals do to me?"** (Hebrews 13:5b-6)

We should be diligent in praying for our missionaries daily.

September 17

Because of our $18 trillion national debt, and other terrible things going on in our world, we hear of a financial crisis that will soon hit our nation, as well as the rest of the world.

The news is so bad that many choose not to listen anymore. You know, the ostrich who sticks his head in the sand. That may cause it to disappear from his mind, but it doesn't make it go away.

The only way to handle such news is to hand it over to God and ask His guidance. He's the *only* One who is big enough to handle it. The way we do that is simply to pray (and believe):

We should pray, "Lord, I know you may allow poverty and even famine to come our way *because* we have allowed laws that go against your laws. (Abortion and same sex marriage, to name a couple). We have given our lives to serve things money can buy. We deserve your wrath. I pray you'll forgive us, and give us wisdom. Help us endure what comes to us and use it to draw us closer to you."

We are like little kids who are willing to trade a dollar bill for 2 quarters. What we have invested our lives in amounts to this same kind of foolish thinking. If our lives are invested in heavenly things, no amount of financial doom can destroy us. God promises to meet all our *needs*!

"And this same God who takes care of me will supply all your needs from his glorious riches, which have been given to us in Christ Jesus." (Philippians 4:19)

So, instead of hoarding up dollar bills, grab a notebook and fill it with: Romans 8:28; Proverbs 3:5-6; Isaiah 55:8; Philippians 4:13 & 19; 2 Timothy 1:7; 2 Corinthians 12:9; & Philippians 4:6-7. Add to that any other verses that God may show you which will sustain you through difficult times. You may also want to add James 5:1-3. It isn't not a sin to save money, in fact, we should. But we can't trust in it! And we should be willing to use it for God's glory.

September 18

How God cares for each one of us! Sometimes we feel it; sometimes we don't. Nevertheless, His love surrounds us continually. His protection is available for us, like the wings of a mother hen, protecting her young.

Yet, many times, we run out into the rain and storms. **"O, Jerusalem, Jerusalem, the city that kills the prophets and stones God's messengers! How often I have wanted to gather your children together as a hen protects her chicks beneath her wings, but you wouldn't let me."** (Matthew 23:37)

God endeavors to teach us His ways. He gave Moses the Ten Commandments to show us how to live a good life. They are His laws that carry the death penalty for disobedience. (Much like Adam and Eve's disobedience in the garden).

God knew none of us could keep all these laws perfectly, and that breaking only one, only once, would label us *sinner*. So He sent His Son.

Romans 6:23 presents the results of and the protection from our disobedience, **"For the wages of sin is death, but the gift of God is eternal life through Jesus Christ, our Lord."** He offers this protection under His wings.

Many think that because we have accepted His gift of eternal life, we don't have to obey any longer. You don't. But He has warned us not to run out from under His wings. **"Don't be misled. Remember that you can't ignore God and get away with it. You will always reap what you sow."** (Galatians 6:7)

September 19

We all have difficulty with discrimination, whether we admit it or not. This may not have anything to do with *racial* discrimination.

"For instance, suppose someone comes into your meeting dressed in fancy clothes and expensive jewelry, and another comes in who is poor, and dressed in shabby clothes. If you give special attention and a good seat to the rich person, but you say to the poor, 'You can stand over there, or else sit on the floor'—well, doesn't this discrimination show that you are guided by wrong motives?" (James 2:2-4)

None of us are perfect, but we should strive for perfection. **"Be ye perfect, even as you Father, who is in heaven, is perfect."** (Matthew 5:48)

We are all so imperfect that if we focus on all our sins at once, we will become discouraged. But as God points out one of them to us, let us empty our lives of that clutter. (See 1 John 1:9) When we do that, we open ourselves up to that abundant life Jesus desires for us.

"The thief's purpose is to steal, and kill, and destroy. My purpose is to give life in all its fullness." (John 10:10)

September 20

I've always been a *fixer*. I've spent many hours *spinning my wheels*, trying to connect something that has come undone. I get so close, *so close* . . . then it slips and I'm back where I started!

Most people would just give up and walk away. But I always think, "*Where there's a will, there's a way.*"

I spend several minutes thinking, "I've just about got it. I can do it." Then desperation sets in and I realize I've invested too much time to give up, but I'm not going to be able to do it. Finally, I ask for God's help. He lets me struggle a little longer, then it slips into place!

This is all small stuff that doesn't *amount to a hill of beans*. But I learn from these struggles that I am not *alone*.

We burden ourselves with so many small problems that when *something big* comes along, the stress is more than we can bear.

I don't know why we can't just see life from God's perspective, and know it may be a long hard struggle, but it will be okay.

The sooner we lean on the Lord, the sooner we get relief. **"I will not leave you comfortless; I will come to you."** (John 14:18)

September 21

When you're employed by a company, you are theirs for those hours. You have assignments that aren't written, but you understand.

Because God created us and bought us back again, we belong to Him; not just for 40 hours a week, but every moment of every day.

We don't realize it, but as we wake every day, we get our assignments. We can either get frustrated or realize that He is in control and has every right to issue and carry out His plans in our lives.

"We can make our plans, but the Lord determines our steps." (Proverbs 16:9)

He supplies all we need, even the strength and wisdom to do His will. At least one of His assignments is concern for others; to pray for them, especially if they are having problems, need to come to Him for salvation, or to turn loose of their rebellion in order to receive His blessings, etc.

His assignments *never* include worry! That's what we do when we want things to be done our way. **"My thoughts are completely different from yours, says the Lord, And my ways are far beyond anything you could imagine."** (Isaiah 55:8)

When we see a child who demands his way, we can visibly see how much better it would be for him if he would just obey!

"Trust and obey, for there's no other way to be happy in Jesus, but to trust and obey."

Why do we struggle like that stubborn child? As God has brought a concern to our attention, He wants us to be still and listen for His assignment. He wants us to let Him do it His way, and for us to assist Him as He instructs. (See Philippians 4:6-7). He is teaching us how to be useful to Him and to give us peace, at the same time, as we bring problems to Him.

September 22

There are those among us that seem to struggle through life. They have repeatedly heard God's Word, but can't seem to allow His Truth to become a part of them.

As they hear it, their minds keep saying, "Yeah, but. . ."

I was reading this morning, **"The Lord is my strength and my song; he has become my salvation. He is my God, and I will praise him; my father's God, and I will exalt him."** (Exodus 15:2)

You can't sing praises and struggle with worry at the same time. You know you should have joy, but you don't! Even when you cry out for joy, it doesn't come. Something is blocking it. What can you do?

James 4:7-8 says, 1. **Humble yourselves before God**. 2. **Resist the Devil and he will flee from you.** 3. **Draw close to God.** 4. **God will draw close to you.**

When we admit how small and helpless we really are, we are humbling ourselves before God. We can resist the Devil by admitting our weakness and asking forgiveness for our pride and trying to be in control.

We come close to God by laying our burdens at His feet. He then is free to work in our lives *as we release control to Him.*

We can trust that He wants to bless us. We can never feel worthy, but He loves us anyway. He sees us like an animal trapped in a snare. He wants to help us, but we keep struggling and He can't come near. He knows the answer that will free us.

"So I tell you, don't worry about everyday life. . ." (Matthew 6:25a) And **"So don't worry about tomorrow, for tomorrow will bring its own worries. Today's trouble is enough for today."** (Verse 34)

"So humble yourselves under the mighty power of God, and in his good time he will honor you. Give all your worries and cares to God, for he cares about what happens to you." (First Peter 5:6-7)

September 23

God spoke to me this morning through the beautiful sunrise, saying, "Here I am!"

I went out with my camera to capture its beauty. My pictures fell way short! Nothing can capture all of God's beauty! So many sunrises have come and gone without my awareness. All of life is like that. We're too busy just living life to acknowledge God, His beauty, His grace, His peace, mercy, wisdom, power, love, faithfulness, provisions, protection, guidance, etc., I could go on forever! You can add your own.

He's so very awesome! Yet, He wants to spend time with *me*! He has always wanted this, but *this little nobody* didn't have time for Him. What have I missed out on by being so preoccupied with other things?

When we focus on *The Giver*, all His gifts unfold before us. We opt instead, to worry and struggle in our own efforts.

"Be still and know that I am God; I will be exalted among the nations, I will be exalted in the earth." (Psalm 46:10)

"Every good gift and every perfect gift is from above, and cometh down from the Father of lights, with whom is no variableness, neither shadow of turning." (James 1:17)

September 24

Some problems we have are hard to understand. That's where *trust* comes in. You can see it in a baby's eyes. He knows you love him. Even when you take him to the doctor to get a shot.

He doesn't understand why you subjected him to this pain, but he forgives you and puts it all behind him.

We have to forgive God because He loves us and knows the pain we have to endure will work for our good.

Our trust in His love is essential. We may not understand while we're hurting. But, like the baby, we have to put the pain behind us and go on.

As time passes, we may vividly remember the experience, but the pain begins to subside, (more slowly for some than for others).

We can reach into our *bag of scriptures*, and pull out our *Romans 8:28* and *Proverbs 3:5* to find comfort.

"Let us hear the conclusion of the whole matter: Fear God and keep his commandments; for this is the whole duty of man." (Ecclesiastes 12:13)

We can take all that has happened as God's planning, (to bring us peace and joy.)

"Now unto him who is able to keep you from falling, and to present you faultless before the presence of his glory with exceeding joy." (Jude 24) *The finished product!*

September 25

Daily, I'm actually watching two little babies become toddlers. They are unsure of themselves as they attempt taking steps. They currently use a *walk-behind* toy to assist them, but they will soon be on their way!

As we slowly learned to walk, physically, it is also a slow process as we learn to turn our backs on our physical walk and depend on God for our spiritual growth.

It's easy for an old *walker*, like myself to get frustrated with the younger Christians, unless I allow myself to remember how far Christ has brought me, (through *thick and thin*).

"You must crave pure spiritual milk so that you can grow into the fullness of your salvation. Cry out for this nourishment as a baby cries for milk." (First Peter 2:2)

We can't make ourselves crave this nourishment, but God sure can! That's why He, in His wisdom, allows difficult situations to come our way. He provides the nourishment for our spiritual growth. We must learn to release the hold our flesh has on us in order to grow spiritually.

"So I advise you to live according to your new life in the Holy Spirit. Then you won't be doing what your sinful nature craves. The old sinful nature loves to do evil, which is just the opposite from what the Holy Spirit wants . . ." (Galatians 5:16-17)

"It's like this: When I was a child, I spoke and thought and reasoned as a child does. But when I grew up, I put away childish things." (First Corinthians 13:11)

September 26

Be blessed today! I'll just let God speak directly to you today the words He spoke through Peter. **"If you want a happy life and good days, keep your tongue from speaking evil, and keep your lips from telling lies. Turn away from evil and do good. Work hard at living in peace with others. The eyes of the Lord watch over those who do right, and His ears are open to their prayers. But the Lord turns his face against those who do evil."** (First Peter 3:10-12) I also read in one of my devotionals this morning: **"The Lord . . . hears the prayers of the (consistently) righteous (the upright, in right standing with Him)."** (Proverbs 15:29)

It also said that to be *consistently righteous* is to refuse to compromise. When we know what is right, we should stubbornly refuse to be swayed.

"Remember, it is better to suffer for doing good, if that is what God wants, than to suffer for doing wrong!" (First Peter 3:17)

September 27

We all know people who have gotten themselves into a bind. And, many times, we lay awake at night, going over their problems in our minds. We have a desire to come to their rescue. But we need to seek God on their behalf.

It may be that God has allowed this situation in order to get their attention. If we jump in to ease their pain, we may just be getting in God's way, as He seeks to draw them to Him.

If we focus on God, He will direct us, either to help, and how we can help, or to stay out of it and allow Him to work it out for them.

There are those who take advantage of people's compassion and *use them up*. But there are also those whose problems are not of their own making. God can see hearts; we can't!

Our Heavenly Father desires us to ask Him for help. His loving arms are outstretched, as He says, **"Come unto me, all ye that labor and are heavy laden, and I will give you rest."** (Matthew 11:28)

I once wrote a poem that contained this verse:
"He watches as we struggle,
And it surely breaks His heart.
But His mighty hands are tied,
And He can't do His part,
Unless we open the door,
And let Him come inside.
And the thing that keeps us from it
Is just our foolish pride."

September 28

We've seen on Nat. Geo. how a lion crouches as he sneaks up on his prey. He watches them as they lay down to rest or become unaware that danger lurks nearby.

Immediately after we've battled against Satan and are licking our wounds, we begin to relax and let our guard down. We soon forget to be alert to the devil's desire to steal, kill, and destroy. (See John 10:10)

When things are going great, we let up on our prayers. By doing this, we become vulnerable. Suddenly, something bad happens and we attack the problem. If we're not careful, we fight against it by using only our own ability. We're no match for the devil!

When we realize we're losing the battle, we call out to God. He comes to our rescue! How foolish to delay turning it over to Him quickly, releasing it completely.

It's like *tag team* wrestling. Only when we reach out to *tag* God, can He jump into the ring and take over for us. We must then get out of the ring and let Him do the fighting.

Discouragement can set in quickly, so we must train ourselves to turn our hearts to God at the first sign of it.

Again I share, **"Be careful. Watch out for attacks from the devil, your great enemy. He prowls around like a roaring lion, looking for some victim to devour."** (First Peter 5:8)

Also, **"So humble yourselves before God. Resist the devil and he will flee from you. Draw close to God and God will draw close to you. Wash your hands, you sinners; purify your hearts, you hypocrites."** (James 4:7-8)

September 29

The secrets of the Universe are far from us! But slowly, they are being unfolded as God reveals His truths to us. Each of us are at a different learning level.

As I was praying a while ago, God revealed that there are some on my prayer list that are winding down and need to down-size their physical responsibilities.

Even in my Bible reading, Peter was saying, **"But the Lord Jesus Christ has shown me that my days here on earth are numbered and I am soon to die. So I will work hard to make these things clear to you. I want you to remember them long after I am gone."** (Second Peter 1:14-15)

Peter was also telling me that God is with each of us in our own learning level, helping us to advance to the next level of maturity. **"So make every effort to apply the benefits of these promises to your life. Then your faith will produce a life of moral excellence. A life of moral excellence leads to knowing God better. Knowing God better leads to self-control. Self-control leads to patient endurance. And patient endurance leads to Godliness. Godliness leads to love for other Christians, and finally, you will grow to have genuine love for everyone."** (Second Peter 1:5-7)

When we finally learn to love everyone, even the most unlovely, we have become one who is able to carry out fully God's plan for production and usefulness.

September 30

I was reading today that God told Jeremiah, **"Go down to the shop where clay pots and jars are made. I will speak to you while you are there. So I did as he told me and found the potter working at his wheel. But the jar he was making did not turn out as he had hoped, so the potter squashed the jar into a lump of clay and started again."** (Jeremiah 18:2-4)

How do you suppose Jeremiah heard God speak? Did he hear a voice with his ears? Did God put the thought in his mind? Or did God lead him by His Spirit?

I don't know. But He speaks to me through His Word, and leads me by His Spirit. A lot of what I *hear* seems to be coming from my mind, but God speaks to our heart, which communicates to our body through our mind.

"Salvation that comes from trusting Christ - which is the message we preach - is already within easy reach. In fact, the Scriptures say, the message is close at hand, it is on your lips and in your heart. For if you confess with your mouth that Jesus is Lord and believe in your heart that God raised Him from the dead, you will be saved. For it is by believing in your heart that you are made right with God, and it is by confessing with your mouth that you are saved." (Romans 10:8-10)

My mind wants to automatically control my body because it always did before Jesus came to live in my heart. My heart automatically spoke worldly things to my mind. And my mind automatically said, "Okay."

Now I can switch off *auto-pilot* because my heart now knows what is right. **"We can gather our thoughts, but the Lord gives the right answer."** (Proverbs 16:1)

I guess I'm saying, (*from Mary only*) that my mind controls my actions, but the Holy Spirit in my heart influences my thoughts and, therefore, leads me to follow what is right. (When I listen to my new heart).

OCTOBER

October 1

There are so many truths we haven't yet discovered. If we were born in a dark prison cell and remained there all our life, we wouldn't long for light, because we wouldn't even know it exists.

We don't live in physical darkness. We're daily exposed to light. So much so, that we have to wear sunglasses!

But do we live in spiritual darkness, without any knowledge of The Light that's available? We don't hunger for God's presence because we've never experienced it. Once we have, it's all that really matters. All the *stuff* that has kept our attention fades in importance.

There are certainly things we need, but God is our Source. We all have jobs and are responsible to work. So, I'm not saying to lay around the house all day with a Bible in your hand, and God will make sure you have everything you need.

I am saying that, in His presence, fear and anxiety are gone because you have *The Source* of all you need right there in your heart!

His love will provide, protect, comfort, encourage, strengthen, guide, and supply anything else you may need.

"Why be like the pagans who are so deeply concerned about these things? Your heavenly Father already knows all your needs, and he will give you all you need from day to day if you live for him and make the Kingdom of God your primary concern." (Matthew 6:32-33)

October 2

I was reading this morning about a missionary who strapped her baby on her back as she went about her day.

Just as the missionary doesn't see her baby, she can sense his presence and is aware at all times that he is there. The Holy Spirit wants us to learn to sense His presence as certainly as this woman senses that her child is with her.

Jesus isn't *strapped on our backs*, but He lives in our heart. He knows us intimately and can see our future needs.

I have been praying for the Lord to reveal His presence to those at church who are battling cancer.

Many times when we experience difficult situations, He gets us through them in His own way and reminds us of His love. This strengthens our faith and prepares us to overcome even bigger problems we may have to face on down the road.

Jesus loves us even more than we love our children. He *is* love!

"**. . . God is love, and all who live in love live in God and God lives in them.**" (First John 4:16b)

I pray we can sense God's love *strapped on our back* as we go about our day!

October 3

When we began our *wobbly walk* with the Lord, we often relied on, "I've always thought," . . . "All the intelligent people," . . . or "I've always done it this way."

If these thoughts and actions line up with scripture, keep them. But if they don't, discard them.

Getting ready for a garage sale isn't enjoyable. You have to *take time to decide* what to keep, what to throw in the trash, and what someone else may want.

There are often items that don't exactly fit in one category or another.

As we look through our spiritual life, we can come across the same problems. We don't have time to think about them right now, so we decide to hang onto them for a while.

Since God is involved in every aspect of our life, He will guide us into His truth. **"And ye shall know the truth, and the truth will make you free."** (John 8:32)

If we don't live in peace, we may have kept a belief or practice that should have been discarded. **"I am leaving you a gift--peace of mind and heart. And the peace I give isn't like the peace the world gives. So don't be troubled or afraid."** (John 14:27)

October 4

The sinful nature in us is still strong, especially when we feel we're being mistreated or misunderstood. It doesn't want to go the direction of *calm*.

"Be still and know that I am God. . ." (Psalm 46:10a) To be still at a time like this, we have to *empty ourselves*.

I used to carry a large purse with several compartments. To clean it, I unzipped all of them, turned it upside down, and shook it. When it was empty, I was able to clean it.

We want to hang onto our *rights* and *pride*, (which is spiritual clutter). We can't fully experience His peace while we secretly hang onto these *war weapons*.

"(For the weapons of our warfare are not carnal, but mighty through God to the pulling down of strongholds), casting down imaginations, and every high thing that exalteth itself against the knowledge of God, and bringing into captivity every thought to the obedience of Christ." (Second Corinthians 10:4-5)

October 5

Does *Russian roulette* paint a picture in your mind? The bullet is real and you never know which pull of the trigger will be the final one!

It is foolish, and deadly, to *play with guns* in this way. But many *intelligent* people think they can out-smart life by partying all their life, until just before the end. Then, decide to accept Christ and go to heaven. (This way, they think they can have the *best of both worlds).*

This intelligent fool doesn't take into consideration that *he* isn't the one who determines the timing of the end!

"How do you know what will happen tomorrow? For your life is like the morning fog--it's here a little while, then it's gone." (James 4:14)

"So be prepared because you don't know what day your Lord is coming." (Matthew 24:42)

October 6

Romans 8 is a *promise-packed* chapter for Christians. It begins, in Verse 1, by telling us we're no longer condemned for our sins since we're in Christ Jesus. It ends with Verses 38-39, by assuring us that *nothing* can ever separate us from God's love.

Verse 3 reveals how God planned to save us.

Verse 11 promises us that we will be resurrected by the same mighty power that raised Jesus from the dead.

Verse 15 assures us that we don't have to live in fear any longer because God has adopted us into His wonderful Family.

Verse 17 promises that we are *joint-heirs* with Jesus.

Verse 18 assures us that all our sufferings will bring future glory.

Verse 26 lets us know that when we don't know how to pray, the Holy Spirit assists in expressing our concerns to God.

Verse 28 is a *Rock-Solid* promise that God has everything under control and has a purpose for all that He allows.

Verse 31 reminds us that since God is on our side, nothing can prevail against us.

Verse 37 promises that whatever we have to endure, we will come out of it victoriously.

God is so good!

October 7

I just read about a missionary who was car-jacked. The Holy Spirit told her to *sit back and enjoy the ride*; that He had everything under control.

That would be hard to do! But she sang praises and they eventually stopped and threw her out. She was safe!

I pray none of us ever get into such a situation. But we know there's all sorts of problems out there looking for us. (See 1 Peter 5:8)

We can be *on guard* for one thing and something completely different slams us. There's only *one* person we can call on who is able to give us wisdom to handle *whatever*. He's always available so we never get a *busy signal*, when trying to get in touch with Him.

We can never be ready to handle *whatever* unless we handle it like *a hot potato* and immediately whisper, "Jesus", and place it in His hands.

"Commit everything you do to the Lord. Trust him, and he will help you." (Psalm 37:5)

"Show me the path where I should walk, O Lord; point out the right road for me to follow." (Psalm 25:4)

Whatever you need; a mechanic, a doctor, or a plumber, you can ask God's direction and He will instruct you.

"My eyes are always looking to the Lord for help, for he alone can rescue me from the traps of my enemies." (Psalm 25:15)

October 8

When we see someone daily, we don't notice the changes that are taking place. A person changes and develops more slowly than a plant. Once the plant comes up, we can see it change almost daily.

We have a purpose for planting the seed and know it will go through many stages before it can produce *fruit*. We don't become discouraged when we have to wait. We know it will take time for God to do His work.

As surely as we watch that plant grow daily to make sure it remains healthy, we can know that God watches each of us and sees our lives unfold.

He's not in a hurry because He can see the end already. He not only watches, He cares for us by meeting our needs. We sometimes get thirsty before He sends the rain. By allowing this, He is teaching us how much we depend on Him, and to appreciate His loving care.

He's a *Master Gardener*, and has planted each of us for His own pleasure. And our purpose is to glorify Him with our lives.

"And I am sure that God, who began a good work within you, will continue his work until it is finished on that day when Christ Jesus comes back again." (Philippians 1:6)

He knows the stages we will go through and is ever present to pour out His grace when He sees us struggling.

When we lose track of our purpose, He 'reminds us', sometimes not so gently.

"No discipline is enjoyable while it is happening - it is painful! But afterward, there will be a quiet harvest of right living for those who are trained this way." (Hebrews 12:11)

October 9

On Nat. Geo., we see the predator seeking to separate his prey from the herd. Once it's alone, it is defenseless!

That's why it's so vital to stay in church, surrounded by those who love us and can encourage us when we feel overwhelmed.

Satan's ploy is to discourage us; to get our eyes off our Father and turn the focus on all the problems we're bombarded with so frequently.

Within *the herd*, those who aren't discouraged can help those who are. There's strength in numbers.

Discouragement is a huge tool of the enemy. We can get to the point that we don't *feel* like praying. We find excuses for staying home on Sunday.

Because we focus on our problems instead of our Lord, the reality of His presence, His power, love, and mercy seems to fade. We become separated from *the herd*!

We simply have to keep our *pockets,* (hearts), loaded with *ammunition*, (scripture).

I pray Jeremiah 29:11, to remind myself that God has plans to bless me, not to harm me. He will give me a future and a hope.

Also, I remember God's promise to work all this together for my good since I love Him and have been called according to His purpose. (See Romans 8:28)

As Satan continues to throw doubt at me, I quote Proverbs 3:5, **"Trust in the Lord with all thine heart, and lean not unto thine own understanding."**

Finally, I conquer Satan by telling him that God doesn't do things the way we do. He thinks differently than we do. (See Isaiah 55:8)

I realize that I have posted most of this before, but it bears repeating and repeating until it becomes part of us.

October 10

Isaiah 55:8 says, **"My thoughts are completely different from yours, says the Lord, and my ways are far beyond anything you could imagine."**

We certainly agree with this statement when we read what Jesus said in the Sermon on the Mount, **"But I say unto you Love your enemies. Pray for those who persecute you."** (Matthew 5:44)

Since we are instructed to pray for them, we're tempted to pray, "Get'em, Lord! Show them a thing or two!"

More than likely, they are lost - walking in darkness, and need Christ's love to show them the way.

Jesus prayed for those who put Him on the cross, **"Father, forgive these people, because they don't know what they are doing. . ."** (Luke 24:34a)

If they get saved, they will be forever on the side of righteousness. Any other way, you may *win the battle but lose the war.*

October 11

Anyone who suits up for football knows the challenge before him. As baby Christians, we don't see how difficult our challenge is. But like a toddler unsure of his first steps, continues to get back up each time he falls, we are to be determined to *stay the course*.

The football player is handed the ball and realizes that all the players on the opposing team will do everything in their power to chase him down, tackle him, and strip the ball from him.

In the *game of life*, Christ has handed the ball, (gospel) off to us. Our goal is to take it with us and share it wherever we go. (See Matthew 28:19-20)

James is our cheerleader as he states in James 1:2-3, **"Dear brothers and sisters, whenever trouble comes your way, let it be an opportunity for joy. For when your faith is tested, your endurance has a chance to grow."**

Our enemy, though invisible, is like those opposing players. But we have a greater Hero who is not only our quarterback, but coach and fullback or lineman who blocks for us so we can be successful.

"But you belong to God, my dear children. You have already won your fight with these false prophets, because the Spirit who lives in you is greater than the spirit who lives in the world." (I John 4:4)

October 12

How solid is our walk with the Lord? If He returned today, would He find us faithful? Would we wish we had more time to set *all* things in our life straight with Him? Are we simply hearing and not doing what we know to do?

In school, we took several *timed tests*. There was some sort of signal when time was up. We all wanted more time so we could get better grades, but . . . it was *over*.

I believe the signal that time is up for all of us will be the sound of a trumpet. **"For the Lord Himself will come down from heaven with a commanding shout, with the call of the archangel, and with the trumpet call of God. . ."** (First Thessalonians 4:16a)

Just as in the days of Noah, people will be going about their day as usual. **"People didn't realize what was going to happen until the flood came and swept them all away. That is the way it will be when the Son of Man comes."** (Matthew 24:39)

(The people had heard Noah preaching destruction, but didn't believe it).

October 13

We act on signs daily: The setting sun means night is near; our gas gauge on "E" means it's time to refill. "Battery low" means our phone is about to die, etc. We take these signs seriously.

The disciples asked Jesus for a sign of His coming and the end of the age. He told them there would be wars and rumors of war; that nations would rise up against nations, there would be famines, pestilences, and earthquakes, but these were only the beginning of sorrows.

He said in Matthew 24:10, **"And then many shall be offended, and shall betray and shall hate one another."**

This world won't get better. Satan will tempt us with a better life, if...

It will get harder and harder to be a Christian. **"Sin will be rampant and the love of many will grow cold."** (Verse 12)

God will separate His sheep from the goats. (See Matthew 25:33-34 & 41)

Persecution will test our faith. The *fence straddlers* will fall the wrong direction. True Christians will remain faithful.

We should all check our *fuel gauge* often to see how full of God our hearts and lives really are!

October 14

As I was reading James 1:2-4 today, it seemed that God was saying that the problems we face produce *growing pains*. Each problem is an opportunity to draw closer to God as we seek His help to get us through it.

Once it has passed, we realize we are able to endure more than we thought we could. But only because we *unloaded* on our Father, who delights in us. He desires to show His love and power in our lives as He meets our needs.

These needs are problems for us, but they aren't problems for Him! As we grow in Him, He strengthens our faith so that life's burdens don't overwhelm us. We learn the way to handle them is to turn them over to Him.

"Come to me, all of you who are weary and carry heavy burdens, and I will give you rest." (Matthew 11:28) He will give us wisdom to handle each problem.

"If you need wisdom - if you want to know what God wants you to do - ask him, and he will gladly tell you. He will not resent your asking." (James 1:5)

He bids us to come to Him. How He loves us!

As I grow weaker, physically, I am able to take more time to see His love unfold. In my *busy-ness*, I have only allowed it to *bounce off* me. There really is a great message in Psalm 46:10, **"Be still and know that I am God; I will be exalted among the nations. I will be exalted in the earth."**

October 15

Why do some people sit in dark prison cells when the doors are unlocked? **"For he has rescued us from the one who rules in the kingdom of darkness and he has brought us into the kingdom of his dear Son."** (Colossians 1:13)

"The thief's purpose is to steal and to kill and to destroy. My purpose is to give life in all its fullness." (John 10:10)

Why do they sit at the King's table and munch on crumbs? We must stand up to this bully because,

". . . You belong to God, my dear children. You have already won your fight with these false prophets, because the Spirit who lives in you is greater than the spirit who lives in the world." (First John 4:4)

"No, despite all these things, overwhelming victory is ours through Christ, who loved us." (Romans 8:37)

"And you will know the truth, and the truth will set you free." (John 8:32)

October 16

When we're totally committed to honor the Lord, (*no matter what!*), we can only fail if we turn away from that commitment. We cannot let fear be our guide.

I was reading about the report of giants in the land that God had promised to give Israel. He told them in Deuteronomy 1:29-30, **"But I said to you, 'Don't be afraid! The Lord your God is going before you. He will fight for you just as you saw him do in Egypt'."**

Basically, He was saying, "Don't worry about the giants, I'll handle them."

When we're going through a *valley of giants*, we can become mesmerized by them. If fear grips us, we're defeated!

But, like a small child, whose hand is in his Daddy's, we can be courageous!

There are *giants* everywhere that threaten and roar. While we can't completely ignore them because they make sure they are positioned in our path, we can avoid them by going around them, remembering our *Constant Companion.*

We may temporarily tense up, just as we do when watching a movie we've already seen. But because we know how it turns out, (for good), we can ignore fear.

When we have *power* by the hand, we can hear, **"For God has not given us a spirit of fear and timidity, but of power, love, and self-discipline."** (Second Timothy 1:7)

October 17

If we could actually see Jesus, as He is always present with us, how different would we act? When we made a snide remark, He would raise His eyebrows and give us a *"Really?"* look.

Would He eventually become *just another person in the room*? Or would we become more like Him as we guarded our thoughts and attitudes?

Martha *told on* Mary because she wasn't helping her with the meal. **"But Martha was worrying over the big dinner she was preparing. She came to Jesus and said, Lord, doesn't it seem unfair to you that my sister just sits here while I do all the work? Tell her to come and help me."** (Luke 10:40)

James and John wanted the best seats in heaven. **"In Your glorious Kingdom, we want to sit in places of honor next to you, they said, one at your right hand and the other at your left."** (Mark 10:37)

It seems as though these were still selfish, even though they could *see Jesus* in their presence. *Self* will try to control us until the day we die. But it will die with us.

Revelation 21:4 mentions some things that will be absent in heaven. It doesn't mention selfishness, but it, too, will be gone!

October 18

When you carve a pumpkin, you first, hollow it out, getting rid of what's inside. (To make room for the light). Then, you put a face on it.

When you look inside, there's nothing to see. It's just an *empty* pumpkin, with a face. But when you put a candle inside and light it, it seems to *come alive*.

This is a good illustration of the difference Christ makes in our lives. Without Him, we have no *light*. There's no *meaning*; no *message*. He places His Truth, (Light) in our heart when we accept His salvation.

We find we're not alone. We can *light up our world* with His presence. As one *Jack-o-lantern*, (among many empty pumpkins), I should desire to share my light so that others can receive life, (meaning and purpose), and a *message to share*.

"You are the light of the world - like a city on a mountain, glowing in the night for all to see." (Matthew 5:14)

And when we see a fellow Christian, whose light is *getting dim*, we should pray for God to *trim his wick*, so His message can shine bright, again.

October 19

The foundation is the strength of the building. Our belief system is the foundation of our life. All of us started life on the shaky foundation of *self*. We learned that we can't depend on ourselves to do what we know to do. What's more, there's so much that we don't know or could ever learn. We can get the best education there is and try to pattern our lives after wise and successful persons, but we still fall short.

Our faith in Christ is the only sure foundation. Paul said in 1 Corinthians 3:11, **"For other foundation can no man lay than that which is laid, which is Jesus Christ."**

Even as we build on this foundation, we are to purposely live a life that pleases God.

"Don't copy the behavior and customs of this world, but let God transform you into a new person by changing the way you think. Then you will know what God wants you to do, and you will know how good and pleasing and perfect his will really is." (Romans 12:2)

This insures that we don't get to heaven *by the skin of our teeth*, (foundation only). Our lives should not only bless God, but others, as well as our own selves.

This *building material* will pass the test of fire mentioned in 1 Corinthians 3:14-15, **"If the work survives the fire, that builder will receive a reward. But if the work is burned up, the builder will suffer great loss. The builders themselves will be saved, but like someone escaping through a wall of flames."**

Even though we know Christ as Savior, if we don't yield control to Him, our lives will be wasted.

October 20

Sometimes God's promises are so loud and clear that we can almost hear His voice. We think of people who are hurting and wish they could *hear* them, too. We whisper their names in prayer.

Other times, we are hurting and confused. We can't *hear* them well, until we pause and focus on our Redeemer.

He is still as close as He ever was. Our focus has pushed Him into a blurred background. How we need to remain focused on Him!

"And I am convinced that nothing can ever separate us from his love. Death can't, and life can't. The angels can't, and the demons can't. Our fears for today, our worries about tomorrow, and even the powers of hell can't keep God's love away." (Romans 8:38)

October 21

When we *think* we know what God wants us to do, we may blunder on ahead without consulting Him at all. We've done this so often that it has become a way of life. We even think that if we pause 10 or 15 seconds, to ask His direction, we have yielded our will to Him.

We don't *really* want to listen. We want to be in control! The problem is *pride* within our heart.

If we humble ourselves to see how short our *wisdom* comes, we would readily stop, listen, and yield. We would *know* that His ways are much higher than ours. (See Isaiah 55:9)

We would trust Him so much more than we trust our own selves.

"So humble yourselves under the mighty power of God, and in due time, he will honor you." (First Peter 5:6)

"He gives more and more strength to stand against such evil desires. As the Scriptures say, God sets himself against the proud, but shows favor to the humble." (James 4:6)

October 22

Have you ever tried to prepare a meal that turned out to be a *mess*? You actually had to scrap it and start over?

Well, at one point of my life, that's just what I had made of my life - a *mess*! When I acknowledged that it was my fault, my pride, and my decisions that had led to that point, I fell at Jesus' feet, confessing my sins and turning it all over to Him.

I remember praying, "You gave me a great life with opportunities to do good things and to be a good person, but I completely blew it. Here - You can do with me as you please. I just can't go on like this any longer. Take my life if you want, just please help me." (Maybe not exact words.)

He picked up the broken pieces and gently put them, (*me*) back together. He did the *impossible* for me. **"Therefore, if any man be in Christ, he is a new (creation); old things are passed away; behold, all things are become new."** (Second Corinthians 5:17)

Now, I can sing the words of the song, "*Something beautiful; something good. All my confusion, He understood. All I had to offer Him was brokenness and strife. But He made something beautiful of my life!*"

October 23

When God sees our hearts, He knows what is missing. His love can fill all the gaps. When we're saturated with His love, deep down - joy is produced, (which causes a natural smile to show up on our face.)

He wants us to live in Him, (become a part of His Family and His Kingdom). But we can't live in Him if He doesn't live in us. That's why He stands at the door and knocks.

"Look! Here I stand at the door and knock. If you hear me calling and open the door, I will come in and we will share a meal as friends." (Revelation 3:20)

Trying to live a joyful life without Christ is as empty as the fake smile produced for the photographer. If joy is not on the inside, it can't show up on the outside.

As Jesus stands at the door, He is holding an armload of fruit to offer you. **"But when the Holy Spirit controls our lives, he will produce this kind of fruit in us: love, joy, peace, patience, kindness, goodness, faithfulness, gentleness, and self-control. . ."** (Galatians 5:22-23)

This is the fruit His love produces. They are all necessary for the health of our soul.

October 24

We were never photographers, but my sister and I enjoyed our cameras so much! We took foliage trips and delighted in old barns and windmills.

My husband often remarked about one of us taking pictures of the other one *taking pictures*!

Our cameras didn't have *automatic focus* features, so we experimented with *depth of field* and *macro* settings. We were amazed at the beauty of a single dandelion when it was brought into focus against the blurred green background. (It took very little to entertain us!)

How often do we walk over these dandelions without giving any thought to their beauty? We have to *intentionally* draw our attention to them and focus on their individual beauty by pushing into the background the other things that vie for our attention.

God's beauty is all around us. Not just the visible beauty that delights us, but the special quiet inward beauty of His peace as we commune with Him, *one on one*.

It seems that our lives have an *automatic focus* feature that is always focused on busy, stressful things. We are being *jerked around* by the things of this world. So, we have to be determined to sense God's presence or we miss it.

"Draw near to God and he will draw near to you. Cleanse your hands, ye sinners; and purify your hearts, ye double-minded." (James 4:8)

October 25

Jesus told us in John 14:1-2a, **"Don't be troubled. You trust God, now trust me. There are many rooms in my Father's home, and I am going to prepare a place for you..."**

I realize as I have entered the door of *old age* that I have passed through many *rooms* in my life. It sometimes feels like I'm in the *waiting room*.

I have time to reflect on many things that have happened, that are now happening, and that may soon happen.

The *whirlwind of life* has landed me here. Each day I wonder "How much longer?"

I believe the task at hand is simply to take each day as it comes and rejoice in it. To do what I can to help those in need of help and to do as Jesus would.

Many days I have to fight for strength to do *my things* that need to be done. But that is life!

I praise God that I don't have to endure pain, both physical and emotional. I've experienced both, first hand, so I can pray compassionately for those who have to endure it.

I don't know how much longer it will be before Jesus comes back. I pray it will be soon. I may live another 20-25 years, but each day, I'm aware that I'm in the *waiting room*.

May I be an encouragement to those around me.

October 26

When you know you've lost the battle, you lay down your arms. You have a choice of either being discouraged and depressed or handing it over to the Lord in prayer. He knows the source of conflict and is working to bring good out of the whole situation.

There's a peace that passes understanding when we *let go and let God*.

"If you do this, you will experience God's peace, which is far more wonderful than the human mind can understand. His peace will guard your hearts and minds as you live in Christ Jesus." (Philippians 4:7)

Your *engagement* in the battle has changed to prayer instead of actively fighting against the will of someone you love, when you feel they're heading in the wrong direction."

When you see there's no progress, you *bow out* of the action, but you don't give up! You simply channel your compassion in a different direction.

"... Do not be afraid! Don't be discouraged by this mighty army, for the battle is not yours, but God's." (Second Chronicles 20:15b)

It's like you're battling a fierce consuming fire that has gotten out of hand. When you're completely exhausted, you finally fall on your face and begin to pray.

Now there's power far beyond anything you're capable of!

"Now glory be to God! By his mighty power at work within us, he is able to accomplish infinitely more than we could ever dare to ask or hope." (Ephesians 3:20)

October 27

Yesterday presented its problems. Today will present its answers.

Since we have the Lord, we have the answers. He will reveal them to us as we seek His wisdom. **"I love those who love me, and those who seek me early shall find me."** (Proverbs 8:17)

His pockets are full and His heart is full! Walking hand-in-hand with Him, we do not fear. Though Satan *nips* at our heels, our Lord will rebuke him and scoop us up to safety. It's difficult to completely ignore Satan's threats, but we can peacefully do just *that* because we are God's children and His plans for us are for good and not evil.

"For I know the plans I have for you, says the Lord, They are for good and not for disaster, to give you a future and a hope." (Jeremiah 29:11)

"Why be like the pagans who are so deeply concerned about these things? Your heavenly Father already knows all your needs, and he will give you all you need from day to day if you live for him and make the kingdom of God your primary concern." (Matthew 6:32-33)

October 28

I don't like to look back on the years of my wandering, helpless and alone, destitute, and so in need of a heap of love to be *dumped* on me.

I was even a child of God at the time, because in V.B.S., I had accepted Jesus as my Savior when I was about 12 years old.

But I never *grew* as we didn't attend church. All I knew was that I would go to heaven when I died. I thought that life here on earth was mine to bear alone.

Needless to say, I was a *miserable mess*! After I had *painted myself into a corner*, I finally looked *up*, and called on the Lord. There, that *heap of Love*, was dumped on me!

I began to understand that those who seemed bent on destroying me were dealing with life the same way I was - the best way they knew how.

We don't have to live like that! **"Take my yoke upon you and learn of me; for I am meek and lowly in heart, and ye shall find rest unto your souls."** (Matthew 29:11)

People in our world who *bump* into us constantly are either lost or are immature Christians who need Love and guidance, not judgmental scorn.

Jesus told us how to handle them in Matthew 5:44. He said for us to love them and pray for them, (as they are in the dark).

In verse 45, He said, **"In that way, you will be acting as true children of your Father in heaven. For he gives sunlight to both the evil and the good, and he sends rain on the just and on the unjust, too."**

October 29

I was reading *the back of the Book*, this morning and saw how all this ends.

Chapter 19 says the One riding the white horse, (V. 11), has a sharp sword in His mouth. (V.15)

Ephesians tells us that the sword of the Spirit is the Word of God. **"Put on salvation as your helmet, and take the sword of the Spirit, which is the word of God."** (Ephesians 6:17)

All the evil in the world is destroyed by this Word. **"Their entire army was killed by the sharp sword that came out of the mouth of the one riding the white horse. . ."** (Revelation 19:21)

In the beginning, God created everything. He spoke the heaven and earth into existence. And in the end, He replaces them with a new heaven and a new earth. (See Revelation 21:1).

The *stuff* we see now and strive to fill our lives with won't matter then. It will all disappear with the old earth.

The wise thing for us to do is to change our emphasis, seeking to fill our hearts more so than our hands.

October 30

Because the twins were 3 months premature, I didn't have much contact with them, as they needed to be protected from anyone who might bring germs and cause sickness.

When they were about 6 months old, I began to *help out*. When one was tired and restless, I sang to him as I rocked and patted him.

(Anyone who has heard me sing knows I don't have *a voice* for it.) But the babies didn't care. It was a peaceful, soothing reminder that they were in loving arms. They immediately closed their eyes as if to say, "This feels so good."

God sings His *love song* to us continually: "I am here, call on Me. I can help."

As the twins get older, they fight sleep and don't listen as well.

We, too, don't listen. We want to be in control. Our *voice* demands its own way and drowns out God's voice. How much better it would be if we just listened to His voice!

"The heart is deceitful above all things, and desperately wicked. Who can know it"? (Jeremiah 17:9)

October 31

Well, when we watch the news, we are disturbed by the lawlessness and disrespect for authority that is becoming so prevalent. And those who hate God have expressed that they are *offended* by Him. Their *right not to be offended* out-weighs our right to admonish Him.

Our rights and freedoms are gradually being taken away and the shape of our future looks dismal indeed.

But I read Revelation 21 today and I know it will *all come out in the wash*. The evil demons will be *offended* when their leader is dealt with. **"He seized the dragon - that old serpent, the devil, Satan - and bound him in chains for a thousand years."** (Revelation 20:2)

Even at that moment, we don't have to be afraid of the lawlessness because I also read in "Open Windows", that God is an anchor for our souls, keeping us steadfast and secure in Him.

In another devotional, I read, **"Do not be afraid of the nations there for the Lord your God will fight for you."** (Deuteronomy 3:22)

Again, I read where King Solomon had come to the end of himself and declared that the reason for his dissatisfaction was his disobedience toward God. (See Ecclesiastes 12:13).

God has a path of blessing for us if and when we yield our allegiance to Him. (See Psalm 23).

NOVEMBER

November 1

God's grace is the help we need in order to get through life. It is the very power to endure, the strength to overcome, the insight to see as God sees. It is the ability to receive love and forgiveness, and to pass it on. It is the very *love* of God in action.

He sees our struggles and reaches down to assist us and to *give us a hug* for encouragement.

He is especially pleased when we pass on what we have received. In order to do that, we must first receive from Him.

"I am the vine, ye are the branches. He that abideth in me and I in him, the same bringeth forth much fruit; for without me, ye can do nothing." (John 15:5)

November 2

Some look at life through only what their eyes can see. (They are driven by the flesh). They think we who walk by faith, are foolish - passing up all the *good things* in life to go through *rituals* like prayer and church attendance.

"That is why we live by believing and not by seeing." (Second Corinthians 5:7)

But we can see that they're the ones who *don't get it*. They are forever restless, wanting more and more, never completely satisfied.

God fills our hearts with His love, which cannot be improved upon. The more we live for Him, the more content we become.

"I know how to live on almost nothing or with everything. I have learned the secret of living in every situation, whether it is with a full stomach or empty, with plenty or little." (Philippians 4:12)

We don't find ourselves fighting to get in front of the line, because we know there's enough of God to go around. In fact, we feel obligated to share Him with those we love, in order that they, too, may have the peace we've found.

"I am leaving you with a gift - peace of mind and heart. And the peace I give isn't like the peace the world gives. So don't be troubled or afraid." (John 14:27)

November 3

The Lord has given us so much to be thankful for! He loves to see us enjoy His creation and all the gifts He has given us. **"Whatever is good and perfect comes to us from God above, who created all heaven's lights..."** (James 1:17a)

He is involved, not only in giving us joyful, peaceful lives, but He keeps us humble by rebuking our pride. When we rush to get the glory that belongs only to Him, we'd better have a *Band-Aid* handy, because discipline is on its way!

"For the Lord disciplines those he loves and punishes those he accepts as his children." (Hebrews 12:6)

We learn through our failures. They are *stair-steps* to maturity and trust. We will eventually learn not to lean on our own understanding, but to yield to God's will and His way. That's a gift in itself!

If we go by the manual, (Bible), we'll find joy and peace a lot sooner, and less painfully.

Different things will become more important to us.

"I once thought all these things were so very important, but now I consider them worthless because of what Christ has done." (Philippians 3:7)

November 4

This world is our classroom and the Holy Spirit, our teacher. Gone are the days of wasting classroom hours, not caring whether we really learn – only cramming for that coming test.

We are beginning to grasp the importance of learning how to live close to God. We've all gone our own way, ignoring God's guidance, and found ourselves *stuck in the mud*! The more we *bang our heads against a brick wall*, the more our heads hurt!

We look out the *window* of our eyes and wonder how some people can be so foolish, yet we can't see that we, too, are one of them.

Still, our flesh continues to coax us into wasting our days. We are continually faced with *multiple choice* questions. Let us listen, intently, to our *Professor*, who lives within us, so that we will get life right and one day be able to hear, **"Well done, good and faithful servant; thou hast been faithful over a few things, I will make thee a ruler over many things. Enter thou into the joy of the Lord."** (Matthew 25:23)

"It's not about me", is one of the many lessons we need to learn.

November 5

THE WINTER OF MY SOUL

When I see a tree, I think of me.
In winter, it seems as if it's dead.
For the life in it has gone to bed.
In spring, I see the life in the tree,
But how often do others see Jesus in me?

God's Spirit in me isn't really gone,
It's just that I haven't yielded to Him in so long.
Oh, God, forgive me for this awful sin,
And stir up Your Spirit that lives within.
This dormant stage is grievous to me.
So bring forth the fruit that I long to see.

Help me to have compassion and care
For needy people in the world out there.
Help me to be humble, and meek, and kind.
And help me to share the love that I find.

(A dear friend requested that I post this poem that was written in 1976).

November 6

I recently purchased an oil-filled heater for another room. It has a knob to adjust the heat, a thermostat, I guess. It also has a knob that turns it on "low" (1), "medium" (2), or "high" (3). I don't understand the difference in these two knobs, but I know that when they are both turned as far to the right as they can go, the heater performs at its highest level.

Thinking on this caused me to consider my level of obedience to Christ. Am I giving the Lord a *low* level of obedience, (every now and then), a *medium* level, (fairly often), or a *high* level, (continually)?

I know the Lord plans to use me to further His Kingdom. He wants me to be filled with oil, (the Holy Spirit), and He determines where and how to use me.

I'm thankful that I don't have to be concerned about that. All I have to do is be willing and *available*.

"Then I heard the Lord asking, 'Whom should I send as a messenger to my people? Who will go for us?' And I said, 'Lord, I'll go! Send me'." (Isaiah 6:8)

"For God bought you with a high price. So you must honor God with your body." (First Corinthians 6:20)

November 7

I don't like clutter in my home, but a little dust doesn't bother me. After a while, it does get my attention!

I'm wondering, as the Lord sees my heart, is there only *a little dust* or a lot of clutter that stands in the way of my being able to sense His presence and marvel in the amazement of who He is and that He wants to have a relationship with me.

When we really clean house, it takes time and isn't enjoyable as we have to get rid of the cobwebs and clutter. But afterward, we are so pleased with our clean house!

We can live in a *lazy body*, ignoring the *dust* that builds or we can *daily* commune with the Lord and allow Him to spotlight the areas that need immediate attention.

I've walked into homes that were so spotless that it was hard to imagine that people really lived there to dirty it up. I've also walked into homes that weren't too far from some of the *"Hoarders"* houses I've seen on T.V.

My home is somewhere between. Most of the time, I can comfortably live here.

Can the Lord comfortably live in my heart?

"Create in me a clean heart, O God, and renew a right spirit within me." (Psalm 51:10)

November 8

When we live in the light of God's love, it's not hard to put away the foolish things that we've clung to in the past.

We live from day to day, not making solid plans, knowing that God may show us a different plan. For instance, if we're on our way to an important ball game and come upon a terrible accident. We see that someone really needs our help. We can't turn our backs and go freely on to the game.

Even if we don't stop, we can't go *freely* on to the game. We'll be burdened down with guilt and shame.

This example shows us what we're made of. What's more important, God's plans or our plans? If Love directs us, we can know that we belong to God.

"**He that loveth not, knoweth not God, for God is love.**" (First John 4:8)

"**Dear children, let us stop saying we love each other; let us really show it by our actions. It is by our actions that we know we are living in the truth, so we will be confident when we stand before the Lord.**" (First John 3:18-19)

November 9

I was reading in Isaiah, chapter 9, about an unimaginable hunger for food. This could be in the near future for us, (*if God allows*).

What are we to do about this information? As we put it alongside our everyday worries, we have to include the presence and grace of God. He will be with us in any situation that may arise. Nothing can come against us that God can't help us handle!

Each day is a *new tomorrow*. We don't face it alone.

Satan fills our heads with worries. He tries to erase God's presence and grace out of our minds. So we have to bring every thought captive to the obedience of Christ. (That's in 2 Corinthians 10:5)

"Thou wilt keep him in perfect peace, whose mind is stayed on thee because he trusteth in thee." (Isaiah 26:3)

November 10

Each morning as I read my devotionals and Bible reading, it is easy to sit still and listen to the Lord. I continue to sense His presence as I do the dishes and make the bed. It's when I am interacting with people that His presence seems to fade somewhat.

Only when I encounter problems, do I focus on Him again. And sometimes, it is after have tried to solve them on my own and become frustrated.

"God is our refuge and strength, a very present help in trouble." (Psalm 46:1)

Life is our classroom and God, our Teacher. Just as a toddler has to fall over and over as he learns to walk, we too, experience many failures and bruises before we learn that the Lord is our strength.

"For I, the Lord thy God, will hold thy right hand, saying unto thee, fear not; I will help thee." (Isaiah 41:13)

I believe that patience is my main *homework* for now. I have learned to be patient in some situations, but I am far from it in so many others.

November 11

When we're facing an insurmountable task, and we know we don't have what it takes to accomplish it, we don't have to fear or worry. God is with us at all times and He will come to our rescue.

"And this same God who takes care of me will supply all your needs from his glorious riches, which have been given to us in Christ Jesus." (Philippians 4:19)

Just in the nick of time, our answer, our strength, our means will come to us through Him.

The Israelites needed to cross the Red Sea to escape the Egyptian army who were coming upon them quickly. What could they do? There was no way out! They would be killed by them or drown trying to escape!

Our dilemmas don't compare to this, but the same God that came to their rescue is there to help us. He will give us wisdom and more strength than we normally have.

Though invisible, He is *real*, and He is present. He allows us to get ourselves into trouble by ignoring His laws so that we can learn the error of our ways. But He doesn't abandon us in our foolishness. At any time, we can call out to Him.

"If you need wisdom, if you want to know what God wants you to do - ask him, and he will gladly tell you. He will not resent your asking. . ." (James 1:5)

But, we are not to test or tempt God. **"Jesus responded, the scriptures also say, 'Do not test the Lord your God'."** (Luke 4:12)

November 12

As I was praying for those battling cancer, I was brought back to the reality of my own struggle. I can see that God sent me from one doctor to another who was more familiar with my disease; then to another who may be considered *an expert* in that field. I was near death, but many prayer warriors petitioned God on my behalf.

This was all in God's plan. He took me through all that so that I could testify first-hand of His marvelous grace and power. Also, to give me compassion for those who are fighting this disease and are in need of encouragement.

The scriptures in two of my devotionals today spoke to me of my healing. (I realize they were really speaking of *spiritual* healing).

In "Open Windows" the scripture was Isaiah 35:10, **"Those who have been ransomed by the Lord will return to Jerusalem singing songs of everlasting joy. Sorrow and mourning will disappear, and they will be overcome with joy and gladness."**

In another devotional, **"You have freed me from my chains."** (Psalm 116:16b, NIV)

The healing I received is temporal, but God wants to bring eternal healing to those who are in prisons of sin and guilt. Some are suffering from depression but others are unaware that they are walking around with this fatal disease, (*sin*).

"For the wages of sin is death, but the gift of God is eternal life through Jesus Christ, our Lord." (Romans 6:23)

November 13

Sin is like a river. At first, it seems refreshing and enjoyable. So we jump in to experience what it offers. The longer we stay, the deeper we go. In our enjoyment, we don't see the rapids ahead, or feel the mighty pull that is bigger than we are.

Then, eventually there's that huge "*waterfall*" that ends in eternal death.

Jesus sees all this - the whole picture. He calls to us while we're enjoying sin, but His voice is muffled and though we hear Him, we don't *hear* Him.

As we see the rapids ahead, many will respond to His call. Yet, sadly, there are those who still refuse to reach out to Him for salvation.

He has pulled us, who have responded to Him, ashore to safety. Sin is also here on the shore, but its sting (*death*) has been conquered for us.

We will have to suffer the consequence of flirting with it. **"Don't be misled. Remember that you can' ignore God and get away with it."** (Galatians 6:7)   But we don't have to fear death. **". . . Death is swallowed up in victory. O death, where is your victory? O death, where is your sting?"** (First Corinthians 15:54b)

November 14

We are all numbed by the terrorism in Paris. It's difficult to see God's presence it in.

"My thoughts are completely different from yours, says the Lord. And my ways are far beyond anything you can imagine." (Isaiah 55:8)

I realize the following verses were addressing homosexuality, but I believe they also are relevant in any situation. **"And instead of worshiping the glorious, ever-living God, they worshiped idols made to look like mere people, or like birds and animals and snakes. So God let them go ahead and do whatever shameful things their hearts desired..."** (Romans 1:23-24b)

(*We* worship the *creation* more than the Creator.)

God sees all that is going on and will eventually repay them. **"I will take vengeance; I will repay those who deserve it, says the Lord."** (Romans 12:19b)

It seems that no one is safe from ISIS' cruelty. **"Unless the Lord protects a city, guarding it with sentries will do no good."** (Psalm 127:1b)

The very people who are *offended* by God will have to depend on Him for protection.

November 15

As a mother of small twins and a 3 year old, I was starved for rest. Nights were interrupted and there were few times in the day while they slept that I could refuel. But there were so many things that needed to be done that I felt were more important.

I learned to struggle by with minimal rest. (*On top of this*, we were having marital problems).

Needless to say, my nerves were stretched beyond repair. (I didn't know Jesus was there to help.)

Still today, my nerves are easily shattered. Thankfully, I now have time to push the world aside and bask in the Lord's presence, *unloading* on Him.

Each day has its stress, but we have God's promise that He won't put more on us than we can handle. He comes alongside us to help. (See 1 Corinthians 10:13).

When our hands and minds are full, and even our hearts can't hold any more, He invites us to come to Him.

"Come unto Me, all of you who are weary and carry heavy burdens, and I will give you rest." (Matthew 11:28)

November 16

As I read my Bible reading in Isaiah 16, I saw a bleak picture for Moab. At the same time, the T.V. was on and I heard discussions about what we should do about ISIS. We'd better fall on our knees!

Then, and only then, will we find the wisdom we need to sustain our peaceful way of life.

Then I read a devotion that reminded me that I am being held by God and am completely safe, no matter what happens.

But, what about my loved ones who seem more interested in the ball game than eternal life? Don't get me wrong, God wants us to enjoy life. But first, we must secure our future with God in eternity.

We can't let Satan lull us to sleep thinking we're okay. We have to *know*. **"Not everyone that says unto me, 'Lord, Lord', shall enter into the kingdom of heaven, but he that doeth the will of my Father, who is in heaven."** (Matthew 7:21)

I can't do anything about ISIS, or even to change the hearts of my loved ones, except *pray*. That's what God called me to do.

"If my people who are called by my name, shall humble themselves and pray, and seek my face and turn from their wicked ways, then will I hear from heaven, and will forgive their sin, and will heal their land." (Second Chronicles 7:14)

November 17

When we finally take time to go through all the *stuff* that has been accumulating to see if there's anything valuable enough to continue *occupying the space* that has been *shrinking*, we may come across something that reminds us of a wonderful experience or a relationship almost forgotten.

Daily Bible readings can do that for us because there are things in life that cause callouses; things that cause our love for the Lord to grow cold. As we read His Word, He is able to speak His love to us and call us back to Him. He restores our soul.

Let us stumble, once again, across some familiar verses: **"The Lord is my Shepherd. I have everything I need. He lets me rest in green meadows. He leads me beside peaceful streams. He renews my strength, He guides me along right paths, bringing honor to his name."** (Psalm 23:1-3) (*And the rest of that precious chapter!*)

November 18

As I sit here this morning, the rising sun comes streaming through the window, reminding me that God's face is shining on me. He is pouring out blessing upon blessing!

A little while ago, I could see the T.V., but now the sun is shining so brightly in my eyes that I can only *hear* it. I have to put my hand up to block out the sun if I want to *see* it.

How I pray that God's presence would be so powerful in my life that, *"The things of earth will grow strangely dim in the light of His glory and grace."* And I pray this also for all my loved ones.

How I thank God for His daily protection and provision; for His guidance and peace. His presence is all I need.

"And this same God who takes care of me will supply all your needs from his glorious riches, which have been given to us in Christ Jesus." (Philippians 4:19)

November 19

If we don't get enough oxygen, we can't function properly. We can't help anyone else because we use all our energy on ourselves.

When we were saved, God drew us into His body, the church, to help us become like Him and to give us the ability to love forever.

In our bodies, the blood is pumped into our lungs, where it receives oxygen, which sustains us.

At salvation, we received the Holy Spirit and the message of salvation at the same time. (He gave us *a transfusion*!) His blood and the *oxygen* (gospel) is what energizes us to function as God's body, (*His church*).

We are to carry Him and His message into all the world, (wherever we go).

"Therefore, go and make disciples of all nations, baptizing them in the name of the Father, and the Son, and the Holy Spirit. Teach these new disciples to obey all the commands I have given you. And be sure of this: I am with you always, even to the end of the age." (Matthew 28:19-20)

If we aren't sharing God's love, our world becomes sicker and sicker. So, in essence, we're helping evil to spread. **"He that is not with me is against me; and he that gathereth not with me scattereth abroad."** (Matthew 12:30)

November 20

Knowing the Lord is spiritually akin to owning a bank. Your needs will be supplied. You don't have to fret about today or tomorrow.

It's even better than owning the bank, because you can still get sick and die. When you know the Lord, He knows the answers for all your needs.

His love keeps us from becoming *spoiled brats*. **"For the Lord disciplines those he loves, and he punishes those he accepts as his children."** (Hebrews 12:6). So, we will have problems because of sin in our lives and the lives of others. But our Father's love holds us securely.

If we know Him, we know His Word. We may not be able to find where it is in the Bible, but His Word drew us to Him in the first place and it will sustain us.

He speaks to us continually, and the more we know Him, the better our *hearing* becomes.

When you have a million dollars at your disposal, you're not concerned with any financial need that may arise.

Every need has a spiritual root and our Father has the love, power, and wisdom to meet any need.

"Now glory be to God! By his mighty power at work within us, he is able to accomplish infinitely more than we would dare to ask or hope." (Ephesians 3:20)

November 21

I don't have to stand on a high mountain to look back and see where I was when God took me in His loving arms and endeavored to show me the way.

I have to admit there were many times I didn't want to follow Him. So, He let me stumble and fall, over and over, so that I would finally yearn for His guidance.

Today, I fully trust His love for me. I trust that He has a plan to bless me. **"For I know the plans I have for you, says the Lord, They are plans for good and not for disaster to give you a future and a hope."** (Jeremiah 29:11)

But, I haven't yet arrived. (He's still working on me).

I was reading in Genesis 22 about Abraham's faith when he was instructed to offer his son, Isaac, as a burnt sacrifice upon an altar to God. Even the faith of Isaac, as he realized that he was the sacrifice!

I can't begin to go through the emotions they must have had! But God had prepared both of them for this test. They passed with flying colors!

When I have my hand in His, I know I'm where He wants me to be and that He will guide me and protect me from anything that Satan wants to throw at me.

I sit here in peaceful surroundings and pray for those who live among terrorists and have to flee for safety. Even for those who have not yet trusted my Savior.

"Jesus told them, I am the way, the truth, and the life. No one can come to the Father except through me." (John 14:6)

November 22

A solar light is a perfect example of how we are to take Jesus with us as we go into any situation or place.

It's not really that difficult to share Christ if we're filled with His love. The more time we spend, one on one, with Him, the more we *absorb* Him.

Then, unless we *hide Him under a bushel*, others can see Jesus in us, (feel His love and encouragement).

"Yes, I am the Vine, you are the branches. Those who remain in me, and I in them, will produce much fruit. For apart from me, you can do nothing." (John 15:5)

A solar light that has been stuck back in the closet cannot shine, no matter how well it has been made. People can tell if we have been with the Lord. His love just shines through us. If we ignore Him, we can go to the best college, look better than anyone, drive the best car, even be a super athlete in every sport, but we are unable to effectively share God's love.

Some of God's children (*Christians*), are *solar lights* that have been hanging out in the *dark* (world) and can't absorb the *Son*. They wonder why they can't sense God's presence.

"Though I speak with tongues of men and angels, and have not love, I am become as a sounding brass, or a tinkling cymbal." (First Corinthians 13:1)

November 23

No matter what people did to Him, Jesus was not afraid. He had heaven in mind, (for us).

They beat Him, spit on Him, pulled out His beard, and they pushed a crown of thorns down upon His brow. They stripped off His clothes and hung Him, shamefully, on a cross. At any time He could have turned them into dust!

We can't even imagine all that He endured for us, even though it has been vividly portrayed in movies.

It was His great love for each of us, His children; that caused Him to be willing to go through all that agony. We had been enticed by the enemy and carried away from Him. Satan endeavored to erase all memory of our loving Father. He hypnotized us with earthly pleasures, (*and still does*). Jesus saw our dilemma and that we were unaware of our eternal end. He could see that hell was our destination! We would be eternally out of reach from Him.

Even though we had turned our back on Him, as though He was *nothing* to us, He poured Himself out in order to bring us back to Him. He wouldn't take, "No," for an answer. He gave all He was, and is, for each of us.

That's the basis of Thanksgiving!!

"But God showed his great love for us by sending Christ to die for us while we were still sinners." (Romans 5:8)

November 24

There is good in everything; . . . *we can't see it* . . . but God is working in everything to bring about good. **"And we know that God causes everything to work together for the good of those who love God and are called according to his purposes for them."** (Romans 8:28)

When we know that God is in control, the *sting* is taken out of the bad, because we know His love will win out.

Sometimes, the only good we can see is that, "This, too, will pass."

When bad things happen, Satan takes opportunity to tell us that God is mean, and that He can't be trusted. But God is faithfully, lovingly there, like the sun of a cloudy day. He knows the *why*, though we may not ever understand it.

Some of my favorite scriptures are **"Always be joyful. Keep on praying. No matter what happens, always be thankful, for this is God's will for you who belong to Christ Jesus."** (First Thessalonians 5:16-18),

Some children have to actually touch the stove to learn what *hot* means. But that's a lesson they will never forget!

Not all bad comes to us as consequences of disobedience, though we do bring a lot of it upon ourselves. God doesn't allow us to get by with disobedience; it will eventually *burn* us.

"No discipline is enjoyable while it is happening - it is painful! But afterward there will be a quiet harvest of right living for those who are trained in this way." (Hebrews 12:11)

We can be thankful for God's love; that He never gives up on us!

November 25

The Holidays are so busy that we may not take time to offer thanks, even for Thanksgiving!

I was able, last night, to test Matthew 11:28, **"Come unto me, all ye that labor and are heavy laden, and I will give you rest."**

So much to do today! I needed my rest so I wouldn't get sick. So, I went to bed fairly early but woke at 12:30 am, remembering I hadn't taken my medicine. When I returned to bed, my head was full of things to be done. Around 1:00, I finally got up and read my devotionals, thinking I could get a head start and be able to clear my mind at the same time.

When I returned to bed at 2:00, I had to fight to keep my focus on the Lord and praise Him that I could trust Him to meet my needs. I fell asleep and didn't wake up until 7:30.

As my day is starting later than usual, I am claiming Ephesians 3:20, **"Now unto him who is able to do exceedingly abundantly above all that we ask or think according to the power that worketh in us."**

I'm leaning on Him to help me accomplish today's tasks.

How thankful I am for His presence and promises!

November 26

We have made many preparations for this day. The Lord, also, has prepared a feast of joy for us! **"This is the day the Lord has made. We will rejoice and be glad in it."** (Psalm 118:24)

He plants many little joys in our path each day to remind us of His love and His presence. (They may be hidden, like Easter eggs, but *they're there!*)

Too often, we scurry past these blessings in search of material things that will soon disappear.

Because we live in a temporary world, that seeks to possess us, we have to force ourselves to turn our attention away from things that will fade away and look to eternal matters.

"There are three things that will endure - faith, hope, and love - and the greatest of these is love." (First Corinthians 13:13)

Happy Thanksgiving!

November 27

As we came together to celebrate Thanksgiving, our home was filled with love and laughter. Only one *visitor* came who wasn't invited. He made a quick, evil appearance, but quickly saw he wasn't welcome.

The problem is that he was manifested in *me* over some trivial happening!

How thankful I am that God's love prevailed! I'm thankful for forgiveness during these times of failure.

I was tempted to even stop posting these devotions as Satan accused me before God. I was tempted to slink away and *lick my wounds*; to make excuses for my bad behavior. How can I *encourage others* when I myself need help?

But Satan is not going to win this battle! He accuses us before God, **"But if we confess our sins to him, he is faithful and just to forgive us and to cleanse us from every wrong."** (First John 1:9)

God knows my weaknesses, and so does my family. They can see that we're all on a journey toward righteousness. Though we haven't yet arrived, Love is the power that prevails!

November 28

Most of the time when I come to meet with the Lord for our morning coffee, I am comfortable in His presence. I sense the fruit of His Spirit listed in Galatians 5:22-23. But the last one, (*self-control*) was missing for a short time (only about a minute) on Thanksgiving Day, (of all times!) The thing is that I wasn't all that upset about the mud that was tracked across the carpet. (If you let it dry without smearing it in, it will vacuum up easily.)

Satan used the incident to cause hurt feelings. (I pray these will heal quickly). But God is using it to teach me about the damage the tongue can do when uncontrolled, even for minute! (Not even filth, just unnecessary, hurtful words).

"But no one can tame the tongue. It is an uncontrollable evil, full of deadly poison." (James 3:8)

Sometimes it's us saying them, sometimes they are said to us. If we can remember how hurt we were, maybe we can use that hurt to prevent us from using hurtful words. And maybe we can forgive others for using them against us.

I publically apologize for my lack of self-control and thank God that He is always willing to forgive.

"There is, therefore, now no condemnation to those who are in Christ Jesus, who walk not after the flesh, but after the Spirit." (Romans 8:1)

(That's the end of this matter for me.)

November 29

We don't ever want to be needy - for anything! But need is what *drives* us. The reason I was able to build our house was need. We didn't have the money to buy a house or even to pay the (*then*) $400 for rent. (This was 1970).

The Lord led us to 5 acres with an old house that looked like it didn't even have electricity or running water. The total cost of the land, *and house,* was $5,000. We moved into the house and made $50 monthly payments.

God saw that I could build, showed me how by supplying a book with step-by-step details, and as my husband got paid, we purchased the materials we'd need until he got paid again. He actually used *me* to build the house!

Our need for God causes us to search for Him. We can't get outside ourselves until we see our need.

"Blessed are they who hunger and thirst for righteousness; for they shall be filled." (Matthew 5:6)

"But my God shall supply all your need according to his riches in glory by Christ Jesus." (Philippians 4:19)

November 30

My name is Mary, but I'm really a *Martha* inside. **"Martha, Martha, the Lord answered, you are worried and upset about many things, but only one thing is needed. Mary has chosen what is better, and it will not be taken away from her."** (Luke 10:41-42)

Why am I not like my *name*? I try to do so much that I *fall in a heap*. And when I'm that tired, my *sweet spirit* fades away. God is trying to teach me, but I say, "Okay, I've got it." Yet I don't, and I *flounder* and cry out for His help again!

He picks me up, but I start the whole routine over again.

I'm thankful that He doesn't give up on me. **"No discipline is enjoyable while it is happening - it is painful! But afterward, there will be a quiet harvest of right living for those who are trained in this way."** (Hebrews 12:11)

I have a one-track mind and I can only see what is in front of me. Sometimes I see nothing bad, but other times, I see nothing good - though good is all around me.

I pray that while I'm basking in God's love and enjoying His presence that I may also be aware of my need to be refined by His fire.

"Even though I have received wonderful revelations from God. But to keep me from getting puffed up, I was given a thorn in my flesh, a messenger from Satan to torment me and keep me from getting proud." (First Corinthians 12:7)

DECEMBER

December 1

We experience God every day, whether we acknowledge it or not. **"And be sure of this: I am with you always even to the end of the age."** (Matthew 28:20b)

He loved us even before we were born. He walks with us through each day, experiencing all that we do, and He will take us into His eternal home one day.

It breaks His heart when we become involved in His creation but leave Him out of our joy. He wants us to enjoy life, but to include Him in it. Life is as it should be when we experience God's presence in our joy.

Sometimes we just need to block everything else out and concentrate on His goodness.

"Be silent and know that I am God." (Psalm 46:10a)

"Enter his gates with thanksgiving; go into his courts with praise. Give thanks to him and bless his name." (Psalm 100:4)

December 2

This morning's post will be different. I want to express gratitude for Austin's life. He lived a few short years and left behind a loving wife and two of the most beautiful twin boys ever. There's a *big* hole left here, as he is *face-to-face* with the Lord. This is certainly one of those "Why?" things. We feel lost . . . but there's nothing we can do but accept it and thank God for His purpose, though we don't understand.

(Isaiah 55:8) **"'My ways are not your ways, neither are your thoughts my thoughts', saith the Lord."** (I may not have quoted it perfectly since I don't have my Bible handy).

Now I pray for comfort and strength for those whose hearts are broken, and whose lives have been shattered.

Somehow, we have to still cling to Jeremiah 29:11, **"For I know the plans I have for you, saith the Lord. Plans to prosper you and not to harm you; to give you a hope and a future."** (Pardon me if I miss-quoted it.)

December 3

Emotions are like the waves of the ocean. Sometimes they take us up; sometimes down. That's why we need to cling to our *Rock*. He never fails us, though the enemy tells us that we can't trust Him.

This *liar* is against us and wants to tear us away from all that we need - Jesus.

Many times we feel all alone, but we're *never alone*. "... **I am with you always, even to the end of the age.**" (Matthew 28:20b)

We are *strong*. "**... For when I am weak, then I am strong.**" (Second Corinthians 12:10b)

We can be *bold*. "**For God has not given us the spirit of fear and timidity, but of power, love, and self-discipline.**" (Second Timothy 1:7)

We can be *certain* that it will be okay. "**And we know that God causes all things to work together for the good of those who love God and are called according to his purpose for them.**" (Romans 8:28)

We *are equipped* with everything we need to overcome any situation. "**For I can do everything with the help of Christ who gives me the strength I need.**" (Philippians 4:13)

We can find *comfort* when we are hurting. "**Nevertheless, I tell you the truth: it is expedient for you that I go away, for if I go not away, the Comforter will not come unto you; but if I depart, I will send him unto you.**" (John 16:7)

We are equipped to face *whatever* . . . (because of Jesus). Let's always remember that and go forward boldly with the strength of His love and presence.

December 4

We are not to be dismayed when things happen that we couldn't foresee. God has been training us to be able to endure any situation He allows.

"**. . . It is not by force nor by strength, but by My Spirit, says the Lord Almighty.**" (Zechariah 4:6b)

Nothing takes God by surprise. He is in complete control and is ready to help us as we trust His wisdom.

Our lives are woven together like colors in a fabric to create a design. God uses one spirit to minister to another who is hurting. Much like our blood sends white corpuscles to help in the healing of a wound in our bodies.

Somehow, we just know to flock to the one who is hurting. It's God's design to restore us when we have nothing left to fight with and are tempted to give up.

"**. . .but God is faithful, who will not permit you to be tempted above that you are able, but will, with the temptation, also make a way to escape that you may be able to bear it.**" (First Corinthians 10:13b)

God has a plan. We may not like it, but we will rebound when we place our faith in Him. Jesus, too, was a man of sorrows and acquainted with grief. (See Isaiah 53:3) He understands and will see us through.

December 5

When God created us, He made us to be an *eternal spirit*, out of the same substance of Himself. **"So God created people in his own image; God patterned them after himself; male and female, he created them."** (Genesis 1:27)

He put us in a temporary earthen vessel. **"And the Lord God formed a man's body from the dust of the ground and breathed into it the breath of life. And the man became a living person."** (Genesis 2:7)

He knew we would always need Him, that we would get *dirty* from living in this sinful world. He knew that our health would fail and that we would get broken.

He didn't just put us on a shelf to be seen and heard. He put us out in the *field*, to trust His love, follow His leadership, and become a blessing.

He doesn't just come and visit us from time to see how we're doing - He lives with us - and is aware of all our needs.

When we get dirty, we look to Him for cleansing. (He's our *Washing Machine*, if you will).

When we get sick, we look to Him for healing. (He's our *Great Physician*.)

When we are broken, we look to Him for mending. (He's our *Repairman*).

When we don't know which way to turn, we look to Him for guidance. (He's our *Leader* and *Counselor*).

No matter what we need, He's our *Everything*. He's always there for us.

How can we go through life only seeing what our eyes allow?

"Anyone who is willing to hear, should listen to what the Spirit is saying. . ." (Revelation 2:11a)

December 6

Many of us set an alarm to wake us so we can prepare for the day. We moan when it goes off because it demands obedience. This happens most every day for many, whether we like it or not.

God sometimes sounds alarms to wake us from a *spiritual slumber*. He can't allow us to sleep away important time - time for us to prepare (ourselves or our family) for eternity.

Satan keeps us so busy with foolish or even seemingly important things. Time just gets away from us and we never know how much we have left!

The most important things are God and family. When we love our family, we're loving God. **"He that loveth not knoweth not God for God is love."** (First John 2:8)

My personal *opinion* is that family is our first mission field. **"And this commandment have we from him, that he who loveth God love his brother also."** (First John 4:21)

December 7

Satan wants to separate us from the trust we have in our God. After he has come against us, he tells us that our *loving God* allowed this to happen because He doesn't really love us, that He isn't really there. . .He begins to build doubt on top of the pain and confusion that we're experiencing.

Although our Lord *is* in control and, indeed, allowed this to happen, He is *love*. He has a plan for good that we can't understand.

Prayers have gone up in our behalf, asking God to give us strength and comfort to get us through this dark time.

If we stay in touch with God through this trial, He will make peace possible and give us courage to endure. (See Philippians 4:7 & 13).

We *have* to trust and run to God. He will guide us with His wisdom through the confusion we're experiencing. He will heal our hurts. (See Luke 4:18).

We are not instantly healed, but the pain and confusion gradually subsides.

It's like when your child gets hurt, he runs to his mommy for comfort and encouragement. You open your arms to receive him and give your love in the most powerful way.

Our biggest need is God, for He is *Love*.

"Love never gives up, never loses faith, is always hopeful and endures through every circumstance." (First Corinthians 13:7)

December 8

You can go to a person's house, read books about him, and even see a movie of his life, but until you've actually met him, you don't know him.

You only get to really know him when you meet and have fellowship with him. As you hear him tell you about his experiences, ideas, and goals, you become friends.

God knows each of us intimately. **"O Lord, you have examined my heart and know everything about me."** (Psalm 139:1) He wants us to know Him that well, also.

But, unless He allows some catastrophic event, we're just not that interested.

Our focus is on ourselves and our needs, not on Jesus, His love, and His plans. But when we meet Him *and* get to know Him, our focus begins to change and joy enters our heart. We begin to understand why He came to earth. **"God did not send His Son into the world to condemn it, but to save it."** (John 3:17)

"My goal is that they will be encouraged and knit together by strong ties of love. I want them to have full confidence because they have complete understanding of God's secret plan, which is Christ himself." (Colossians 2:2)

Have you noticed that even at Christmas, we have placed our focus on earthly, temporary things, instead of the *reason* we are celebrating?

December 9

If we knew the length of our days, would we think it more expedient that we carry the *Words of Life* with us to share with our loved ones? If we had only two more tomorrows, I know our focus would change drastically!

If we are saved, we have these *Words* in our heart. They sustain us in troublesome times. They give us strength when we're weary. They comfort us when we're broken. They give us so much more than salvation alone!

But if that was all that Jesus gave us, it would be sufficient. It will last for all eternity. We will be forever free from Satan's grasp.

If our cup is truly running over, let us *spill* it on those we love and those who need a drop of this precious gift of Love in their lives.

"You prepare a feast for me in the presence of my enemies. You welcome me as a guest, anointing my head with oil. My cup overflows with blessings." (Psalm 23:5)

December 10

We endure the long, cold, hard winter, knowing that spring will come and our *black and white* world will again be filled with color. We will again rejoice and frolic in God's wonderful creation!

This is a picture that gives us hope. When we are going through dark times, we can't imagine that life can again be joyful. But God is there! With Him, anything is possible. Nothing is too hard for Him.

"He will feed his flock like a shepherd. He will carry the lambs in his arms, holding them close to his heart. He will gently lead the mother sheep with their young." (Isaiah 40:11)

We can't allow Satan to rob our joy. He hands us a *bleak picture*, but we can turn it over and see the other side.

As we search for understanding, we fall short. But our faith will sustain us.

"That is why we live by believing and not by seeing." (Second Corinthians 5:7)

December 11

Long ago, the world was in turmoil . . . much like it is today.

Israel looked forward to the coming Messiah. They waited . . . they yearned . . . and He finally came! (Though many didn't *recognize* Him as Messiah.)

Just as Abraham and Sarah waited 25 years after the Lord promised they would have a son. She was 90 years old when Isaac was born! It seemed way too late for that to happen.

We don't like to wait, but sometimes that's what we have to do. We wait and trust. It's a test of our faith.

The tragedy is that, though Israel waited for so long for their Messiah, (They thought He would be different). They *continue* to wait and look for Him today.

We recognize Him and have received His salvation.

Now we wait and yearn for His 2nd coming. We have faith, (which is basically *trust that knows*), that Jesus is *Truth*.

"Jesus told him, I am the way, the truth, and the life. No one can come to the Father except through me." (John 14:6)

The *Truth* said, **"When everything is ready, I will come and get you, so that you will always be with me where I am."** (John 14:3)

December 12

God had the perfect gift! He saw our dilemma. We were imprisoned in sin, (wallowing in it by our own choice) and headed for hell.

"For the wages of sin is death", (*eternal separation from God*), **"but the Gift of God is eternal life through Christ Jesus our Lord."** (Romans 6:23) (Parenthesis are mine.)

Centuries before He came, His birth was predicted.

"But you, O Bethlehem Ephratah, are only a small village in Judah, yet a ruler of Israel will come from you. One whose origins are from the distant past." (Micah 5:2)

God planned this *Precious Gift* even before Adam and Eve fell under Satan's curse. (See Genesis 3)

"In the beginning was the Word and the Word was with God, and the Word was God." (John 1:1)

Christmas is our celebration of the birth of *God's Salvation*. Easter is our celebration of the *victory* He came to give.

"O death, where is thy sting? O, grave, where is thy victory?" (First Corinthians 15:55)

December 13

Our conscience acts on our knowledge. If we *know* it's wrong, our conscience warns us about it. But if we don't *know*, we will *learn* from our mistakes. We will, then, have a *guilty conscience*.

We should immediately admit, not only to ourselves, but to God and others, that we were wrong. We shouldn't try to hide or excuse our faults.

"Confess your sins to each other and pray for each other so that you may be healed. The earnest prayer of a righteous person has great power and wonderful results." (James 5:16)

If we're not saved, we won't confess our faults. This leads us further in the wrong direction. We eventually get ourselves into such a mess that we cry out to God. All along, we've known that He is *real*. (We just didn't think we needed Him!)

But when we acknowledge and come to Him, He forgives and accepts us into His loving Family. We establish a relationship of Father and child. We feel secure in this relationship and allow it to grow.

Each day of our life is a step toward death's door. We don't know how long our journey will be, but we can make sure of our eternal destination when we eventually arrive at death's door.

We establish this Father/child relationship by inviting Jesus to come into our lives and welcome Him to walk with us *toward death's door*. (This may seem a *morbid thought*, but it's a truth we can't ignore.)

December 14

As long as he had his eyes on Jesus, Peter could do the impossible - he was walking on water! But then...

When life demands more than we have in us, then Jesus...

I reflect back on the days when my dear, sweet sister was dying with cancer. I knew I was losing her though I prayed I wouldn't. I didn't have the strength to endure this loss! She was so dear to me, (*"My heart"*, I've often said.) We helped each other hurdle the *junk* in our path.

God assured me that He would be with me to help me through my emptiness. **"Each time He said, 'My gracious favor is all you need. My power works best in your weakness'..."** (Second Corinthians 12:9)

I'm still leaning on His grace and power, though I get my eyes off Him from time to time.

But when I begin to *sink*, I call out to Him and He's there for me. He comforts and encourages me as He speaks to me through the promises He recorded in His precious Word.

"For the Word of God is full of living power. It is sharper than the sharpest knife, cutting deep into our innermost thoughts and desires..." (Hebrews 4:12a)

I feel secure and strong as I snuggle in His loving arms. I find encouragement in the truth He reveals as He guides me through what He promises in His Word.

December 15

When I began these devotions, it seemed the Lord was saying, "I have given you this tool. I want to bless my people, but they're so busy! Many don't take time to read My Word, but they *always* carry their cell phones. They will take time to look at *Facebook*."

God leads me to write these *text messages* to you, but they are only *junk food*. You can *grab it on the go*, but you need at least one *real meal* a day.

Go directly to God's Word. Take time to fellowship with Him. Speak your needs to Him and listen as He speaks to you. He has a lot to say to you.

Satan shows us what's in front of us and tells us that's more important at the moment. Then we never get around to *one-on-one* time with God.

"Unless the Lord builds a house, the work of the builders is useless. Unless the Lord protects a city, guarding it with sentries will do no good." (Psalm 127:1)

If we don't get instructions from *The Boss*, we can stay busy *building* life, but if we're building it wrong, our efforts are wasted. It has to be torn down and rebuilt.

"Your Word is a lamp for my feet and a light for my path." (Psalm 119:105) Our path gets pretty dim if we try to live only on *junk food*.

If you don't know where to start reading, begin in Proverbs. Since this is the 15th, read Chapter 15. Tomorrow, read Chapter 16, etc. When you finish Proverbs, start over or go to another Book; (Maybe Matthew).

Reading one chapter each day doesn't take that much time and you'll be blessed by hearing *The Boss* say, **"Well done, thy good and faithful servant."**

December 16

God became like us so we could become like Him. **"For God made Christ, who never sinned to be the offering for our sin, so that we could be made right with God through Christ."** (Second Corinthians 5:21)

But... **"Even in his own land and among his own people, he was not accepted."** (John 1:11)

In order for us to become like Him, we have to *accept Him*.

I'm thinking about when our country was established. It was founded on *Christian principles*. On our currency, *"In God, we trust."* We pledge allegiance to *"One nation, under God."*

At this time, we allow babies to be killed for the convenience of their mothers. This goes directly against God's law, **"Do not murder."** (Exodus 20:13)

God's Word warns about homosexuality in Romans 1:16, yet we find it *politically incorrect* to speak against it.

We hear of teachers and coaches being fired for praying!

We are definitely heading in the *wrong* direction as a nation! Repent means to stop going that way, *turn around*, and go the other way.

We're approaching the end of the age. Time is running out. If we were heading toward God, that would be good news. But...

We have gradually slipped to this low position. (*Grandma would turn over in her grave!*)

Let us quickly open our eyes and speak up. God offers joy but Satan offers hell. His pleasure turns sour at the end. It's not a hard choice to make.

I can't change the world, but I can change mine by keeping my eyes on Jesus.

December 17

When we've developed a lifetime of habits, we may recognize that some of them are not good. But they've become a part of us and we choose to excuse ourselves with: *"That's just the way I am."* We don't take time to listen as God desires to rid us of them.

"Come now, and let us reason together, saith the Lord, though your sins be as scarlet, they shall be as white as snow; though they be red like crimson, they shall be as wool." (Isaiah 1:18)

As I was reading this morning, God was saying to me, (*once again*), that like Martha in Luke 10:41-42, I get too preoccupied with household things and don't take time to visit and enjoy my kids when they come for Sunday lunch. I eat with them and visit for a short while, then I'm up doing the dishes. These can wait until after the kids are gone. My house is not more important than my guests!

I realize that the scripture in Luke is teaching me to take time to listen to the Lord, to make Him top priority, and to *really* listen to Him.

While other things need to be done, they can wait until I've done the most important thing - spend time with the Master and get instructions for how to bring honor to Him.

December 18

One day our spiritual eyes will be opened *continually*. We'll be able to see the heart of God and touch Him! He's too awesome for us now, to even look upon.

He has to prepare us to gradually get glimpses of His glory. His plans for us are only briefly visible - like a child playing *peek-a-boo*.

There's nothing on earth to describe His glory, but I get a picture in my mind of two little toddlers, gazing in wonder and amazement at the Christmas tree.

They are drawn to it, but are only to *see*, not touch! And if they are allowed to touch, it is only with the tip of their finger. How they want (and *need*) to touch and feel it!

We are instructed to wait. But while we're waiting, we are going through a learning process. **"Dear Brothers and sisters, whenever trouble comes your way, let it be an opportunity for joy. For when your faith is tested your endurance has a chance to grow."** (James 1:2-3)

This leads us to realize Romans 8:18, **"Yet what we suffer now is nothing compared to the glory he will give us later."**

The pain of our suffering is producing joy eternal - just one of the things we'll be able to touch and feel when we get to the heart of God.

December 19

When I was saved, I received the greatest *Christmas Gift* ever!

Because of the *power* of this Gift, I am able to do anything I set my mind to.

Because of the *love* of this Gift, I am forgiven when I act like *myself* instead of like Him.

Because of the *wisdom* of this Gift, I know I'm headed in the right direction.

Along with this Gift, came *assurance* that everything will be okay because He is in control. I don't have to depend only on what I know. I can trust Him to lead me into all truth, because He is *Truth*.

When confronted with cancer, He assured me that I couldn't *lose for winning*! (It was a *win/win* situation).

It's becoming clear that because He lives in me, I can't *really* fail because *He is able* to use my failures and turn them around for good.

"And we know that all things work together for good to them that love God, to them who are the called according to his purpose." (Romans 8:28)

"What can we say to these things? If God be for us, who can be against us?" (Romans 8:31)

December 20

God didn't look for the most beautiful, richest, or most brilliant girl to be the mother of His Son. He chose a common, ordinary, probably plain, person. The spotlight was to be on Jesus, not on His mother.

The place He chose to be born wasn't an elegant, well-furnished home. These choices show He preferred the *common*.

By these choices, He shows us that we don't have to be *good enough* to be accepted by Him. He reaches out to the young and the old, the rich and the poor, the homely and the beautiful, the skinny and the fat, the brilliant and the slow, alike.

He doesn't choose us because of our *qualification*, but because of our *need*. **"For there is no respect of persons with God."** (Romans 2:11)

He sees our need for Salvation above any other thing about us and His Gift is *available* to each of us alike.

December 21

Silently, a picture is being painted. There's a *Hand*, guided by Love, putting purpose and fulfillment in our lives. If we go through life with our eyes closed, we can't see the effect of each stroke as it completes the picture of who we are and are becoming.

When something unexpected happens, we want to take the brush out of the Master's hand and create a different picture. We think He *purposefully* messed it up. But, if we sit still and allow His hand to move, we'll soon be able to see that He knows what He's doing!

He shows us strength we never knew we had. It's not really our strength, but His as He holds us together through each difficult situation.

We think, "How could love act this way?" But His love works through Wisdom that we can't understand. **"For just as the heavens are higher than the earth, so are my ways higher than your ways and my thoughts higher than your thoughts."** (Isaiah 55:9)

If we can't trust His Love, His Wisdom, and His Power, then we're destined to live in fear, depression, and defeat. That's Satan's desire for us - *not God's*!

"For I know the plans I have for you, says the Lord, They are plans for good and not for disaster, to give you a future and a hope." (Jeremiah 29:11)

December 22

The routine of the normal lulls us to sleep, spiritually. We seem to just *follow our nose* through life, doing the *necessary*.

God is not asleep during these times. He is actively supplying us breath, energy, and thoughts to direct us. He allows another *voice*, but gives us discernment.

At the end of the day, when we reflect on our accomplishments, we may or may not give Him credit. But He is living life in and through us. He is only *with* those who don't know Him, speaking constantly. But they can't hear Him. He isn't living in their hearts because He hasn't been invited.

"Look! Here I stand at the door and knock. If you hear me calling and open the door, I will come in and we will share a meal as friends." (Revelation 3:20)

He directs events that are designed to speak to our needs. Some need salvation, some need Spiritual growth. He doesn't enjoy using it, but pain is His most effective tool to get our attention. Our need for relief draws us to Him with open hearts.

Much of the "*Why?*" we experience is because He desires fellowship with us, (for our good, as well as His). We ignore this need so easily.

Let us lovingly come to Him so that He can bless us as He desires, and isn't forced to allow extreme measures.

Christmas reminds us of the joy He came to bring!

December 23

Jesus was born and grew up like a *'nobody'*. **"He was despised and rejected - a man of sorrows, acquainted with bitterest grief. We turned our backs on him and looked the other way when he went by. He was despised, and we didn't care."** (Isaiah 53:3)

He was treated much like a homeless, dirty beggar. No one understood who He really was and why He came.

He was a Human Being who deserved to be treated fairly - to be loved. He gave His life for us out of Pure Love.

Many still regard Him as nothing.

Of the many gifts He brought to us, one is compassion. We have the capacity to care for those *nobodies* out there. Each has a story, but our attitude usually is "They brought it on themselves."

Even if they did, they need to be loved. *WWJD? WWJWUTD?* (What would Jesus want us to do?)

As we celebrate Christmas, let us open our hearts to receive compassion for those who may be starving for love and understanding.

How we praise God that Jesus was far more than He seemed to be! Let us be thankful and show Jesus how truly thankful we are for His unspeakable Gift!

December 24

Today we celebrate *with family*, the birth of our Savior! He is invited and will be here, though we have to see Him with our hearts, instead of our eyes.   He's just like our parents, grandparents, and those in our family who have moved to heaven. Our minds tell us they're not here, but our hearts cling to the hope they are.

Hope is something that is not *yet* sure, but is near! Its *reality* is taking shape behind the scenes of our earthly existence.

"Don't be troubled. You trust God, now trust in me. There are many rooms in my Father's home, and I am going to prepare a place for you. If this were not so, I would tell you plainly. When everything is ready, I will come and get you, so that you will always be with me where I am." (John 14:1-3)

It's like when we've applied for a job and have been hired, but haven't received our first paycheck. We know *it's coming*!

Eternal life is so much *surer* than that! It has been promised by the One who created and owns all the earth - the One who can't lie. (See John 14:6)

His existence can't be seen with our eyes. But with our hearts we can see this Savior who was born in a stable, lived a perfect life, and taught us how to live. This is the One whose death paid the penalty we deserve to pay for ourselves.

His power overcame death and He's alive today to offer gifts that can encourage us in the face of fear, comfort us when we're broken, and guide us through each day.

These gifts aren't wrapped and placed under the tree, but they are there when we open our hearts to receive them. They are supernatural, everlasting, and free for the taking!

December 25

We weary ourselves each year searching for the perfect gift for our loved ones. It's been given, once and for all, through Jesus - *Love*! It has been in our hearts all this time.

To be with someone we love, sharing smiles, even laughter, is more enjoyable than the many presents we open.

"There are three things that will endure - faith, hope, and love - and the greatest of these is love." (First Corinthians 13:13)

"Greater love hath no man than this; that a man lay down his life for his friends." (John 15:13)

God's *Love* came to earth as a Babe in a manger. He went to the cross to fulfill our greatest need. (To become one with God).

His love caused Him to give all He had for us - *His very life*!

His Light shines in the darkness. It's been there all the time. . . .MERRY CHRISTMAS!

December 26

We struggle to become. As I look back to see how much I've changed since I acknowledged God's love and daily presence, I'm amazed!

"Therefore, if any man be in Christ, he is a new creation; old things are passed away; behold, all things are become new." (Second Corinthians 5:17)

Yet, as I sit here smugly reveling in what I've learned and now understand, I am also amazed at the creature I still am - so steeped in hidden selfishness!

I've labeled the things I've overcome as *sin*, yet, I am embarrassed to admit what I still need to overcome. I hide these faults from myself and try to hide them from others.

If God opened my eyes completely, (all at once), and allowed me to see the wretched creature I still am, I would be overwhelmed beyond relief!

How can I judge others? My plate is so full just trying to overcome my own faults!

"And why worry about a speck in your friend's eye when you have a log in your own." (Luke 6:41)

It's true - the more we learn, the more we realize what we *still yet need to learn*.

Yet, we are accepted!

December 27

I'm so grateful that God accepts me, (*warts and all!*) He hasn't given up on me. He sees, not what I am, but what I can (and will) become.

I desire to be tender and loving. But I am harsh, (and loving).

I prefer to look upon the grace that God has already bestowed on me, rather than focusing on the areas that still need work.

Yet, if I don't see myself as I really am, I'll see no need for improvement, no need for God to do any further work on me.

In the past, He pointed out a weakness to me in a dream. Since then, my plea is, *"Show me, Lord, but be gentle!"*

Had the dream been reality, it would have been *devastating!*

Any good in my life comes from God. **"Whatever is good and perfect comes to us from God above..."** (James 1:17) ... because on my own, I'm not capable of it!

"As it is written, there is none righteous, no not one." (Romans 3:10)

"Come here and listen to me! I'll pour out my Spirit of wisdom upon you and make you wise." (Proverbs 1:23)

December 28

We make our plans and hope they'll turn out. Sometimes they do! But we're never sure until afterward.

God's plans are sure! He planned our life even before we were in our mother's womb. **"You saw me before I was born. Every day of my life was recorded in your book. Every moment was laid out before a single day had passed."** (Psalm 139:16)

Jesus said, **". . . I go to prepare a place for you. . ."** (John 14:2) His plans are for us to be with Him in eternity. The things He allows to happen to us during this lifetime are preparing us for that place.

We don't understand the pain He allows to come our way. But a mother has to inflict pain of some sort in order to discipline and strengthen her children. A mother's love is the closest example of God's love.

We're in the path of God's love and we don't to have to fear because (1 John 4:18) says, **"There is no fear in love, but perfect love casteth out fear, because fear hath punishment. He that feareth is not made perfect in love."**

December 29

Our trust in God places our hand in His as we walk through this life. When something happens to shake our faith, do we continue to trust Him though we can't understand?

Or do we release our grip on His hand and turn our backs on Him?

Even if we do, He still has us in His hand and heart. Though it grieves Him, He still cares.

"And grieve not the Holy Spirit of God, by whom ye are sealed unto the day of redemption." (Ephesians 4:30)

Nothing we do *or don't do* can change His love for us. (See Romans 8:38-39). But it can change our awareness of His continual presence and concern for us.

When we come to our senses and turn back to Him, we will find He has been waiting with out-stretched arms.

He allows us a choice to live as *spiritual orphans*, though we are His children. (But this is not His choice for us.)

When our lack of trust removes our hand from His, it is like unto a child of the King living in the city dump, searching for something that satisfies.

This spiritual void causes us to yearn for a bath as well as for food.

We can't let any *emotional* or *material* need draw our attention away from His continual love and provision.

"But my God shall supply all your need according to his riches in glory by Christ Jesus." (Philippians 4:19)

December 30

Determination is a powerful force! It's that power *we give ourselves to*. When dealing with the strong-willed child, we realize they are determined to do what they want, no matter what!

But we are also determined to teach them to obey in order to prevent the painful consequences. That battle causes pain on both side.

"If you refuse to discipline your children, it proves you don't love them; if you love your children, you will be prompt to discipline them." (Proverbs 13:24)

It seems we're never free of this battle. The child grows up, and even old, while still clinging to his selfish determination.

Our determination for control clashes with his determination for control!

Only when we realize that we can't *make* them obey, and turn control over to the Lord, can we have peace in the midst of this struggle.

God doesn't *make* us obey. He simply makes us *wish we had*! (By allowing us to *suffer the consequences*). **"There is a path before each person that seems right; but it ends in death."** (Proverbs 14:12)

When we realize that we actually have *no control*, we go to the Lord. **"And I will ask the Father, and he will give you another counselor, who will never leave you."** (John 14:16)

He is teaching us while we teach our children.

December 31

"Unless the Lord builds the house, the work of the builders is useless. Unless the Lord protects a city, guarding it with sentries will do no good." (Psalm 127:1)

No amount of tornadoes, flooding, fires, or earthquakes will be able to destroy the house built by the Lord. (See Romans 8:38-39).

We are completely safe and secure there.

We don't put our faith and trust in *the house*, but in the Lord who keeps watch over it.

Here and now, God is on the scene!

He promises His continued presence.

". . . I will never leave thee nor forsake thee." (Hebrews 13:5b)

That means, in the coming year, no matter how difficult life may become, we're never alone! His presence is a *given*!

Printed in the United States
By Bookmasters